Buick V-8 Engines

HOW TO REBUILD 1967–1980

Mike Forsythe

CarTech®

CarTech®

CarTech®, Inc.
6118 Main Street
North Branch, MN 55056
Phone: 651-277-1200 or 800-551-4754
Fax: 651-277-1203
www.cartechbooks.com

Edit by Bob Wilson
Layout by Connie DeFlorin
ISBN 978-1-61325-774-6
Item No. SA539

Library of Congress Cataloging-in-Publication Data Available

Written, edited, and designed in the U.S.A.
Printed in China
10 9 8 7 6 5 4 3 2 1

DISTRIBUTION BY:

Europe
PGUK
63 Hatton Garden
London EC1N 8LE, England
Phone: 020 7061 1980 • Fax: 020 7242 3725
www.pguk.co.uk

Australia
Renniks Publications Ltd.
3/37-39 Green Street
Banksmeadow, NSW 2109, Australia
Phone: 2 9695 7055 • Fax: 2 9695 7355
www.renniks.com

Canada
Login Canada
300 Saulteaux Crescent
Winnipeg, MB, R3J 3T2 Canada
Phone: 800 665 1148 • Fax: 800 665 0103
www.lb.ca

SA
S·A DESIGN

INTRODUCTION

It's a common misconception that an engine overhaul is beyond the capability of the average do-it-yourself (DIY) mechanic. Sure, it's a time-consuming task that requires attention to detail and effort. However, if you take your time and thoroughly study each step of the process, it is possible. It helps if you're a detail-oriented person. If you're not a detail-oriented person, this is your chance to learn! It is important to be meticulous when cleaning, measuring, and reassembling the engine. Don't rush any part of the overhaul. Hurrying the process can lead to forgetting to tighten a bolt or installing a piston ring upside down. Seemingly small mistakes can have serious consequences.

My approach in writing this book considers that decades have passed since the last Buick V-8 engine was built. Many readers, I assume, are Buick enthusiasts who plan to restore their collector cars. Others may just want to breathe new life into their tired, old friend. In either case, an engine inspection is likely to reveal extensive wear to many components. The information in this book helps DIYers identify the extent of that wear and presents overhaul options for the cost-conscious rebuilder as well as the spare-no-expense restorer.

Many tasks in this book can be carried out in more than one way. I always present the best method. In some cases, alternative methods can be used that have advantages, such as being quicker or not requiring a special tool. In these cases, I document the alternative method(s) as well. All of the methods that I discuss are safe and follow accepted shop practices.

BUICK SECOND-GENERATION V-8 ENGINES

In 1967, the final generation of Buick V-8 engine production (400- and 430-ci big-blocks) began. Buick's new engine design took advantage of the latest manufacturing technology, which included thin-wall castings to reduce weight as well as cylinder heads that had better flow characteristics than its Nailhead V-8 predecessor.

For the 1968 model year, the small-block 350 engine joined the lineup. By 1970, the big-block had grown in displacement to 455 ci, and a Stage 1 version was available for those who wanted to dominate the street. While the engine was rated at 360 hp, it is generally accepted that the Stage 1 455 was significantly underrated.

Sadly, 1970 was the high-water mark for Buick performance. Plans for production cylinder heads with improved flow and other performance parts never materialized. The "smog era" forced Buick to lower compression ratios and add performance-sapping emissions equipment. Nevertheless, Buick continued producing its venerable 350 V-8 through the 1980 model year. The 455 had already been dropped in 1976, as fuel prices rose and government-mandated fuel-economy standards were on the horizon.

Identification

Before beginning the rebuild process, identify your engine. Buick engines are unique and somewhat

In 1967, when the second-generation Buick V-8 was launched, the smooth, powerful engine was the best of Detroit's offerings. Refinements in subsequent years improved power and durability. Sadly, production of this iconic power-plant was cut short. It was in Buick's lineup for a mere 13 years, which was the shortest run of any GM V-8 from the same period.

rare when compared to more popular General Motors (GM) V-8 engines, such as those from Chevrolet, Oldsmobile, and Pontiac. Engines from those manufacturers were installed in many Buick cars beginning in 1975. Additionally, it is important to know whether you're dealing with a small-block or a big-block Buick engine. There are many differences between the two.

Buick V-8 engines can be quickly distinguished from engines that were manufactured by other GM divisions. To determine this, follow the information that is listed below:

1. The distributor on a Buick engine is mounted in the front and is angled toward the driver's side at a 30-degree angle. The only other GM V-8 engine that had a front-mounted distributor was Cadillac. Use the characteristics below to distinguish a Cadillac engine from a Buick engine.
2. Buick engines have five bolts that secure each valve cover. Cadillac engines have nine.
3. If the car has air conditioning (A/C) and the A/C compressor is still installed, it will be attached to the passenger's side of the engine, outboard of the alternator. This further distinguishes Buick engines from Cadillac engines of the era, which had the compressor mounted above the passenger-side valve cover (1967) or on top of the intake manifold (1968 and later).
4. The oil pump is integral to the aluminum front engine cover and is on the lower passenger's side. The oil filter is attached to the pump. Note that Cadillac engines have a similar oil pump and filter location.

This view of a Buick V-8 shows two distinctive characteristics: 1) the distributor is mounted on the driver's side in the front and 2) the A/C compressor is mounted outboard of the alternator.

5. The thermostat housing on Buick engines has a unique design. In addition to the large radiator hose fitting on the thermostat housing, Buick engines also have an additional small-diameter hose fitting.

GM Corporate Engines

Not every Buick vehicle had a Buick engine. Beginning in 1975 and continuing into the 1980s, GM commonly mixed engines among its four major divisions (Buick, Chevrolet, Oldsmobile, and Pontiac). While some Buick engines were used in cars from other GM divisions, it is much more common to find Buick vehicles with an engine from one of the other divisions.

From 1975 to 1980, the Chevrolet small-block (305), Oldsmobile small-block (260 and 307), and Pontiac 301 engines were commonly installed in Buick cars. GM commonly (and confusingly) referred to the Chevrolet 305, Oldsmobile 307, and Pontiac 301 generically as "5.0 liter" engines. However, few characteristics of these three engine designs are similar, aside from their approximate metric displacement.

The quickest and easiest way to ensure that you have a Buick engine is to review the list in the "Identification" section.

VIN Details

The engine can be identified by referencing the vehicle identification number (VIN). The VIN is

Buick thermostat housings have a small hose fitting that is below the large radiator hose fitting. Another identifying characteristic is that the thermostat housing is mounted to the front vertical surface of the intake manifold. On other GM engines, the thermostat housing is mounted on the upper (horizontal) surface of the intake manifold.

On 1968-and-later models, the vehicle identification number (VIN) can be seen in the lower corner of the driver's side of the windshield from outside the vehicle.

found in one of two places, depending on the year in which it was manufactured. On a 1967-or-earlier vehicle, the VIN plate is in the front driver-side doorjamb and is visible when the driver's door is open. On 1968-and-later vehicles, a VIN plate is visible from the outside of the vehicle when looking through the driver's side of the windshield at the base of the dash.

GM VINs were in different formats over the years. All 1981-and-later models use a standardized 17-digit VIN. The 8th digit identifies the engine, and the 10th digit identifies the model year.

Prior to 1981, GM VINs were not as standardized and took multiple formats over time. On 1971-and-earlier models, the VIN did not include information related to engine identification. On these models, a data plate was riveted on the firewall inside the engine compartment. The information on this plate only identifies whether a V-8 or a 6-cylinder engine was installed

Buick 1972-and-Later V-8 Engine VIN Codes

VIN Letter	Engine Displacement	Notes
1972		
G	350 2V	Dual exhaust
H	350 4V	—
J	350 4V	—
K	350 4V	Dual exhaust
T	455 4V	—
U	455 4V	Dual exhaust
V	455 4V	Stage 1
W	455 4V	Stage 1
1973		
H	350 2V	—
J	350 4V	—
K	350 4V	Dual exhaust
T	455 4V	—
U	455 4V	Dual exhaust
V	455 4V	Stage 1
W	455 4V	Stage 1
1974		
G	350 2V	Dual exhaust
H	350 2V	—
J	350 4V	—
K	350 4V	Dual exhaust
P	455 2V	—
R	455 2V	Dual exhaust
T	455 4V	—
U	455 4V	Dual exhaust
V	455 4V	Stage 1
W	455 4V	Stage 1
1975		
F	260 2V	Oldsmobile*
H	350 2V	—
J	350 4V	—
T	455 4V	—
1976		
F	260 2V	Oldsmobile*
H	350 2V	—
J	350 4V	—
T	455 4V	—

VIN Letter	Engine Displacement	Notes
1977		
H	350 2V	—
J	350 2V	—
K	403 4V	Oldsmobile*
L	350 4V	—
R	350 4V	—
U	305 2V	Chevrolet**
Y	301 2V	Pontiac***
1978		
H	305 4V	Chevrolet**
K	403 4V	Oldsmobile*
L	350 4V	—
R	350 4V	—
U	305 2V	Chevrolet**
W	301 4V	Pontiac***
X	350 4V	Chevrolet**
Y	301 2V	Pontiac***
1979		
G	305 2V	Chevrolet**
H	305 4V	Chevrolet**
K	403 4V	Oldsmobile*
L	350 4V	—
R	350 4V	—
W	301 4V	Pontiac***
X	350 4V	Chevrolet**
Y	301 2V	Pontiac***
1980		
H	305 4V	Chevrolet**
R	350 4V	—
W	301 4V	Pontiac***
X	350 4V	Chevrolet**
Y	307 2V	Oldsmobile*

* These engines were manufactured by Oldsmobile and are not covered in this book.
** These engines were manufactured by Chevrolet and are not covered in this book.
*** These engines were manufactured by Pontiac and are not covered in this book.

On 1971-and-earlier GM cars, the VIN does not indicate the type of engine that was installed in the vehicle. A body-code plate (such as this) is attached to the firewall. Although the plate does not provide much detail regarding the engine that was installed, it identifies whether the car was originally equipped with a V-8 or a 6-cylinder engine.

at the factory. No specifics about the engine are provided. On 1972–1980 models, a 13-digit VIN code is provided. On these models, the fifth digit identifies the engine type, and the sixth digit identifies the model year.

VIN Derivative on the Engine Block

The 1968-and-later Buick V-8 engines have a small-font number that is stamped onto a machined surface on the engine block. On early models (typically 1968–1970), the number is stamped onto the block's deck surface between the number-1 and number-3 spark-plug locations. To see it, look down deep, through the scalloped area at the bottom edge of the cylinder head. This area usually has an accumulation of gunk on top. If the engine's deck surface was machined during a previous rebuild, the number will most likely be completely gone.

On 1971 and 1972 models, the number is on the driver-side front face of the cylinder block, slightly below the block deck surface.

On 1973-and-later 455 engines, the number is stamped vertically on the passenger's side adjacent to the water pump. On 1973-and-later 350 engines, the location was unchanged. It is still on the driver's side below the cylinder-head gasket surface.

The first digit of the VIN derivative number is the division code.

On most later models, the VIN derivative is stamped onto the front of the engine block, just below the cylinder head (right arrow). On 1973-and-later 455 engines, the VIN derivative is stamped vertically on the passenger-side front surface of the engine block which is adjacent to the water pump (left arrow).

Code	Division
1	Chevrolet
2	Pontiac
3	Oldsmobile
4	Buick
6	Cadillac

The VIN derivative number uniquely identifies an engine to its chassis. On this early model, the block deck was machined, so most of the number is indecipherable. The number "4" is visible, but the rest of the characters can't be determined. Engines have four scalloped openings such as this (two on each side). Depending on the year and engine type, the stamped numbers may be shown at other openings.

The division code identifies the vehicle line in which the engine was installed—not the engine type. Engines from other GM divisions were sometimes installed in Buick cars, so the division code can't be used to confirm an engine's origin.

The second digit identifies the year in which the vehicle was manufactured. On 1979-and-earlier models, this is the last digit of the year in which the vehicle was manufactured (9=1969, 0=1970, 1=1971, etc). On 1980-and-later models, a letter is used instead of a number (A=1980, B=1981, etc.).

The third character is a letter code that identifies where the engine was manufactured. The six numbers that follow the three-digit code should match the last six numbers of the VIN, which is known as the "sequence number." If the last six numbers of the VIN match these six numbers, it means that the engine was originally installed at the factory. In other words, it's the "numbers-matching" engine for the car.

Cylinder Block Casting Numbers			
Casting Number	Displacement	Type	Years
1231738	455	Big-block	1970–1971
1238861	455	Big-block	1970–1971
1241735	455	Big-block	1972–1976
1242694	455	Big-block	1970–1976
1381624	400	Big-block	1967
1381625	430	Big-block	1967–1969
1383424	430	Big-block	1967–1969
1383434	430	Big-block	1968–1969
1383790	400	Big-block	1968–1969
1384790	400	Big-block	1967–1969
1393444	400	Big-block	1968–1969
9773524	400	Big-block	1967–1969
1241748	350	Small-block	1972–1980
1231447	350	Small-block	1971–1972
1233472	350	Small-block	1970–1971
1237650	350	Small-block	1970–1972
25504744	350	Small-block	1972–1980
1241748	350	Small-block	1972–1981
3182201	350	Small-block	1968–1980

Engine Casting Number

All engines that are covered in this book have a casting number at the top rear of the engine block behind the intake manifold. On big-block engines, the engine displacement is displayed in this location. For 350 engines, the casting number does not indicate displacement, as all small-blocks from 1970 onward were 350s.

For those who are building a big-block for maximum performance, the so-called "blue block" is considered by many to be the strongest because it had thicker casting walls. These engines carry casting number 1241735 and were painted blue at the factory.

The casting number is located behind the intake manifold and just forward of the transmission-mounting surface at the rear of the engine. With the engine installed, you can use a mirror to see it.

Engine Code

Buick provided a two-letter engine identification code that can be used to specifically identify all of its V-8 engines. Unfortunately, this code can often be difficult to locate and read. Also, if the engine block has been previously rebuilt and the cylinder head mounting surface was machined (decked), the identification code is most likely gone.

The engine code is stamped onto the engine block deck, which is the top surface where the cylinder head is mounted. When the cylinder heads are installed, the code is visible below one of the four scalloped areas at the bottom edge of the cylinder heads. (See the VIN derivative on the engine block, which was discussed previously). The scalloped areas (two on each head) are below the pairs of spark plugs. The number-1 and number-3 pair of spark plugs as well as the number-5 and number-7 pair of spark plugs are on the driver's side. The number-2 and number-4 pair of spark plugs as well as the number-6 and number-8 pair of spark plugs are on the passenger's side.

Usually, the engine code is on the driver's side. If the engine is an early model where the VIN derivative is between the number-1 and number-3 spark plugs, the code will likely be between the number-5 and number-7 spark plugs. If it is a later model and the VIN derivative is on the front of the engine block, the code will likely be between the number-1 and number-3 spark plugs.

Engine Codes						
Year	Code	Displacement	Compression ratio	Torque	Horsepower	Carburetor
1967	NR	400	10.25:1	440	340	4V
1967	MD, ND	430	10.25:1	475	360	4V
1967	NE	430	8.75:1	N/A*	N/A*	4V
1968	PO	350	9.0:1	350	230	2V
1968	PP	350	10.25:1	375	280	4V
1968	PW	350	7.6:1	N/A*	N/A*	2V
1968	PR	400	10.25:1	440	340	4V
1968	PD	430	10.25:1	475	360	4V
1968	PE	430	8.75:1	N/A*	N/A*	4V
1969	RO	350	9.0:1	350	230	2V
1969	RP	350	10.25:1	375	280	4V
1969	RW	350	8.0:1	N/A*	N/A*	2V
1969	RR	400	10.25:1	440	340	4V
1969	RS	400	10.25:1	440	350	4V
1969	RD	430	10.25:1	475	360	4V
1969	RE	430	8.75:1	N/A*	N/A*	4V
1970	SB	350	9.0:1	375	285	4V
1970	SO	350	9.0:1	350	230	2V
1970	SP	350	10.25:1	410	315	4V
1970	SF	455	10.0:1	510	370	4V
1970	SR	455	10.0:1	510	350	4V
1970	SS	455	10.5:1	510	360	4V
1971	TB	350	8.5:1	360	260	4V
1971	TC	350	8.5:1	350	230	2V
1971	TD	350	8.5:1	360	260	4V
1971	TO	350	8.5:1	350	230	2V
1971	WC	350	8.5:1	270	155	2V
1971	TA	455	8.5:1	455	330	4V
1971	TR	455	8.5:1	450	315	4V
1971	TS	455	8.5:1	460	345	4V
1972	WC	350	8.5:1	265	150	2V
1972	WB	350	8.5:1	275	180	4V
1972	WC	350	8.5:1	285	190	4V
1972	WF	455	8.5:1	360	225	4V
1972	WF	455	8.5:1	375	250	4V
1972	WS	455	8.5:1	390	270	4V
1972	WA	455	8.5:1	380	260	4V
1973	XC	350	8.5:1	265	155	2V
1973	XC	350	8.5:1	265	150	2V
1973	XB	350	8.5:1	270	175	4V
1973	XB	350	8.5:1	285	190	4V
1973	XF	455	8.5:1	360	225	4V
1973	XF	455	8.5:1	375	250	4V
1973	XS	455	8.5:1	390	270	4V
1973	XA	455	8.5:1	380	260	4V
1974	ZC	350	8.5:1	270	150	2V
1974	ZP	350	8.5:1	270	150	2V
1974	ZM	350	8.5:1	260	175	4V
1974	ZB	350	8.5:1	260	175	4V
1974	ZI	455	8.5:1	355	175	2V
1974	ZH	455	8.5:1	370	190	2V
1974	ZF	455	8.5:1	335	210	4V
1974	ZK	455	8.5:1	355	230	4V
1974	ZS	455	8.5:1	370	255	4V
1974	ZA	455	8.5:1	360	245	4V
1975	AB	350	8.0:1	270	145	2V
1975	AM	350	8.0:1	260	175	4V
1975	AF	455	7.9:1	345	205	4V
1976	PA	350	8.0:1	270	140	2V
1976	PE	350	8.0:1	280	155	4V
1976	SA	455	7.9:1	345	205	4V

Parts Interchange

With the exception of the pistons and valvetrain components, most parts interchange among big-block engines (the 400, 430, and 455). In addition, almost all parts interchange among 350 engines. The main exceptions to interchange among big-blocks and among small-block 350 engines are the rocker-arms and shafts, lifters, and pushrods. The 1967–1969 rocker arms, rocker-arm shafts, pushrods, and lifters do not interchange with 1970-and-later engines.

Few parts interchange between the small-block and big-block engine families. Parts that do not interchange include the cylinder heads, crankshafts, camshafts, connecting rods, intake manifolds, front covers, oil pans, etc. While small-block and big-block engines have a similar appearance, they are completely different engines.

The internet is flooded with information regarding parts swapping among engines to achieve greater strength and performance. If you're building a budget performance engine, do further research. Most Buick engines are gone from junkyards, and those who are selling used high-performance parts are usually aware of their value. If you plan to purchase used parts, consult with an automotive machine shop to make sure that the parts are worth using, especially after any necessary machine work is carried out.

There is a large variety of new parts that are available for Buick engines at a reasonable price. It's usually best to go with new, high-quality parts instead of taking a chance on decades-old parts.

Engine Overhaul

To overhaul an engine means to restore the internal parts to new-engine specifications. At a minimum, an overhaul involves replacing the piston rings and reconditioning (honing or re-boring)

* Low-compression engines for export only. Horsepower and torque specifications are not available.

the cylinder bores. If the cylinders are re-bored, new pistons need to be installed. The main and connecting rod bearings need to be replaced, and if there is any damage to the crankshaft bearing journals, the crankshaft needs to be re-ground, which requires installing oversize bearings.

In addition, the cylinder heads need close attention. The sealing surfaces of the valves and seats need to be resurfaced, and the valve oil seals need to be replaced. The valve guides, springs, retainers, and seals must be inspected and replaced as needed. The camshaft and valvetrain components (rocker arms, pushrods, and lifters) need to be carefully inspected.

At the time of the overhaul, it is wise to replace the water pump, distributor, alternator, and starter. The goal is to have everything under the hood fresh and ready to deliver many years of trouble-free service.

There are no strict rules regarding mileage before an overhaul is needed. A Buick engine that has been driven normally, has had regular oil changes, and has not overheated can achieve 200,000 miles before an overhaul is needed. Conversely, an engine that has been neglected or has seriously overheated can fail very early in its life. Use diagnosis, which is covered in chapter 3, to determine the condition of the engine.

Overheating is the most common cause of early engine failure. For this reason, it's essential to replace cooling-system components at the time of the overhaul to make sure that the new engine will last. Always replace the cooling-system hoses, water pump, and thermostat. Service the radiator or replace it with a new one.

Before beginning the overhaul, read through this book and become familiar with the requirements and scope of the process. An engine over-

Used Buick engines are available at some salvage yards. While they provide a quick and inexpensive solution, assessing the condition of the internal components is usually a guess. In addition, there are many small variations among engines of different years and models that can provide potential headaches.

haul is straightforward with the correct tools and equipment. However, the job is time-consuming. Even if you think the overhaul will be simple, plan on the vehicle being unusable for several weeks. Overhauls almost always take more time than expected, as there are often unforeseen delays with scheduling machine work and obtaining parts.

Overhaul Alternatives

Sometimes, inspecting and reconditioning the original parts is not the best option when accounting for the cost of the parts, machine work, and time. If the engine block, heads, and crankshaft are in reasonably good condition, the overhaul can usually be performed at a low cost. However, if a major component is badly worn or damaged, the job will be much more costly and time-consuming. If this is the case, consider other options.

Engine parts suppliers frequently sell reconditioned kits that include a re-ground crankshaft, connecting rods, pistons, bearings, and rings. The kits are ready to install and may also include the gaskets and seals needed to reassemble the engine block. Some machine work on the block is still required, such as a cylinder re-bore, align-honing the main bearing journals, and resurfacing the cylinder-head gasket surface, which is commonly known as "decking."

A short-block is a complete engine-block assembly, including the crankshaft, pistons, connecting rods, bearings, rings, camshaft, oil pump, timing chain, and seals. The existing cylinder heads and valvetrain can be bolted into place (assuming that those parts are in good condition).

Long-blocks are basically short-blocks with new or rebuilt cylinder heads installed. Long-blocks have the valvetrain components installed and correctly adjusted. If a long-block is purchased, the only work that needs to be performed is installing the engine covers and external components. In addition, long-blocks frequently have warranties, which is another good reason to go this route.

Salvage yards regularly have used engines available and may provide a brief warranty so you can verify that the engine runs normally after it has been installed into the vehicle. You can usually save a significant amount of time and money by selecting a used engine, but there is also a risk of major engine problems arising in a short time. If possible, try to find an engine that can be inspected before it has been removed from the vehicle so that you can verify the mileage and the condition of the fluids as well as hear and see how it runs. In addition, if the vehicle has been wrecked, this shows that the engine was running prior to the crash and is more likely to be in good condition.

TOOLS, EQUIPMENT, AND SUPPLIES

An engine overhaul requires a significant investment in tools and equipment. Some items can be rented or borrowed, but it is possible to spend hundreds of dollars on tools and equipment by the time the job is complete. This chapter helps you understand the tools of the trade because access to these tools is a factor to determine the level of work that you can do on your own.

Only purchase the tools and equipment that reflect your future plans and interest in engine overhauling. If this will be your only engine overhaul and/or you are on a budget, purchase only the basic tools and equipment and borrow or rent the rest. If you're interested in learning more about overhauling an engine and may overhaul another engine in the future, you may want to buy some items that aren't essential but that you might reuse.

When it comes to hand tools that will receive heavy use, make sure they are good quality, made of forged steel, and are sold by a reputable manufacturer. Look at brands such as Craftsman, Stanley, Gearwrench, SK Tools, and Icon (a Harbor Freight

Wear safety glasses whenever you're working. Most eye injuries happen when they are least expected. Wear a mask whenever there's debris in the air, such as when cleaning parts.

brand). It isn't necessary to buy the best of the best, but you also don't want to buy bargain-basement quality. If you do, you will regret that decision.

Access to a full workshop or even a garage is not required to perform an overhaul, but a workspace is essential. The area must be organized, safe,

When doing heavy work, such as engine removal, wear gloves. Mechanic's gloves are lightweight and offer protection from grease and scratches. Latex gloves provide protection from grease and harsh chemicals.

and clean. It is best if the work area is indoors, but a sheltered outdoor area can be enough if there is an indoor area available to store parts.

When working with flammable materials, especially gasoline and solvents, be prepared by having a fire extinguisher in the vicinity. When an engine is fired up for the first time, small fires can occur from fuel leaks and backfiring.

A disassembled engine takes up more space than you might expect. Be sure there is plenty of shelf space to store the parts—preferably not a closet! Parts that have been removed from an old engine are very dirty, and shouldn't be stored in a living space. Inexpensive cabinets with plastic drawers are available, and cardboard boxes work well too. Label all of the parts and store related items together wherever possible.

It's almost impossible to carry out an engine overhaul without a workbench. The bench should be capable of handling about 100 pounds because it needs to support heavy components, such as the crankshaft and cylinder heads. Inexpensive benches are available, or a workbench can be easily built with 2x4 lumber and 1/2-inch plywood. A bench vise is a great accessory that will be used frequently.

Work should not be done without the appropriate safety equipment. Whatever job is being performed, first think about what type of protection is needed. Use safety glasses and gloves frequently. In addition, a fire extinguisher and respirator should be available whenever you are working with hazardous or flammable liquids.

General-Purpose Tools

A basic set of general-purpose tools is required to do any level of work during an overhaul. Many of these tools are essential, while others are nice to have but are not essential. The following basic tool list is required for an engine overhaul. Additional tools will likely be needed, depending on the issues that are encountered.

- Society of Automotive Engineers (SAE) combination wrench set (3/8-inch through 1-inch sizes)
- Adjustable wrench (10 inch)
- Flare-nut wrench set
- 3/8-inch-drive SAE socket set (3/8-inch through 1-inch sizes)
- 1/2-inch breaker bar
- 1/2-inch-drive to 3/8-inch-drive reducing adapter
- Torque wrench (1/2-inch drive with a range of 20 to 120 ft-lbs)
- Screwdrivers (various sizes, lengths, and tip types)
- Allen wrenches
- Slip-joint pliers
- Locking pliers
- Long-nose pliers
- Ball-peen hammer
- Rubber mallet
- Feeler gauge set (flat and wire type)
- Gasket scraper
- Small wire brushes and plastic-bristle brushes (for cleaning oil passages)
- Small machinist's ruler (measures in 64ths of an inch)
- SAE tap and die set
- Floor jack (can sometimes be rented)

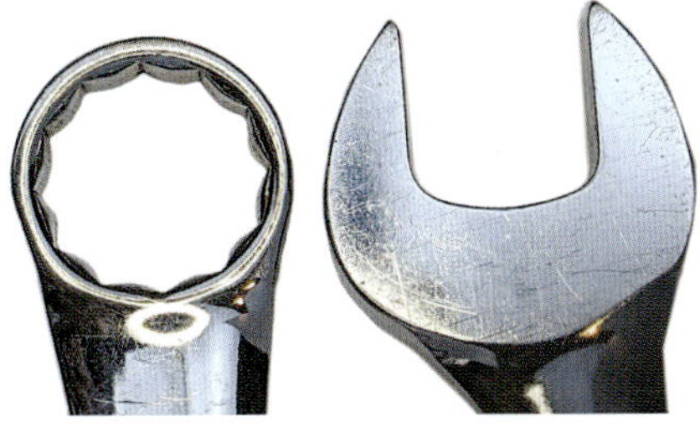

A box-end wrench (left) engages a hex head on all six sides. Use it whenever there is sufficient access around the head. An open-end wrench engages only two flats and is, therefore, more prone to slipping and damaging fasteners. Use it only when access is limited or on square-head fasteners. These are two of the most useful types of wrenches.

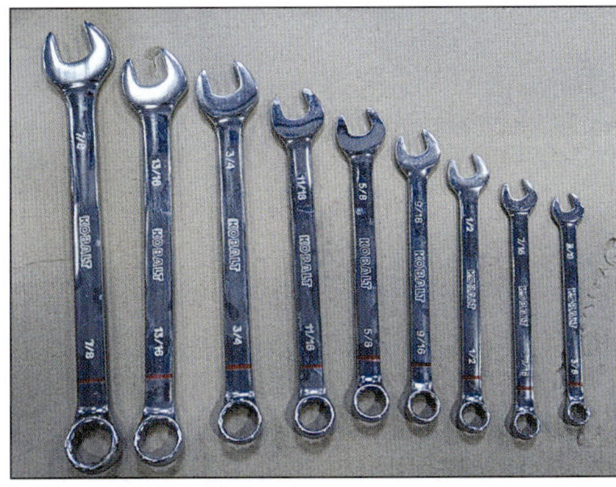

Start with a quality set of combination wrenches. Beginning in the early 1970s, Buicks used some metric fasteners, so it's best to buy both SAE and metric wrenches.

A machinist-type vise is one of the most useful and versatile tools in a shop. A good one is expensive, but it will last a lifetime and be helpful for many types of projects.

Wrenches and sockets are available in 6-point or 12-point designs. Six-point wrenches provide a stronger grip on the fastener but have fewer engagement angles than the 12-point design. Use 6-point wrenches and sockets whenever possible. Buick connecting-rod nuts that have a 12-point head and need a 12-point 9/16-inch socket are a notable exception.

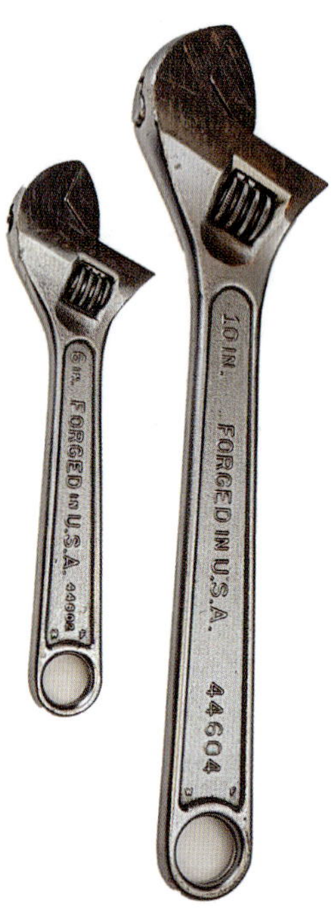

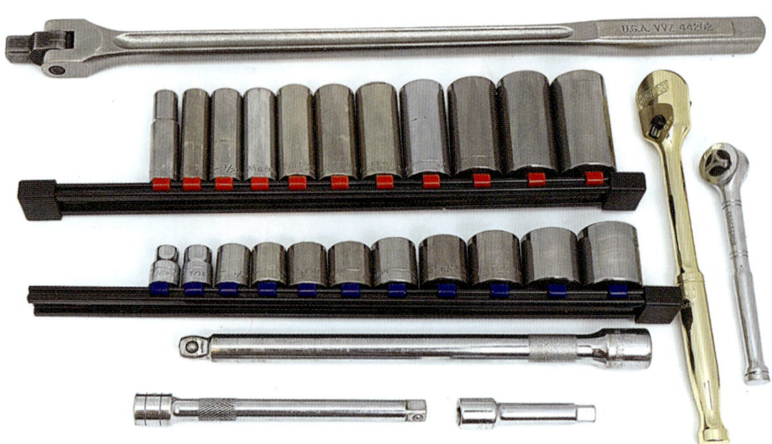

The majority of the fasteners that are involved with a Buick engine overhaul can be removed with 3/8-inch-drive standard sockets. Most of the bolts on Buicks are SAE sizes, but starting in about 1973, there was a slow integration of metric fasteners. So, metric sockets are needed for later-model vehicles.

Adjustable wrenches are handy but do not grip fasteners very tightly. They can be used as backup wrenches when tightening bolts that have nuts on the other end or when bolts don't need to be very tight. During use, turn the wrench in the direction where the pressure is against the permanent jaw.

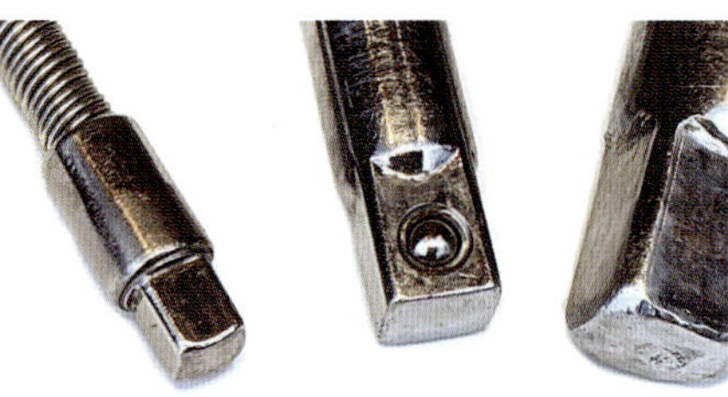

Three socket drive sizes are commonly used: 1/4 inch, 3/8 inch, and 1/2 inch. The 3/8-inch drive (in the center) is the most common. For a starter set, get a 3/8-inch drive and build onto it when you have the budget for more tools. A 1/2-inch-drive breaker bar and an adapter to a 3/8-inch drive is convenient and can be used to remove extremely tight bolts.

A torque wrench is essential. It must be used when tightening critical fasteners, such as the main bearing cap bolts, connecting-rod cap nuts, cylinder-head bolts, and intake manifold bolts. The click-style wrenches (shown) are reasonably priced and have good accuracy. In addition, digital-style torque wrenches are available, but they are more expensive.

This type of wrench is called a flare-nut wrench, a tubing wrench, or a line wrench. It's used for threaded fittings on fuel lines, transmission-fluid lines, and power-steering lines. Don't try to loosen line fittings with an open-end wrench because it will damage the fitting.

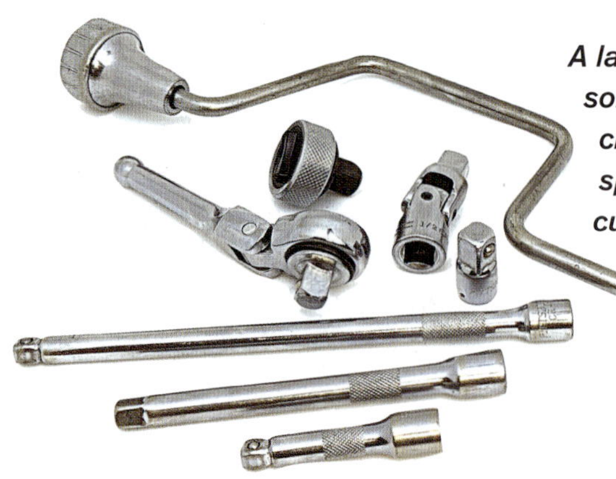

A large variety of socket drive accessories are available to extend reach, change the angle, or increase the speed of the removal process. The curved speed handle shaves off some time when a job requires removing many bolts, such as removing the oil pan.

A beam-type torque wrench is the cheapest option. If you purchase one from a quality brand, it will usually do the job well enough. However, the digital- or click-type torque wrenches are more accurate and are highly recommended. A torque wrench will likely be used for other jobs after the overhaul has been completed.

Use pliers and other gripping tools only when wrenches or sockets are not appropriate. Do not use these tools to tighten or loosen nuts or bolts, unless you are using it as a last resort on a damaged fastener.

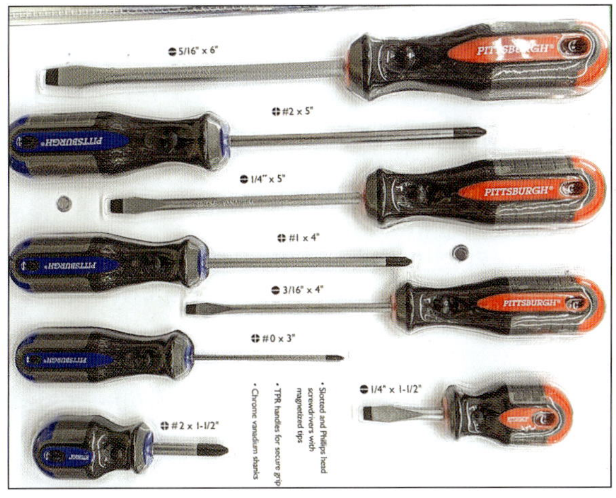

Screwdrivers are relatively cheap, so get a set with a wide variety of lengths and sizes. Spend a little extra for a quality brand, such as Craftsman, Stanley, etc.

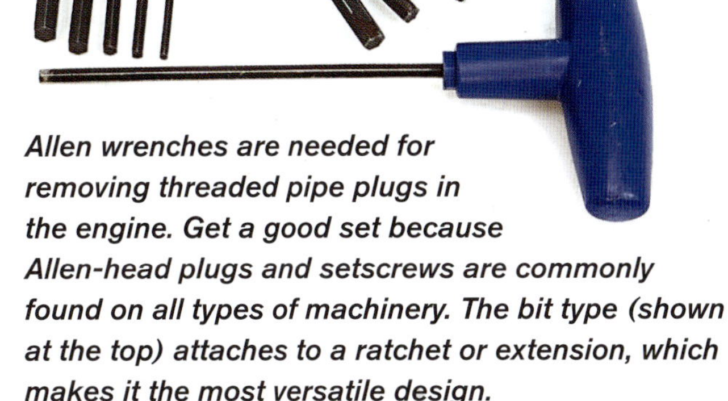

Allen wrenches are needed for removing threaded pipe plugs in the engine. Get a good set because Allen-head plugs and setscrews are commonly found on all types of machinery. The bit type (shown at the top) attaches to a ratchet or extension, which makes it the most versatile design.

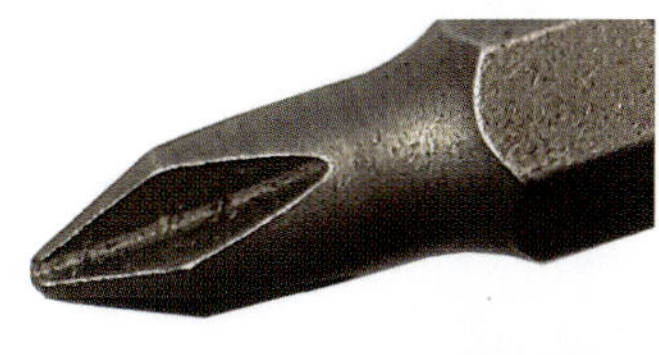

Phillips screwdrivers are not all the same. It's important to select the correct tip size that matches the screw. From top to bottom are size numbers 1, 2, and 3. This range of sizes covers most automotive work. Test the various sizes until the best fit is found and make sure that the tip is not worn. Phillips screw heads are easily stripped.

A wide variety of hammer sizes and types are available. A medium-size steel hammer is required, and a ball-peen hammer and a soft-face hammer are preferred.

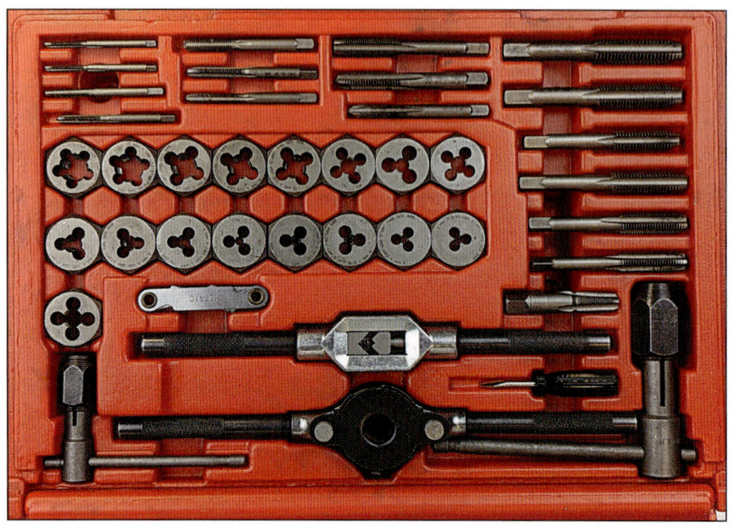

A tap-and-die set is needed to clean the threads on critical engine fasteners. It is common to need them to repair damaged threads, which is often encountered on older engines.

A quality floor jack works well to access the underside of the vehicle. During an overhaul, it is needed to support the transmission when the engine is being removed. Use jack stands whenever you're underneath the vehicle. Never rely solely on the jack.

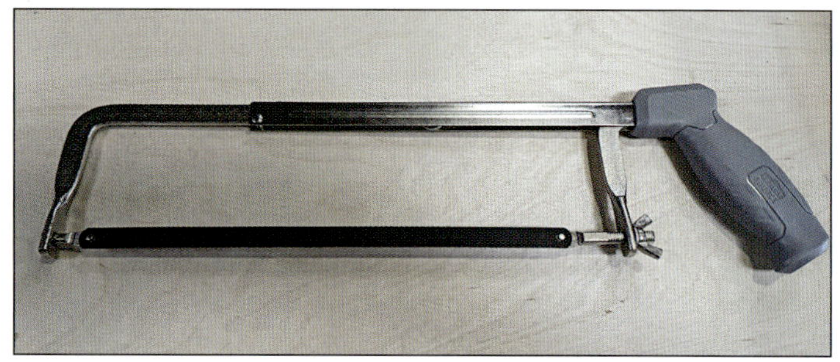

Although a hacksaw may not be needed for an engine overhaul, it is helpful for tasks such as cutting oversize bolts to length.

Feeler gauges are manufactured to precise thicknesses and are used to measure clearances between surfaces. To use them, slide gauges of different thicknesses into the gap that you want to measure. One will slide through with a bit of resistance. The number on the gauge is the clearance. Wire-type feeler gauges are used to measure spark-plug gaps, but I use them to measure hydraulic-lifter preload.

A variety of brushes and scrapers are needed to clean the engine.

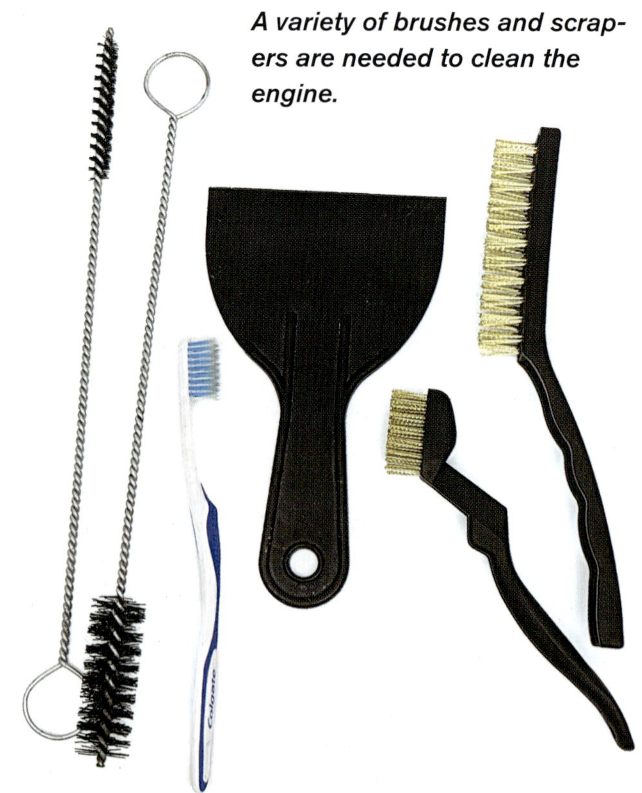

Punches and chisels will likely be necessary during the overhaul, and it's economical to buy them in a set. Make sure that they are designed for metal work. Wood chisels become dull very quickly.

Broken bolts require a variety of solutions. A nut splitter (top) works when a nut is stuck. Bolt extractors (center left) can unscrew a broken bolt after a hole has been drilled into the bolt. The round tool (center right) grabs a broken bolt's shank. External extractors (bottom) grab the outside of a bolt's broken shank.

If you replace the power-steering pump, this type of special puller will likely be needed to remove the pulley and transfer it to the new pump.

If the bolt holes become stripped or damaged, they can be repaired with threaded inserts. The most popular brand to use is HeliCoil. To use a threaded insert, drill the bolt hole oversize, use the tap as the instructions specify, and then spin the threaded insert into place. It is a permanent repair that uses the same bolt size.

While files are not always necessary during an engine overhaul, they are useful for deburring after cutting and machining operations.

A jaw-type puller may be needed to remove the crankshaft timing gear. A variety of pullers are available, but I recommend getting a three-jaw type. They are the most commonly available and are strong and versatile. Two-jaw pullers can get into tighter places, but they are not as strong.

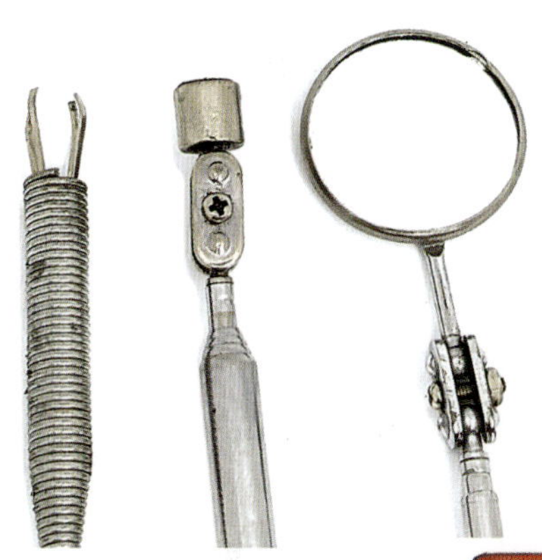

Pick-up tools with long telescopic handles are inexpensive and can be used when a fastener or tool is dropped into an otherwise-inaccessible area. The magnetic tool (center) is easier to use than the claw (left). A mirror on a telescoping handle (right) can help you locate a fastener that has been dropped.

For removing small components from blind holes, a slide-hammer puller set is extremely valuable. During an engine overhaul, it's most commonly used for removing lifters that are stuck in their bores and pilot bearings from the rear of the crankshaft.

Power Tools

Power tools increase efficiency, and they may be required for various situations encountered during an overhaul. If a fastener breaks, it likely will need to be drilled out. With an impact gun, it is much easier to deal with stubborn bolts in rotating components.

If you're on a budget, wait until the need arises for power tools.

Using a die grinder with abrasive pads makes the job of cleaning gasket surfaces easy. A pneumatic die grinder is shown. Electric die grinders are available if you don't have an air compressor.

Electric or air-powered impact tools increase the speed of the disassembly process and are great for removing fasteners at the center of rotating components, such as the camshaft and crankshaft. Since they deliver a rapid pulse of impacts, the bolt will break loose before the shaft can turn. Do not use impact tools during reassembly.

A drill and drill bits may be needed to deal with broken fasteners, and the type of bit matters. Bits need to be high-speed steel (HSS), black-oxide coated, titanium coated, or cobalt coated. The higher-quality bits are more expensive but do the job better and last longer. Never use woodworking bits.

A bench grinder is an essential tool for any well-equipped shop. In addition to grinding metal parts, wire-wheel attachments can be a massive help to clean small parts. Use a wire wheel with extremely fine bristles to clean the engine.

Pneumatic tools can be used with an air compressor. In addition, high-pressure air can be used to clean or dry parts. Place a nozzle on the end of an air hose to create the perfect tool for blowing out the various passages in the cylinder block and heads. Be sure to wear safety glasses.

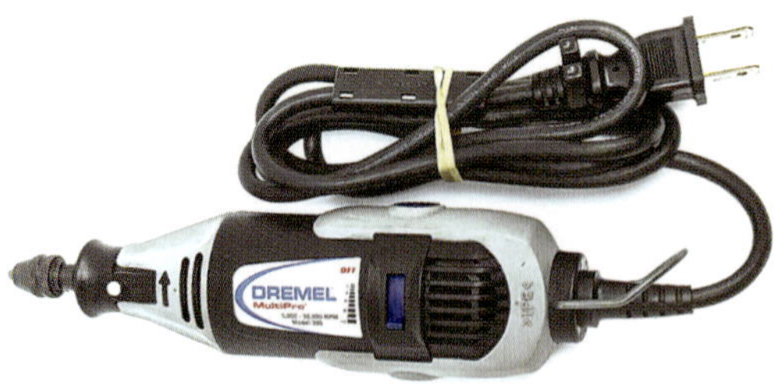

Although rotary tools are commonly used by hobbyists, they are also used by mechanics. They work well for cleaning small parts and for cutting off stuck fasteners in areas that are difficult to access.

Grinding wheels are designed to be used on steel and iron, which shed molten bits (sparks) during grinding. Don't grind aluminum with a grinding wheel, as it does not shed the metal. Instead, the aluminum adheres to the wheel, ruining it.

Special Tools and Equipment for an Overhaul

Several specialty tools and equipment are specifically used to overhaul engines. Depending on how much of the disassembly and reassembly you plan to do yourself, not all of them may be needed. An engine hoist and stand will be needed, and both can be rented.

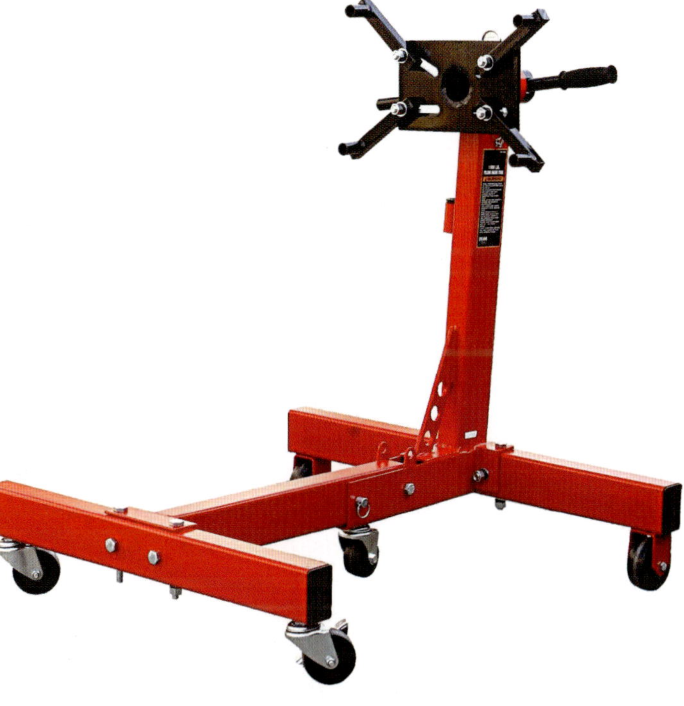

An engine stand is required. It must be rated to hold at least 500 pounds. Engine stands are available to rent, but it often makes more financial sense to buy one because you may need the stand longer than you anticipated. If you purchase a stand, you have the option to sell it after completing the overhaul.

An engine hoist is required for removing and installing an engine. Engine hoists are commonly available from equipment rental companies. Do not attempt to remove the engine using an A-frame hoist or by attaching a chain to a roof rafter.

If you plan to disassemble the cylinder head yourself, a valve-spring compressor is needed. The C-clamp type (surrounding the two other compressors) is the fastest and easiest to use, but it's also the most expensive.

If you plan to assemble the cylinder heads, purchase a valve-lapping tool to confirm that the valve work was done correctly.

When removing or installing an engine, an engine tilter can help significantly. Attached between the hoist and the engine, the tilter can move the engine to the exact angle that is needed. Often, the engine needs to be re-angled during the removal process or installation process, and that is difficult to do without this tool.

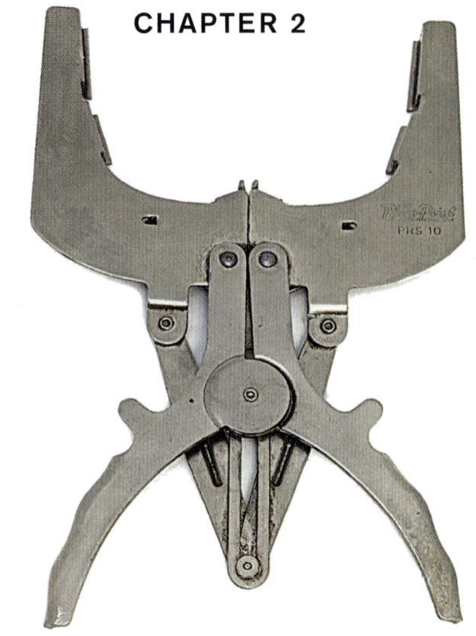

Precision Measuring Tools

The difference between a serviceable engine part and a worn-out engine part is measured in thousandths of an inch. If you've never overhauled an engine before, have an expert take the critical measurements to avoid making any mistakes. If you decide to take the measurements yourself, purchasing the precision tools is expensive. A dial indicator or digital indicator and a micrometer are typically used when inspecting and reassembling an engine.

This tool is used to measure the valve spring's installed height. A caliper can be used to try to measure the installed height, but there's some trial-and-error involved, and readings may not be accurate. This tool is accurate and allows you to perform the job efficiently.

When installing the piston rings on the pistons, they need to be expanded to fit over the piston's head. If you try to do this by hand, some of them will likely break because they're brittle cast iron. Use a piston-ring expander to install the rings.

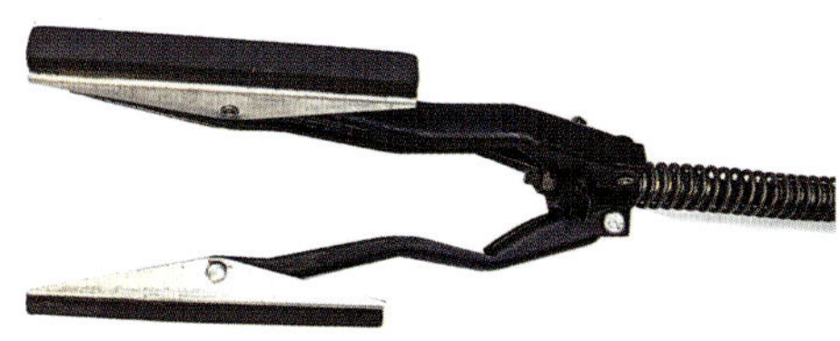

Drill-operated cylinder hones require skill to achieve a proper finish in the cylinder bores. Leave cylinder honing to a professional who has better equipment and skills. If the surface finish is not correct, the rings will not seat correctly.

The piston rings need to be compressed when the pistons are installed in the cylinders. This job cannot be done by hand. A ring compressor is required. Several types of ring compressors are available. The type that is shown uses a ratcheting pliers–type tool to pinch an appropriately sized band around the piston.

While performing inspections, a dial indicator or digital indicator that precisely measures up-and-down movement is needed. Inexpensive indicators are available, but I recommend using a quality indicator to ensure accuracy. Many of the latest designs have digital readouts and are easy to use.

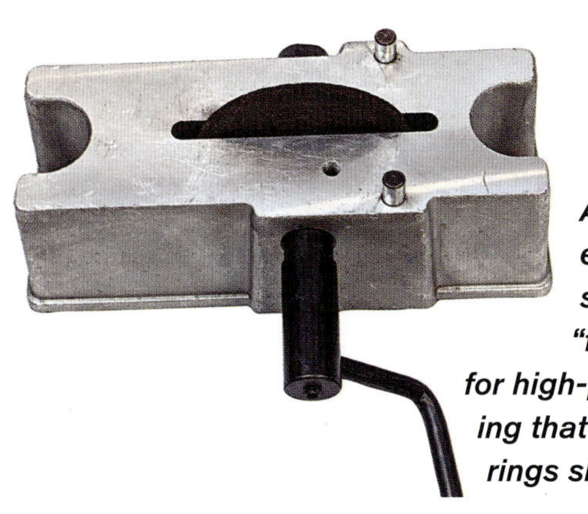

A piston-ring filer is needed when the ring end-gap clearance is less than the official specification. Filing is essential if you use "file-to-fit" rings, which are commonly used for high-performance and racing engines. Assuming that the machine work is correct, standard rings should not require any filing.

A dial indicator or digital indicator can only be as accurate as the stability of its mounting base. Bases have various methods of attaching the gauge to the base and attaching the base to the mounting surface. A magnetic base and a clamp-on base are shown. At the rear are solid rods with pivots that are obsolete. Most mechanics prefer a flexible connector between the gauge and the base.

Micrometers are the ultimate tool for precision dimensional measurements. Quality is important, so don't purchase a cheap micrometer. Many modern micrometers have digital readouts and are easy to read.

Reading a Micrometer

The markings on a traditional micrometer can be confusing and intimidating. Today, those who are learning the basics of precision measuring are likely to purchase a digital micrometer to avoid the process of learning to read a traditional micrometer. However, once you know how to read an old-school micrometer, you'll be glad that you do. They are less expensive than the digital type, and they are more reliable because there is no need to worry about battery failure or damage to the digital display.

A confusing aspect regarding micrometer markings is that there are markings on the thimble (the part that rotates) and the sleeve (the part that does not rotate). Both of these sets of markings are used in conjunction with each other to obtain a measurement.

One full rotation of the thimble (360 degrees) moves the spindle (the moving part that contacts the item being measured) by 0.025 inch. There are 25 marks around the spindle, and each one represents 0.001 inch.

Each mark on the sleeve indicates 0.025 inch of rotation. So, rotating the thimble one full revolution moves the thimble from one mark on the sleeve to the next mark on the sleeve. After every four marks on the sleeve is a number. The number represents 0.1 inch of movement. So, four turns of the thimble equals four marks uncovered on the sleeve, which is 0.1 (one-tenth, or 100 thousandths) of an inch. So, what if the thimble rotates 40 times? It represents 1 inch.

Remembering that one full rotation of the spindle is 0.025 inch, there are 25 graduations on the thimble. What does each of these marks represent? They each represent one thousandth of an inch.

A trick for reading a micrometer is to think of the marks as money. Each mark on the sleeve represents a quarter, and the numbers represent dollars. On the thimble, each mark represents a penny. So, add it up the same way that you would add up the money in your pocket! ■

Starting from zero on the sleeve, there are five lines. That's $1.25 (five quarters). The thimble is rotated past the number three on the thimble. So, add 3 cents to the total, and the equation equals $1.28. Now, take away the dollar sign and move the decimal point one space to the left. The measurement is 0.128 inch.

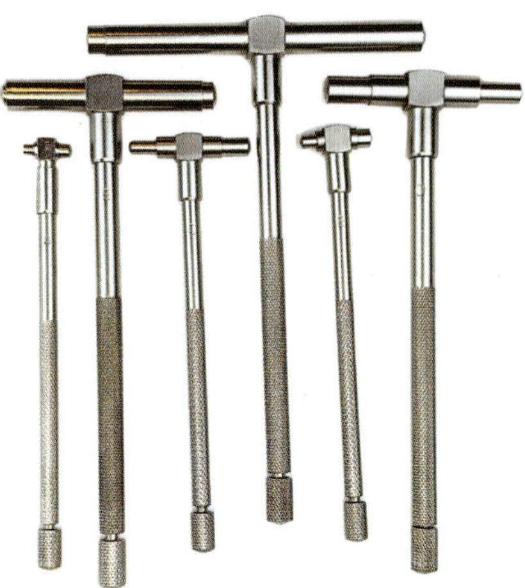

Telescoping gauges make it possible to measure the engine bores without internal measuring tools. The gauge is expanded to the size of the bore and locked. Then, a micrometer is used to measure the gauge. It takes practice to do this precisely.

Even if you have purchased a set of micrometers, you should purchase calipers. Calipers can measure up to 6 inches and can be found at a reasonable price. They allow for quick measurements. However, don't make major machining decisions based on these readings. Calipers are not as accurate as micrometers.

A cylinder-bore gauge is necessary to obtain accurate readings on a worn engine. Cylinders do not wear evenly. Normal wear causes the cylinders to become tapered and out of round. Bore gauges are expensive, and the machine shop will almost certainly have one.

Test Equipment

Before beginning an engine overhaul, gain a thorough understanding of your engine problems. Knowledge of these problems will help to guide the inspections. Be sure to find the problems that were causing the symptoms that led to the overhaul.

After the overhaul is complete, confirm that the engine is in top running condition. Perform a compression test after the first few thousand miles of driving and compare those readings to what was recorded before the overhaul.

Chapter 3 covers the diagnostic methods to employ while using diagnostic tools. Depending on the symptoms, some of these diagnostic tools may be required to confirm that an overhaul is required.

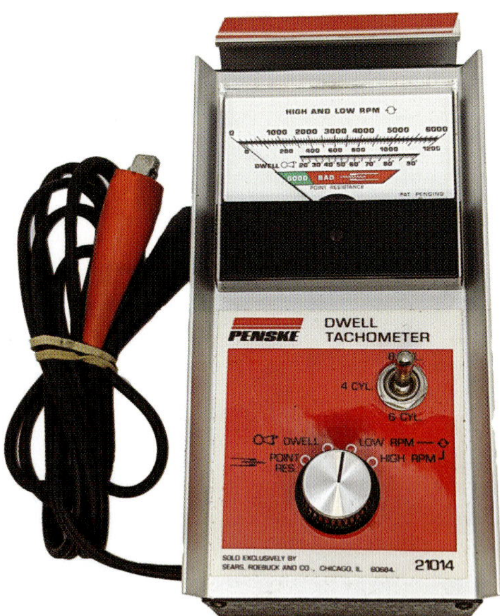

Even if the vehicle has a tachometer on the dash, it's unlikely to be accurate at low RPM. When adjusting the idle speed or looking for small variations in the engine speed (such as during a power-balance test), use a diagnostic tachometer (shown).

A timing light is essential for checking ignition timing, and it can be used to identify problems related to the ignition system. When performance tuning, "dial back" is a great feature to have, which allows you to check the distributor's advance curve.

This small tool is used to confirm that an adequate spark is being delivered to the spark plug. It is useful when diagnosing rough-running or no-start problems.

This inexpensive tool keeps you from getting shocked during a power-balance test. It grips the spark-plug wire terminal securely for removal but is made of plastic, which prevents you from getting shocked. It also helps to keep your hand at a safe distance from the hot exhaust manifolds.

After installing an engine, it's common to find new electrical problems caused by pinched wires or incorrectly installed electrical connectors. An inexpensive multimeter is helpful to diagnose these problems.

A remote starter switch is not required but is very handy when performing a compression test or aligning timing marks. It is connected between the positive terminal on the battery and the "S" terminal on the starter. Squeezing the trigger cranks the engine. Make sure the ignition system is disabled so that the engine doesn't start.

A combustion-leak detector identifies if any combustion gases are finding their way into the cooling system. Combustion gases in the coolant usually indicate a blown head gasket but can also be caused by a cracked cylinder head or engine block.

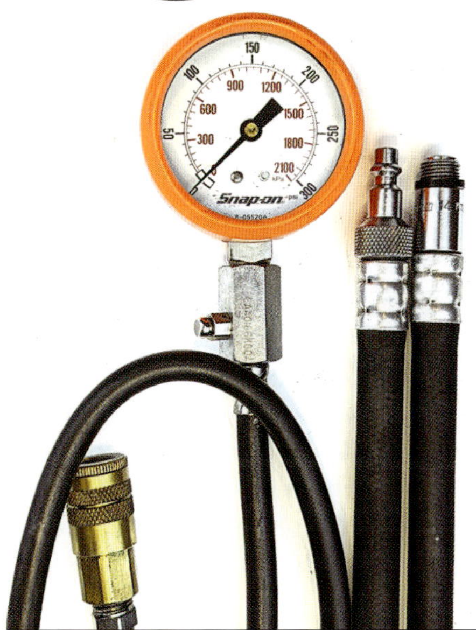

A stethoscope is handy for pinpointing where noises are occurring in an engine compartment.

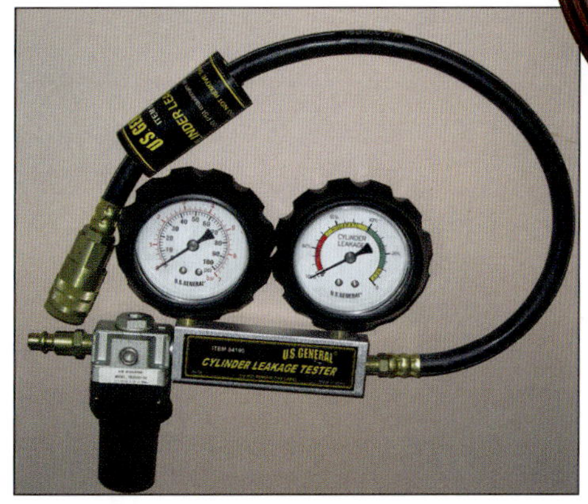

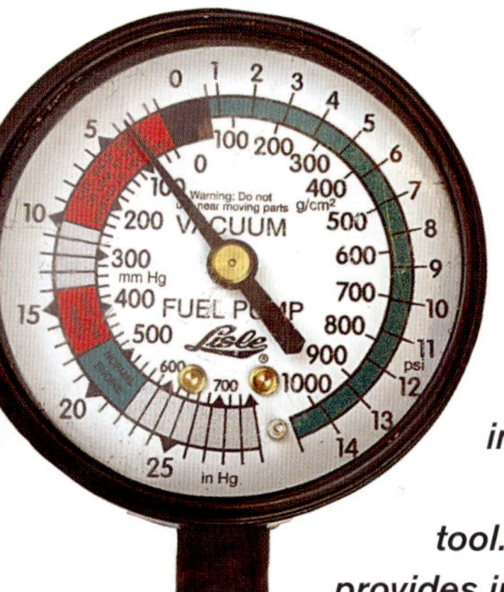

A vacuum gauge is an essential and inexpensive diagnostic tool. Chapter 3 provides instructions regarding its proper use.

A cylinder leakage tester, or leak-down tester, is needed to perform a leak-down test on an engine with low compression. It helps you find the source of the compression leak and indicates the percentage of leakage occurring in the cylinder.

A compression tester is an essential diagnostic tool. It is relatively inexpensive and can reveal many problems within an engine.

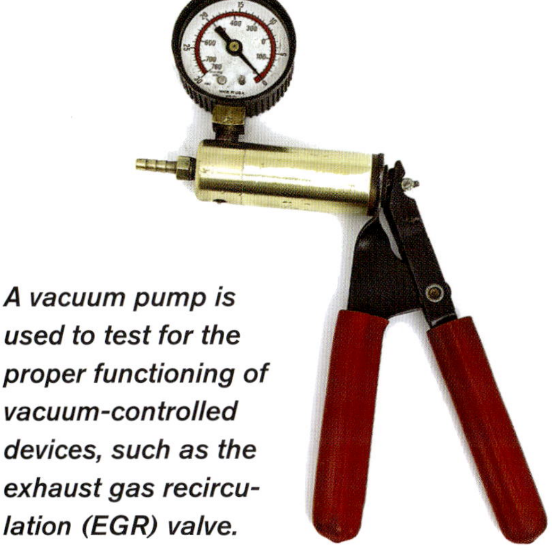

A vacuum pump is used to test for the proper functioning of vacuum-controlled devices, such as the exhaust gas recirculation (EGR) valve.

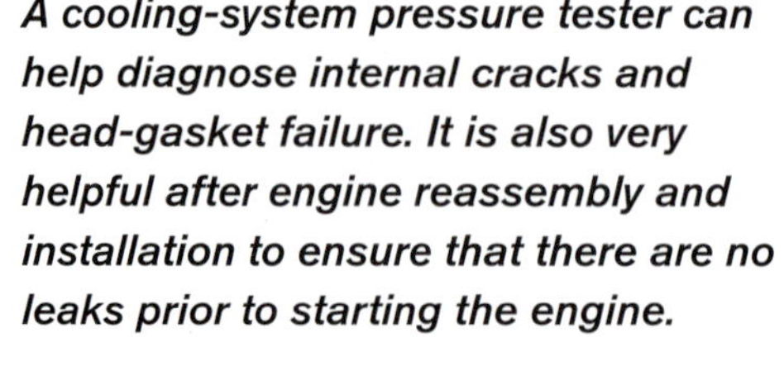

A cooling-system pressure tester can help diagnose internal cracks and head-gasket failure. It is also very helpful after engine reassembly and installation to ensure that there are no leaks prior to starting the engine.

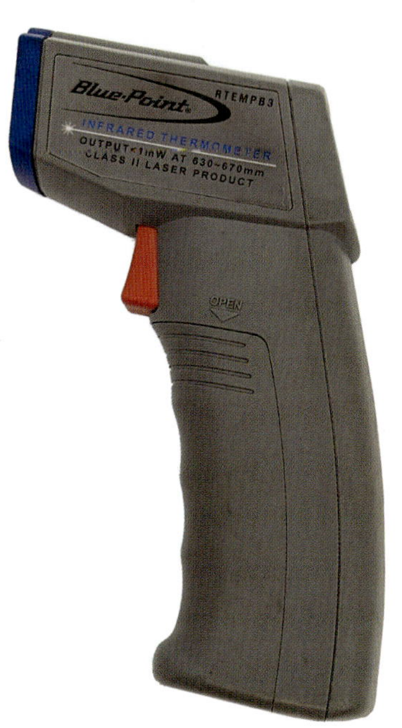

An infrared thermometer allows you to determine the temperature of a component from a distance. It is great for checking the relative temperature of the cylinders. Check each exhaust manifold runner or header tube where it exits the head. The temperatures should be very similar across the board. A cylinder that is not firing will have a lower temperature.

Oil-pressure gauges are commonly available from auto-parts suppliers. One can also be fabricated with a mechanical pressure gauge with a range of 0 to 100 psi—just make sure that the connections and hoses are capable of handling the pressure.

Fastener Sizes

Later-model Buicks have a mixture of standard fasteners and metric fasteners. You must be able to identify the differences so that you can use the appropriate tool.

Bolts are identified by their diameter, thread pitch, and strength rating. A 3/8-16 Grade-5 bolt has a 3/8-inch diameter, 16 threads per inch, and a Grade-5 strength rating. This is a common bolt on a Buick engine. The head of the bolt has three radial lines. Radial lines on the head are the easiest way to identify a standard bolt. However, low-grade standard bolts (Grade 1 or Grade 2) do not have any marks on the head. This makes them easily confused with metric bolts because some metric bolts do not have markings on their heads, either.

Metric bolts are also identified by their diameter, thread pitch, and strength rating. A common metric bolt size is M10-1.5, 8.8. This is a bolt with a 10-mm diameter, 1.5 mm between threads (thread pitch), and a strength rating of 8.8. There are three common strength ratings on metric bolts: 8.8, 9.8, and 10.9. The higher the number, the higher the strength rating. For purposes of identification, the metric strength marking on the head (8.8, 9.8, or 10.9) is the giveaway.

In some situations, it is difficult to determine which wrench or socket to use. On late-model Buicks, there's always a chance of encountering metric fasteners. Don't use a tool that fits too loosely on the bolt or nut head. If you do, it will round off the corners of the fastener. The following information may help when you are selecting the correct tool and/or determining if it's standard or metric.

An SAE bolt is on the left. The six radial lines indicate its strength grade, which is Grade 8. To determine an SAE bolt's strength grade, add two to the number of lines on the head of the bolt. A metric bolt head is on the right. The metric bolt's strength rating (8.8) is indicated by the number on the head of the bolt.

Fastener Approximate Torque Range	
US Size	**Approximate Torque Range**
1/4-20	5 to 10 ft-lbs
5/16-18	12 to 18 ft-lbs
3/8-16	20 to 30 ft-lbs
3/8-24	25 to 40 ft-lbs
7/16-14	40 to 50 ft-lbs
7/16-20	40 to 60 ft-lbs
1/2-13	55 to 80 ft-lbs

Metric Size	Approximate Torque Range
M-6	5 to 10 ft-lbs
M-8	15 to 20 ft-lbs
M-10	30 to 40 ft-lbs
M-12	50 to 70 ft-lbs
M-14	80 to 140 ft-lbs

1. 3/8 inch is slightly smaller than 10 mm. This is usually a close-but-incorrect fit. If the 3/8-inch tool is slightly too small, a 10-mm tool will most likely fit.
2. 7/16 inch is almost exactly 11 mm. Either size of wrench or socket will work interchangeably.
3. 1/2 inch is slightly smaller than 13 mm, and a 13 mm wrench or socket fits too loosely on a 1/2-inch fastener head to be used safely.
4. 9/16 inch is almost exactly 14 mm. Either size of wrench or socket will work interchangeably.
5. The 5/8-inch size is slightly bigger than 16 mm. A 5/8-inch wrench or socket will work on a 16-mm bolt, but the converse does not usually work.
6. The 11/16-inch size is larger than 17 mm but smaller than 18 mm. They are not close. Use the correct tool.
7. The 3/4-inch size is about 19 mm. The tools can be used interchangeably.

Torque

Critical fasteners have torque specifications that must be followed (specifications are listed in the appendix). However, sometimes the torque specifications are not listed. In those cases, the following information may help.

Consider the fastener's strength rating and material when applying a torque value. This is the reason that a range and not a single number is provided. For example, a short, low-strength bolt threading into aluminum should be torqued toward the low end of the torque range, but a long, high-strength bolt going into cast iron can handle torque toward the top of the torque range.

Cleaning Chemicals

Engine degreaser is commonly available from auto-parts stores. It is a heavy-duty solvent designed

Engine degreaser (left) is the harshest of these cleaners. Carburetor cleaner (center) is not as harsh but leaves a slight residue. Brake parts cleaner is the safest of the three. It does not leave a residue and won't damage most plastic or rubber.

to break down the thick accumulation of gunk on an engine. For the best results, use it while the engine is warm and before the engine is removed from the vehicle. Use plenty (two large cans), let it soak in, brush the gunk as much as possible, and use high-pressure water to wash it off.

Two common varieties of spray solvents are available from any auto-parts store: brake parts cleaner and carburetor cleaner.

Brake parts cleaner is best for light cleaning, especially on gasket surfaces. Originally designed to protect the rubber seals in brake systems, it is the preferred cleaner when rubber and plastic are involved. Brake parts cleaner leaves behind a perfectly clean surface, making it ideal for final assembly when gasket mating surfaces have to be perfectly clean.

Carburetor cleaner is another aerosol cleaner solvent. It is more aggressive than brake cleaner and is ideal for removing gum, varnish, and carbon. It also contains a small amount of lubricant that dries and remains on surfaces, even though it's almost impossible to detect. This residue generally doesn't matter for engine-cleaning purposes, but carburetor cleaner should not be used for the final cleaning of gasket surfaces.

Penetrating Oil

A can of penetrating oil is a must-have item for rusted fasteners, particularly on exhaust components that are often frozen in place by heat cycling over the years.

Locking Compound

Locking compounds, commonly known by the brand name Loctite, can be used on external bolts that might vibrate loose during operation. Locking compounds are commonly used on flywheel, flexplate, and harmonic balancer bolts. For these purposes, use the blue variety, which is designed to allow the bolts to be removed later. The red variety is for permanent installations that will never be disassembled.

Lubricants

When assembling an engine, it's essential that all moving parts are protected from wear. When an engine first starts, it is brought quickly to a raised RPM level. Without adequate protection, an initial dry start could ruin the engine.

For main and connecting-rod bearings, a thick assembly lube is required to protect the bearings until an adequate oil film builds up. For camshafts and lifters (especially conventional flat lifters), a special camshaft lubricant is available that provides enhanced lubrication for camshaft lobes and lifter faces, which are under extreme pressure during break-in.

Standard engine oil should be used in cylinder bores and on piston rings. Don't use a thick lubricant in the cylinders because it is good to have some friction between the rings and cylinder walls to be sure that break-in occurs quickly. If the break-in is delayed, a glaze can form on the cylinder walls, which can prevent ring break-in from ever happening.

Sealants

When assembling an engine, care must be taken to ensure that there will be no leaks. Over the years, new sealants and sealing techniques have been developed that are superior to the factory methods. These techniques are included in chapter 7.

DIAGNOSIS

This chapter covers diagnostic checks that must precede engine mechanical work. Engine diagnosis requires a careful, systematic approach to avoid unnecessary work and confirm that there are serious problems with an engine before removing it from the vehicle.

Incorrect diagnosis is common—even by professionals. Always confirm your assumptions with thorough testing. In addition, it's wise to consult with a Buick engine expert. Getting a second opinion is always a good idea.

Some Buick engines were manufactured during a time before electronic control systems. Routine adjustments and other maintenance are required to keep these engines running well. Attention to the spark plugs, plug wires, distributor cap/rotor, ignition timing, and carburetor adjustments can greatly improve an engine's performance and fuel economy.

Oil additives with detergents, such as Sea Foam and Marvel Mystery Oil, can sometimes help a stuck valve lifter break free or solve other issues related to combustion deposits and sludge that has accumulated in the engine over the years. Some oil additives include agents that can make the rubber seals swell and sometimes reduce or eliminate small

When disassembling an engine, the wear and damage may be obvious or subtle. Parts aren't always as mangled as this example. Perform thorough diagnostics before disassembly so that you can properly focus the inspections during the overhaul.

Tune-up parts are inexpensive and relatively easy to install. Performing a basic tune-up is a wise first step in diagnostics because it eliminates potential problems that may be difficult to find. After an overhaul has been completed, these new parts will be needed anyway, so purchase them before the overhaul.

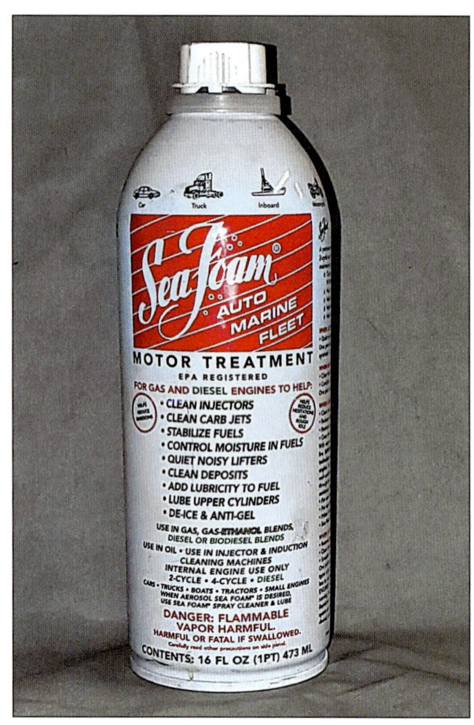

Don't expect to fix serious engine problems with the contents of a bottle, but oil additives can be helpful with certain problems. Additives, such as Sea Foam, can dissolve deposits and potentially help a stuck hydraulic lifter break free.

leaks. If you're on a budget and just want to nurse along the engine until you can afford an overhaul, such additives may be worth considering.

Unless the engine has obvious serious problems, I recommend an oil change and a thorough tune-up before going deep into the diagnosis. Doing so will help to eliminate potential small problems and help focus the diagnostic strategy.

The information in this chapter will help determine if the engine needs an overhaul and also what you can expect to see after the engine has been disassembled.

If you are concerned about the condition of your engine because of decreased performance or fuel economy, perform a vacuum test, a power-balance test, and a compression test. If the problem is not obvious after these tests, check the camshaft-lobe lift and the timing-chain slack. If the engine is making unusual noises, check the oil pressure and make use of the information in this chapter regarding noise diagnosis.

Visual Clues

Your eyes (and ears) are your best diagnostic tools. Thoroughly survey the engine compartment and look for anything suspicious. Many of the problems that were thought to be internal to the engine may actually have simple and obvious solutions.

Smoke

Smoke emitting from the vehicle's tailpipe can indicate the internal condition of the engine. Smoke caused by excessive oil consumption is bluish-gray in color. If smoke of this color leaves the tailpipe, oil is entering the combustion chambers and being burned. This generally indicates internal engine problems, although oil can be drawn into the engine through a malfunctioning positive crankcase ventilation (PCV) system.

Oil burning is often most pronounced during closed-throttle deceleration when vacuum is high. A good test is to drive the vehicle in a low gear at an elevated RPM. Then, take your foot off the accelerator. This should create strong engine braking. Watch for blue smoke. It's often helpful to have someone in another vehicle follow you during this test.

Blue smoke during this test generally points to worn valve guides and/or piston rings. Perform a compression test to identify the issue. Blue smoke only at startup frequently indicates a failure of the valve seals.

Loose Components

Sometimes, loose external components can cause noises that mimic internal engine noises. Check the belts and pulleys on the front of the engine as well as the vibration damper. In addition, check the brackets and engine mounts.

Leaks

Engines are often overhauled because of oil consumption. Before deciding that the engine needs an overhaul due to oil consumption, make sure that oil leaks aren't the culprit. If the vehicle is parked in the same place every day on pavement, look for oil stains or puddles of oil. To check more accurately, place a sheet of cardboard under the engine overnight. Even a few drops can indicate the source of a significant oil loss.

When observing drips from underneath the vehicle, keep in

It's not enough to know that a car is leaking oil. You must know how much it's leaking to determine how much of the oil is disappearing out the tailpipe. Sliding a fresh piece of cardboard under the engine every night provides data about the severity of the leak.

mind that engine oil is only one of the potential sources. Transmission fluid and power-steering fluid can be mistaken for engine oil. These fluids are less viscous (thinner in consistency) than oil. In addition, transmission fluid has a red tinge.

Look carefully under the vehicle to see which component is wet with the fluid. Keep in mind that fluid can be blown rearward during driving, which can make the origin point of the leak more difficult to identify.

If any drips are evident, raise the vehicle and inspect the underside. Sometimes, leaks occur only when the engine is hot, under load, or on a hill. Look for signs of leakage as well as active drips. If a significant oil leak is found, correct it before taking oil-consumption measurements.

Oil Consumption

If an engine is consuming oil, this may be a sign that the cylinders, pistons, rings, valve seals, and/or valve guides are worn. A clogged PCV system can also increase oil consumption.

Modern engines that are in good condition use very little oil, and oil loss between oil changes is frequently undetectable. This is largely attributable to improvements in the design and the materials that are used to make pistons, piston rings, and valve seals. It's important to understand that Buick engines were manufactured during a period when most engines had noticeable oil consumption between oil changes. Don't judge your Buick engine by comparing it to a new, modern engine.

Even for engines that were built during the same era, normal oil consumption rates vary greatly for several reasons. For example, forged

When measuring oil consumption, precision is critical. Check the oil on level ground and do so frequently. For an accurate oil-consumption comparison, check the oil while the car is in the same location as your previous oil check.

pistons, which have more clearance between the piston and cylinder wall, are often used in high-performance engines. It's normal for an engine with forged pistons to consume more oil than an engine with conventional cast pistons.

To measure oil consumption accurately, park the vehicle on a level surface and turn off the engine. Wait several minutes to allow the oil to drain into the oil pan. Then, remove the dipstick. Wipe off the dipstick and reinsert it fully. Pull it out carefully and read the level. Fill the pan to the "full" mark with the correct grade and viscosity of oil and note the mileage. Continue to check the oil level using this same procedure until 1 quart of oil has been consumed. Again, note the mileage. If there is blue exhaust smoke and/or the oil consumption is higher than about a quart in 700 miles, there's certainly a problem.

Noise Diagnosis

When performing a noise diagnosis, use caution and don't get too close to the moving components.

All moving parts can create sounds for various reasons. Often, the engine is blamed when the actual problem is in the transmission or driveline. Be sure to isolate the noise. A knocking sound from under the hood could be loose torque-converter bolts or a damaged vibration damper.

To isolate a noise, first apply the parking brake and place the transmission in Neutral (manual) or Park (automatic). Start the engine with the hood open and determine if the noise is actually coming from the engine. Rev the engine slightly and determine if the noise increases as the engine speed is increased. If the noise seems to be coming from the engine and varies with engine speed, it is probably an engine issue. However, knocking noises that vary with engine speed are sometimes associated with the flywheel, flexplate, or torque converter.

Identify the type of noise. If it's a squealing sound, check the accessory belt tension. Spray belt dressing on the belts. If the noise goes away, the belts need adjustment or replacement. Another test is to remove the drive belts and run the engine for a short time to be sure that the noise is not coming from the accessories (the power steering, water pump, alternator, or A/C compressor pulley).

Does the sound occur at crankshaft speed or half of crankshaft speed? Determine this by connecting a timing light to any spark-plug wire. Listen and watch the flashing of the light. If the sound occurs every time that the light flashes, this is half of crankshaft speed. If the noise is heard twice for every flash, this is crankshaft speed.

Tapping and knocking noises are the most common noise types when diagnosing engine problems. Knocking sounds that occur at crankshaft speed are usually caused by crankshaft problems or connecting rod and bearing problems. If the noise occurs at half of crankshaft speed, the source is likely the lifters, rocker arms, valves, valve springs, or fuel pump. Listen for these sounds near the top of the engine.

A helpful tool for pinpointing the source of a noise is a mechanic's stethoscope. It is also possible to use a long piece of hose or a long screwdriver. Hold the handle of the screwdriver or the end of the hose against your ear and place the tip of the screwdriver or the other end of the hose on areas where a problem is suspected.

The listening device can be moved around to determine where the sound is the most pronounced. Note the cylinder that is closest to the noise. Then, with the engine off, pull the spark-plug wire for the associated cylinder from the distributor cap. Start the engine and determine if the noise changes. If the noise goes away or reduces significantly, that may identify a cylinder that has a bad connecting rod bearing or other problem.

Noises in the upper part of the engine are usually associated with the valvetrain (lifters, pushrods, and rocker arms) and are heard as tapping sounds at half of crankshaft speed. With the valve cover removed from the associated cylinder bank, start the engine and allow it to idle slowly for a brief amount of time. Oil will spray from each rocker arm, so be careful to avoid making a mess. Special tools are available to deflect the spray, but a piece of cardboard that has been stood up at the lower edge of the cylinder head can help catch and direct the oil back into the cylinder head.

While the engine is running, check that the valves are opening the same amount and that the pushrods are rotating slowly. Press your thumb against the top of each rocker arm, directly above the valve. If the noise stops or lessens, it is the source of the noise. First check the valve adjustment (see chapter 7). If that's okay, remove the rocker arm and pushrod, inspecting them carefully for excess wear and damage. If there are no problems with the rocker arm or pushrod, the lifter is most likely the problem.

Knocking is the most common noise from the lower end of the engine. The source of knocking is usually excessive clearance in the main bearings or connecting rod bearings, or the knocking could be due to low oil pressure.

Connecting-rod knock is most pronounced when the throttle is opened briefly and then quickly released. The noise is usually caused by excessive bearing wear or insufficient oil pressure.

A main bearing knock is a low-pitched knock that is deep within the engine. It is the loudest when the engine is first started. It may also be noticed under heavy load. Disconnecting the spark plugs

Sounds tend to echo in the engine compartment, which can create diagnosis errors. A small investment in a mechanic's stethoscope will help you precisely locate engine noises.

from the adjacent cylinders can sometimes help identify the location of the knock.

Piston slap is most pronounced when the engine is cold. As the engine warms up, it gets quieter. Listen at the side of the engine (at each cylinder), just below the cylinder head. A light piston slap sounds dull or hollow, while a heavy piston slap sounds more like a knock or a rattle. Piston slap often decreases or goes away when the associated cylinder's spark plug is disconnected.

Another trick is to slowly retard the ignition timing while listening. If the slap decreases or goes away, the most likely problem is piston slap. Note that high-performance engines equipped with forged pistons have greater piston-to-bore clearance than engines with standard cast pistons. Engines with forged pistons often exhibit some piston slap after a cold start, but that goes away when the engine is fully warmed up.

Piston-pin problems are heard as a double click at idle and low speeds. Disconnecting the associated spark plug often causes the noise to go away.

Piston rings can become loose in their grooves due to wear or breakage. This results in a chattering noise that is loudest when accelerating. A leak-down test helps to identify this problem.

Spark-Plug Condition

If the spark plugs have been in service for an extended period of time, the deposits shown will be cumulative and do not accurately represent the engine's current running condition. If there is anything concerning on the plugs, replace them with a new set, operate the

vehicle for a week or so, and then check the plugs again.

The condition of a spark plug's firing end can provide a great deal of information about what is happening in the combustion chamber. Learning to read spark plugs is a great skill to develop, as it helps in tuning and engine diagnostics.

Before you begin, drive at highway speeds and allow the engine to warm up thoroughly. Do not allow the engine to idle excessively. Turn off the engine and wait until it cools to avoid getting burned by the hot components. Label the spark-plug wires in order so that they can be reinstalled on the correct spark plugs.

To avoid getting dirt into the engine, clean the area around the spark plugs before removing them.

Remove the spark plugs and keep

Mark each spark-plug wire to avoid getting them mixed up. Special labels are available, but using masking tape and a marker works as well.

Use compressed air to blow away dirt from around the spark-plug holes. This prevents the dirt from entering the cylinder when the spark plugs are removed. If you don't have an air compressor, a can of compressed air from an office-supply store works as well.

Keep the spark plugs organized because each one indicates the condition of its associated cylinder. When plugs vary in condition from cylinder to cylinder, it's important to understand the reason why. Take note of the brand and number on each spark plug. Compare this to the factory recommendations to be sure that the spark plug is the correct type and in the correct heat range.

Examine each plug tip. The ideal condition of the spark-plug tip has only a light accumulation of deposits on the insulator, which should have a tan or light gray appearance. In addition, the side electrode should be between light gray and dark gray.

The spark plug on the left has shiny black deposits, which indicate oil consumption in the associated cylinder. The spark plug on the right shows sooty black deposits, which indicate that the engine is running rich or the spark plug's heat range is too cold.

If the spark plug has a bright white insulator, the mixture is too lean or the combustion chamber is excessively hot.

Mechanical damage to a spark plug usually means that its "reach" into the combustion chamber is too deep, causing contact with the piston. Another possible cause is that a foreign object may have found its way into the cylinder and has been bouncing around and causing damage.

them in order. Making an organizer out of a cardboard box helps to prevent the plugs from getting mixed up. Take note of the brand and number on each spark plug. Compare this to the factory recommendations to be sure that the spark plug is the correct type and heat range.

Carefully examine each plug tip. The ideal condition is to have a light accumulation of deposits on the insulator, which creates a tan or light gray appearance. The side electrode should be a shade between light and dark gray.

Plugs that are wet with oil indi-cate that the engine is consuming a large amount of oil in the combustion chamber. This is also associated with bluish smoke emitting from the tailpipe. This level of oil consumption indicates that an engine overhaul is needed.

If the plugs have shiny black deposits, some oil is seeping into the cylinders. The engine is worn. If you're not ready to overhaul the engine yet, try installing a spark plug with a hotter heat range to help burn off deposits and delay the need for repair or an overhaul.

Sooty black deposits on all of the plugs usually indicate that the engine is running rich. If only one plug or some plugs have sooty deposits, it usually indicates a misfire due to an ignition problem or low compression. Sooty carbon deposits are not an indication of oil consumption because oil deposits are wet and/or shiny.

A bright white insulator indicates that the mixture is lean and the combustion chamber is excessively hot. If this is accompanied by the electrode or the insulator being melted, high temperatures have led to detonation. Detonation may have damaged the pistons as well.

If the spark plug has mechanical damage, there could be one of two issues. First, the "reach," or the protrusion, into the combustion chamber is too deep. It could also mean that a foreign object is trapped in the cylinder.

If all of the plugs are the same heat range but there is a large variance in rich/lean indications among the cylinders, it's likely that there is a vacuum leak at the intake manifold. The leak is most likely at the mating surface between the cylinder head and the intake manifold.

Vacuum Gauge

An inexpensive vacuum gauge is a great investment that will help you diagnose a myriad of engine problems. However, careful interpretation of the readings is required because they can be misleading and make you confused easily. Confirm your findings with other tests.

When interpreting the readings, note the reading as well as the amount and rate of needle movement. The details are important. Gauges are usually graduated in inches of mercury (in-Hg). Altitude can cause readings to vary, so note the reading when no vacuum is applied.

Find a vacuum source on the intake manifold (not the carburetor) and "tee" into it with a three-way hose connector.

With the engine warmed to normal operating temperature, put the transmission in Park (automatic) or Neutral (manual). Set the parking brake and chock the wheels.

A vacuum gauge is an essential diagnostic tool. It can indicate a myriad of problems in the engine as well as in the ignition, fuel, and exhaust systems.

Connect a vacuum gauge to the intake manifold vacuum with a T-fitting. Make sure that there aren't any disconnected hoses during the test because they can affect the reading.

A healthy stock Buick engine usually generates about 18 to 22 in-Hg at idle. There should not be any significant fluctuation on the gauge. High-performance engines with long-duration camshafts generate less vacuum than a stock engine. In addition, engines that were manufactured during the "smog era" (1972 and later) sometimes have lower vacuum due to differences in valve and ignition timing. The following paragraphs provide the typical readings that you will encounter when checking the vacuum. Keep in mind that the reading may indicate multiple problems.

If the reading is low and steady, it indicates a vacuum leak, retarded ignition timing, or incorrect valve timing. Vacuum leaks are commonly caused by disconnected or deteriorated vacuum hoses or poor sealing at the gaskets, such as at the carburetor base or the intake manifold-to-cylinder head joint. Check for vacuum leaks and make sure that ignition timing is correct. If the problem still can't be found, check for timing-chain slack, which is described in this chapter.

If the needle is low and fluctuates about 3 to 8 inches, the problem is likely a vacuum leak at an intake port.

If the needle drops several inches at regular intervals, there is likely a valve leak. Check the compression and also perform a leak-down test.

An irregular needle drop is likely caused by an ignition misfire or a sticking valve. Read the spark plugs and perform a compression check.

If the needle rapidly vibrates within a range of about 4 in-Hg at idle, the valve guides may be leaking. This reading is also associated with blue smoke in the exhaust, which is most pronounced on start-up. Other possible causes are a leaking intake manifold gasket, leaking head gasket, ignition misfire, leaking valves, or weak valve springs.

Slight fluctuation of about an inch or so often indicates ignition problems. Check the spark plugs, spark-plug wires, and distributor cap/rotor.

A needle that fluctuates greatly usually indicates a head-gasket leak or a cylinder that has serious problems. Check the compression and perform a leak-down test.

If the needle slowly moves across a wide range, there may be a clog in the PCV system. It could also indicate an incorrectly adjusted idle mixture or a vacuum leak at the carburetor or intake-manifold gasket.

Accelerate the engine to about 2,500 rpm and then release the throttle quickly. Under normal conditions, the needle should drop to almost zero and then rise slightly above the normal idle reading before returning to the normal idle reading. A slow return of vacuum that also does not peak when the throttle is released indicates worn piston rings. If there is a long delay before the vacuum returns, there's a restriction in the exhaust—most commonly the catalytic converter.

Compression Check

A compression check can help you determine the condition of the pistons, piston rings, valves, cylinder heads, and the head gasket. Before performing the check, run the engine until normal operating temperature is reached. If the engine does not run, the test can still be performed but the results will not be as precise.

Exhaust manifolds or headers are very hot and in close proximity to the spark plugs. Be careful so

Compression gauges are commonly available from auto-parts stores. Get one that includes hoses and adapters that fit different vehicles. Purchase a quality gauge because some of the inexpensive gauges provide inaccurate readings.

that you do not get burned. Wearing heat-resistant gloves during the check is a good precaution.

Remove all of the spark plugs from the engine. Open the throttle and find a way to hold it in this position. Usually, it is possible to block it or wire it in the open position.

Disable the ignition system. There are different steps depending on whether it is a high-energy ignition (HEI) or not. On non-HEI systems (1974 and earlier), detach the coil wire from the center of the distributor cap and ground it on the engine block. On HEI systems, disconnect the battery connector from the side of the distributor cap.

Install the compression gauge in the number-one spark-plug hole.

Turn the ignition key to "Start." An assistant may be needed to crank the engine while you

Disable the ignition system before beginning the compression check. If the engine is equipped with high-energy ignition (HEI), which is on 1975-and-later models, the easiest way to disable the ignition system is to disconnect the battery wire connector on the side of the distributor cap.

observe the gauge. Another option is to use a remote starter switch. As the engine is cranked, the gauge needle should rise rapidly on the first compression stroke and then more slowly on successive strokes.

A remote starter switch allows the starter to be operated while you're under the hood and observing the compression gauge. Without it, an assistant is needed to turn the ignition key during the compression test.

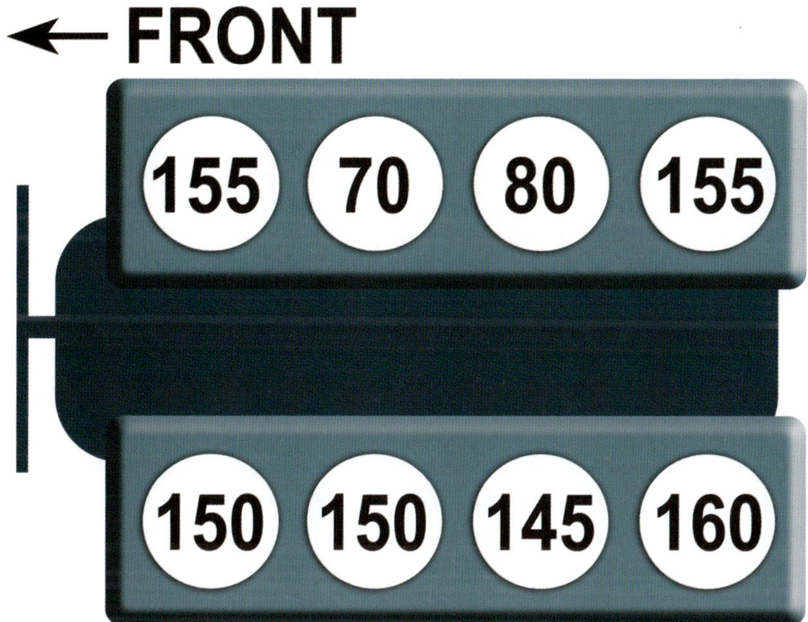

Carefully record the compression readings to compare them. The two low cylinders in this test are adjacent to each other (the number-4 and -6 cylinders). The most likely cause is a blown head gasket between the cylinders.

A "wet test" can quickly determine if low compression is due to worn piston rings or upper-engine problems, such as a blown head gasket or leaking valves. To perform a wet test, add a few squirts of oil to the low cylinder and repeat the compression test.

Crank the engine until the gauge needle stops moving, which is usually about five compression strokes. If the first compression stroke is low and gradually increases with each stroke, the piston rings are likely worn. If the compression starts low and remains low on successive strokes, the problem could be valves that are not sealing, a blown head gasket, or a crack in the cylinder head's combustion chamber.

Repeat the procedure for the other seven cylinders. Record each reading. In a healthy engine, the readings from all cylinders should be within 20 percent of each other. Compression readings can vary significantly from engine to engine, so don't be overly concerned if the readings are different than another engine. Instead, look at how each cylinder compares to the other cylinders.

If any of the readings are low, repeat the test with a few squirts of oil added in each cylinder. This is known as a "wet test." If the oil increases compression, it indicates worn piston rings. If there is no increase in compression, the problem is in the top end of the engine. It could be bad valves, a blown head gasket, or a crack in the combustion chamber.

Adjacent cylinders with equally low compression (much lower than the others) indicate a blown head gasket (blown between the cylinders). Another indication of a blown head gasket is coolant in the combustion chambers or oil pan. Coolant in the oil gives the oil a milky appearance.

If compression is very low (less than 100 psi) or varies greatly among cylinders, perform a leak-down test, which will provide more precise information regarding the source of the cylinder leakage.

Oil-Pressure Check

Engine oil pressure is a good indicator of the condition of the main and connecting-rod bearings. Excessive bearing clearance and/or damage leads to lower oil pressure. Low oil pressure can also be caused by a worn oil pump or low viscosity (thin consistency) oil.

Remove the dipstick and check the condition of the oil. If it's dirty or seems very thin, change the oil before the check.

Remove the oil-pressure sending unit and install a gauge in its place. Run the engine at normal operating temperature and note the reading at idle. In a healthy engine with the correct oil viscosity, the pressure shouldn't drop below 20 psi at idle.

As engine speed increases, oil pressure should rise quickly. There should be at least a 10-psi increase in pressure for each 1,000 rpm.

To check the oil pressure, remove the oil-sending unit and connect a pressure gauge in its place. On Buick engines, the oil-sending units are located on the passenger's side, just behind the oil filter.

Usually, the pressure will rise more quickly than this. The maximum pressure with a warm engine should not go higher than about 80 psi. If the pressure is too high, change to a lower-viscosity oil. The appendix lists

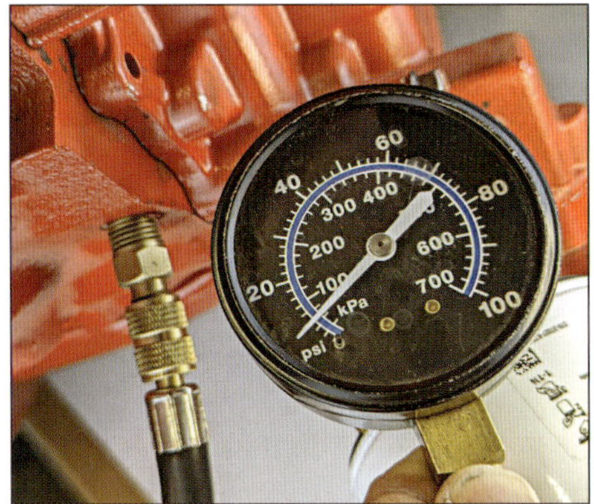

Depending on the oil viscosity and engine temperature, readings may be as high as 80 psi. Don't use ordinary hoses and clamps. Use only high-pressure hoses and threaded fittings.

factory oil-pressure specifications for all Buick engines that are covered by this book.

Camshaft-Lobe Lift Check

Most Buick engines use flat-bottom lifters that wear the camshaft over time. Various conditions can accelerate camshaft wear, including using oil without an anti-scuff additive, such as zinc. During the time that Buick engines were being manufactured, all automotive engine oils contained zinc to deal with the intense friction that was created by flat lifters. Many modern automotive oils do not use zinc due to environmental concerns.

A worn camshaft lobe will cause an engine to idle poorly, have low compression, and make valvetrain noise. A worn lobe or lobes can be identified with a lobe-lift check.

To do a lobe-lift check, remove the valve covers and rocker arms. Mount a dial indicator in line with each pushrod end and zero the indicator. Rotate the engine by hand with a socket and breaker bar on the crankshaft bolt. Rotate two full turns and watch the dial indicator. Write down the highest and lowest reading. Subtract the lowest from the highest and record the reading, including whether it is an intake or exhaust valve.

Compare the lift of all lobes, which should be very close. They usually vary by only a few thousandths of an inch. Generally, a damaged lobe will be much less than the others. Once wear starts, lobes wear down very quickly.

If lobe wear is indicated, replace the camshaft and install a new set of lifters. Never install used lifters on a new camshaft.

Timing-Chain Slack Check

Remove the timing chain cover and reinstall the crankshaft bolt. Rotate the crankshaft counterclockwise to take up the slack in the passenger's side of the chain.

Make a mark on the driver's side of engine block to serve as a reference point for the chain slack measurement.

Rotate the crankshaft clockwise to take up the slack in the passenger's side of the chain.

Pull the driver's side of the chain out by hand and measure the distance between the chain and the reference point.

Slack greater than about 3/4 inch is excessive. A new chain and sprockets should be installed.

As an alternate method, timing chain slack can be checked at the distributor rotor. This method is not as accurate, but it avoids removing the timing chain cover. Simply remove the distributor cap and rotate the crankshaft in each direction until the rotor starts to move. The amount of crankshaft rotation that does not move the rotor is the slack. The crankshaft should not be able to move more than about 1/16 of a turn (12 degrees) without moving the rotor.

Power Balance Test

A power balance test is used to determine if any cylinders are not firing, if they are firing weakly, or if they are firing intermittently. This is done by disconnecting each spark plug (one by one) and noting the change in engine RPM. If there is no change in RPM when a particular plug is disconnected, the associated cylinder is not firing.

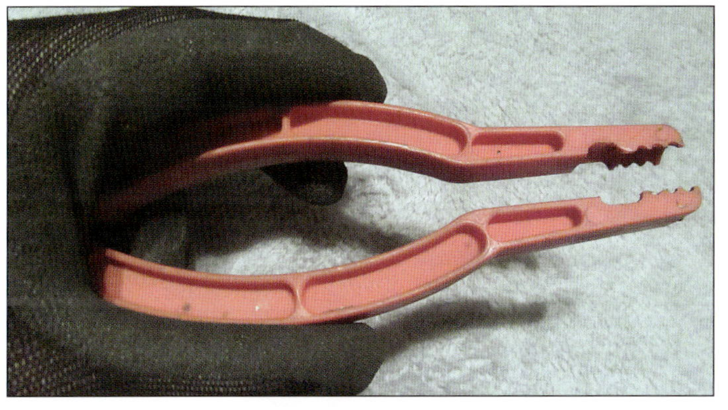

Take special precautions to avoid being shocked during the power-balance test, especially if the engine has an HEI. This insulated tool keeps your hands at a safe distance from the wire while pulling the boot. In addition, you should wear thick rubber gloves.

This test requires the use of an accurate tachometer, as the RPM variations on a V-8 engine can be subtle. Do not rely on the car's tachometer.

Before beginning the test, remove the spark-plug wire from each spark plug and then reinstall them. Do this because the boots frequently adhere to the spark plugs, which makes them difficult to remove. Removing them prior to the test will make removal during the test easier when the engine is hot.

Hook up the tachometer and warm up the engine. Be sure that the transmission is in Neutral (manual) or Park (automatic). Note the idle speed.

Using a special tool and rubber gloves for safety, disconnect the spark-plug wires one at a time and record the RPM drop for each one. If the vehicle has electronic ignition, immediately short the wire to an engine ground to prevent damage to the system.

Caution: If the vehicle is equipped with a catalytic converter (1975-and-later models), do not leave the spark plug disconnected for more than 10 seconds at a time. Unburned fuel in the exhaust system can overheat the catalytic converter.

There should be a reduction of about 50 rpm when each spark plug is disconnected. The amount of the RPM reduction can vary in a normal, healthy engine, so don't be too concerned if the RPM reduction numbers are not all the same. Look for a noticeable drop, not an exact number.

If there is little or no change in RPM when a spark plug is disconnected, that cylinder is not firing, is firing weakly, or is firing intermittently. The cause of this could be an engine mechanical problem or the secondary ignition system. Be sure to check the spark plugs, spark-plug wires, and distributor cap. A localized vacuum leak (usually at the intake manifold) can also cause a misfire.

Cylinders that fail this test should receive a compression test. If the cylinder has normal compression, there is a vacuum leak or a problem in the secondary ignition system (spark plugs, spark-plug wires, or distributor cap).

Cylinder Leak-Down Test

Any time that a compression test identifies one or more weak cylinders, perform a cylinder leak-down test to determine precisely where the problem lies. The test requires a specialized tester and an air compressor. It may be more economical to have the test performed by a repair shop.

A leak-down tester applies air pressure to the cylinder with the valves closed. The rate of leakage is then measured. The steps to perform a cylinder leak-down test are below.

Remove all of the spark plugs. Test each cylinder (one at a time) following the firing order: 1-8-4-3-6-5-7-2.

Disconnect the battery and bring the number-one cylinder to top dead center (TDC) on the compression stroke (see chapter 7).

Thread the tester's air hose into the spark-plug hole and connect the tester. Connect the air compressor and zero the gauge using the regulator knob.

Warning: The crankshaft will try to rotate one way or the other as pressure is applied. Find a safe way to lock the crankshaft in place before beginning the test. For a vehicle with a manual transmission, put it in high gear and set the parking brake. For a vehicle with an automatic transmission, use the special tool that has

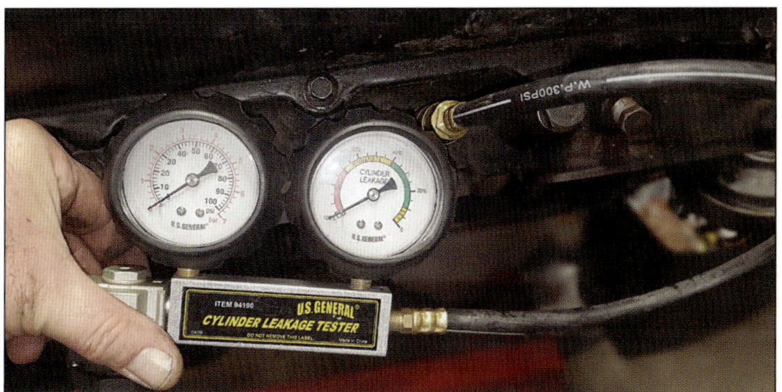

A cylinder leakage tester, or leak-down tester, measures the amount of leakage in a cylinder as well as the origin of the leak. This information helps you determine whether to remove the entire engine or possibly just the cylinder heads.

been designed for this purpose. Some DIYers hold the crankshaft bolt with a socket that is attached to a long breaker bar. While this method usually works, it cannot be considered completely safe.

The leak-down rate should be about 10 percent. If the rate exceeds 20 percent, the engine has problems.

While the cylinder is pressurized, air will leak past the worn/damaged parts. Listen to determine where the air is escaping. If leakage is heard out the exhaust pipe, the exhaust valve is not seating. If air is heard escaping into the intake manifold, an intake valve is not seating. Remove the oil filler cap and listen to determine if air is escaping past the piston rings (commonly known as "blowby").

Test the remaining cylinders. Rotate the crankshaft clockwise exactly 90 degrees to get to the next cylinder in the firing order. Mark the vibration damper carefully to ensure precision of rotation. Inexpensive degree-marking tapes are available that adhere to the outer circumference of the damper.

Cooling System Tests

An engine with a blown head gasket, cracked block, or cracked cylinder head will likely exhibit overheating, steam emanating from the exhaust, bubbling in the coolant reservoir, unexplained coolant loss, and/or coolant in the oil. These problems are usually caused by severe overheating or coolant freezing in the engine block due to inadequate antifreeze protection.

Diagnosis starts with checking the oil on the dipstick. If the oil has a milky appearance, there's almost certainly an internal coolant leak, which also causes an unexplained

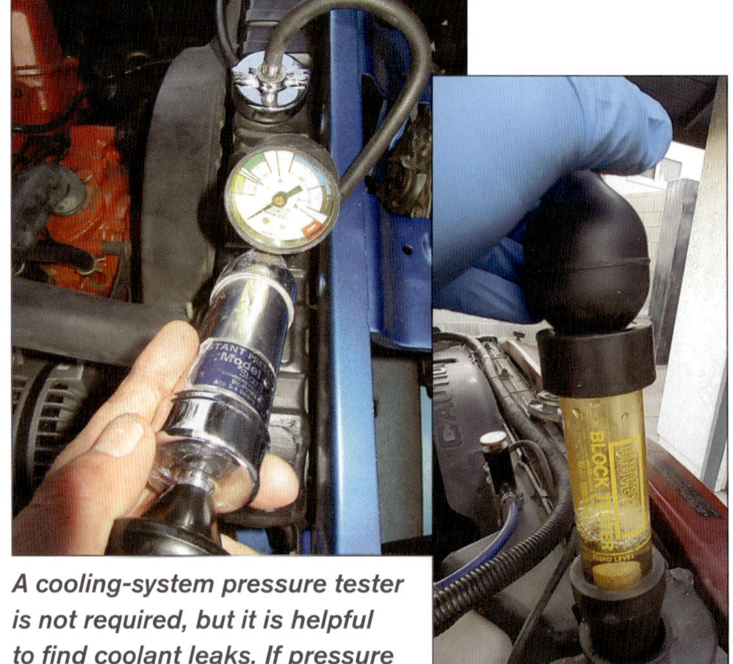

A cooling-system pressure tester is not required, but it is helpful to find coolant leaks. If pressure leaks down, there's a leak. If the leak is not external, it's inside the engine. The most common cause of an internal coolant leak is a blown head gasket.

If a blown head gasket or another internal leak is suspected, perform a combustion-leak test. Testers are commonly available and work on the principle that combustion gases change the color of the special test fluid.

increase in the oil level.

With the engine cold, check the coolant in the reservoir and in the radiator. If oil is floating on top of the coolant, this is a sign of a blown head gasket. With the engine running, observe the coolant in the reservoir (if equipped). If there is bubbling, suspect a blown head gasket or a crack in the cylinder head or block.

Steam coming from the tailpipe after the engine is fully warmed up means that coolant is entering the combustion chamber due to a blown head gasket or a crack in the cylinder head. Some steam is normal during warm-up due to condensation in the exhaust system. It's when the steam continues after warm-up that you should be concerned.

A cooling-system pressure tester is a great diagnostic tool that will help find internal or external coolant leaks. The tester is a hand pump with a gauge that connects to the radiator filler neck. With the engine cold, use the pump to pressurize the cooling system to the pressure that is indicated on the radiator cap.

The gauge needle should remain steady at this reading. If the gauge needle drops, there's a leak. External leaks are usually obvious, but a leak in the heater core may be difficult to identify. If a heater-core leak is suspected, pinch off the two heater hoses to test if the pressure now holds.

A combustion leak detector can help identify a blown head gasket or a crack in the engine block or head. The tester draws gases from the cooling system through a special test fluid. If the test fluid changes color from blue to yellow, there is a combustion leak into the cooling system.

If testing causes you to suspect an internal coolant leak, remove the spark plugs and check their firing tips. If a firing tip is clean and/or wet with coolant, it indicates an internal leak is affecting that cylinder. In that case, the plug tip is being steam-cleaned by the boiling coolant in the cylinder.

If there is an internal coolant leak, remove the cylinder heads and inspect carefully. If the head gasket(s) are blown, be sure to check for cylinder head warpage and cracks in the heads and cylinder block.

ENGINE REMOVAL AND EXTERNAL DISASSEMBLY

Removing an engine is difficult, dirty, and potentially dangerous. When you are under the vehicle, make sure that it's safely supported. When removing a heavy component, be sure to have a solid grip on it before removing the bolts. When removing the transmission-to-engine bolts or the engine-mount bolts, be absolutely sure that the engine and the transmission are safely supported. Never position any body parts underneath heavy components as they are being removed. Wear safety glasses whenever you are under the vehicle, as bits of dirt and grease can fall into your eyes.

Engine removal requires some specialized tools and equipment (see chapter 2) and can only be done on a level concrete or asphalt surface. Concrete is preferable because jack-stand bases tend to sink into asphalt.

This is a messy job. No matter how careful you are, coolant will almost certainly spill along with some transmission fluid and oil. Be prepared with oil-absorbent material (or clay cat litter) and many rags. In addition, it's wise to wear gloves because old engines are greasy.

To make the job a little cleaner, spray down the engine with engine degreaser that's commonly available from auto-parts stores. Allow it to soak in and then spray it off with a pressure nozzle on a garden hose. An even-better option is to use a home pressure washer or the high-pressure spray wand at a self-service car wash. Just make sure that the cleaning methods do not violate any environmental guidelines.

Be organized! When assembling and reinstalling the engine, it is important to remember where all of the components attach and the loca-tions where all of the bolts go. Keep the bolts stored with their associated components. Use labeled plastic bags and boxes. Components are often secured by bolts of different lengths. Keep track of which bolts go into which holes and take many photos.

Before beginning, set the parking brake and chock the rear wheels. Place the transmission in Neutral to prevent a release of tension between the transmission and engine when the engine is detached.

The procedure described is for a typical vehicle with an automatic transmission. For a vehicle with a manual transmission, remove the transmission and the clutch prior to engine removal.

The following photos and captions describe the task. Take your time and make sure that each step is complete before continuing the process.

Removing the Hood and Disconnecting Components

1 *This once-proud 1968 Buick Riviera has become a rusty mess. However, the heart of this cruiser (the original high-compression 430 engine) was overhauled, improved, and transplanted into a special project for this book. Photos of a 1975 Riviera are interspersed throughout this book to show the design differences between early and late engines.*

2 *Before beginning, set the parking brake and block the rear wheels. Place the transmission in Neutral to prevent a release of tension between the transmission and engine when you detach them.*

3 *Disconnect the negative battery terminal and then disconnect the positive battery terminal. Disconnecting the negative terminal first prevents accidental grounding when removing the positive terminal. The style of clamp that is shown was used on early models. Later models have side-terminal batteries that are disconnected by using a 5/16-inch wrench or socket.*

4 *Using a permanent marker or a scratch awl, mark around each hood-attachment bolt so that you can align the hood correctly during reinstallation.*

5 Get help when removing the hood. Place a pad on the rear of the hood to protect the windshield. Hold the hood securely on both sides and remove the front bolts first. The hood is heavy and will move after the last bolts are removed. Move the hood forward and then up. Store it vertically against a wall (front up) with padding at the bottom. Wire the latch securely to the wall. Do not store the hood horizontally. If you do, the hood can be easily dented.

6 After the hood has been removed, disconnect all of the wiring and hoses on top of the engine. The negative battery cable (arrow) is usually connected to the engine. Sometimes, there are secondary ground cables, so inspect carefully.

7 Many of the electrical connectors simply pull off, such as this spade-type connector that is used for the oil-pressure sending unit. These types of connectors tend to become corroded and loose over time. Note any connectors that are loose or damaged so that you can replace them later.

8 Some connectors have tabs that must be pried away with a small screwdriver before the connector can be removed. The battery wire at the HEI distributor used on later models is shown. Models with tachometers also have a "TACH" wire next to it. Both must be disconnected.

Removing the Hood and Disconnecting Components *continued*

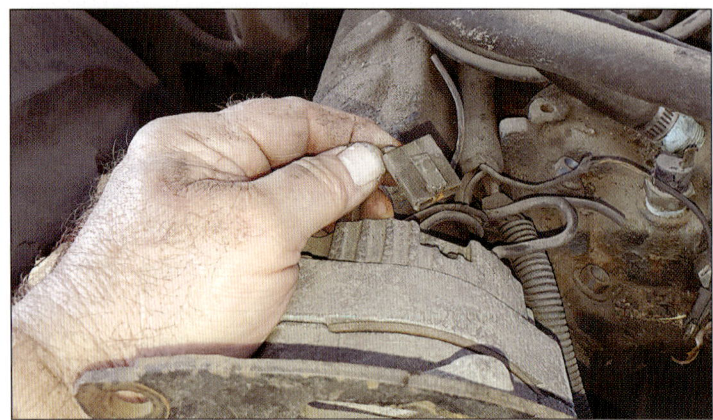

9 Remove this two-wire electrical connector at the rear of the alternator. Squeeze the tab prior to pulling the connector upward. This tab is broken (as many may be) from past mechanics who attempted to remove it. Replace any broken connectors during an overhaul.

10 All alternators have a battery terminal at the back (arrow). Remove the nut to disconnect it. This wire is powered at all times, which is why the factory protected it with a rubber boot. Even though the battery has already been disconnected, further protect yourself from a short circuit by wrapping the wire end with electrical tape. This also helps to locate the wire during reassembly.

11 The 1974-and-earlier models have a separate cylinder-style coil. The large center wire and the smaller-diameter positive wire must be disconnected. This often requires an 11/32-inch wrench or nut driver. Be aware that this size is not included with most wrench sets.

12 The 1971-and-later engines have many vacuum hoses. Label them so that they can be reinstalled correctly. It's wise to replace all of the hoses during reassembly. Old hoses don't seat well after they've been disconnected.

13 Detach the throttle linkage. To do so, most linkages can be easily pulled or pried off. An early type that requires prying up a safety tab on a clip while sliding the clip off is shown. Some automatic-transmission models also have a TV cable. If so, detach both.

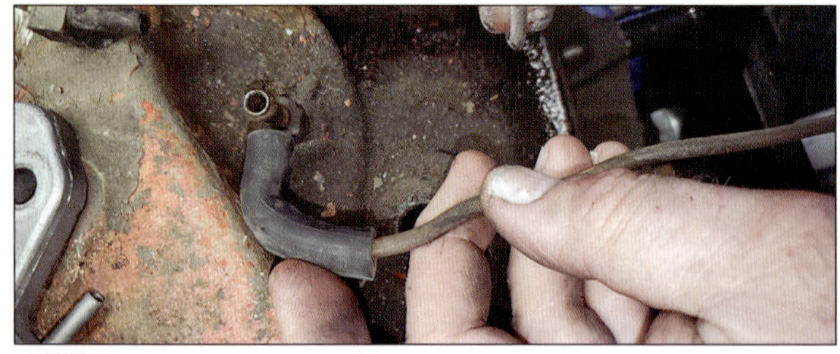

14 Models with TH400 transmissions do not have a TV cable. Instead, they have a vacuum hose on the intake manifold behind the carburetor. Disconnect it.

Draining Coolant and Disconnecting Hoses

1 At least two large drain pans are needed to avoid making a mess. The pan used for coolant should be larger than a standard oil drain pan and have a capacity of at least 2 gallons.

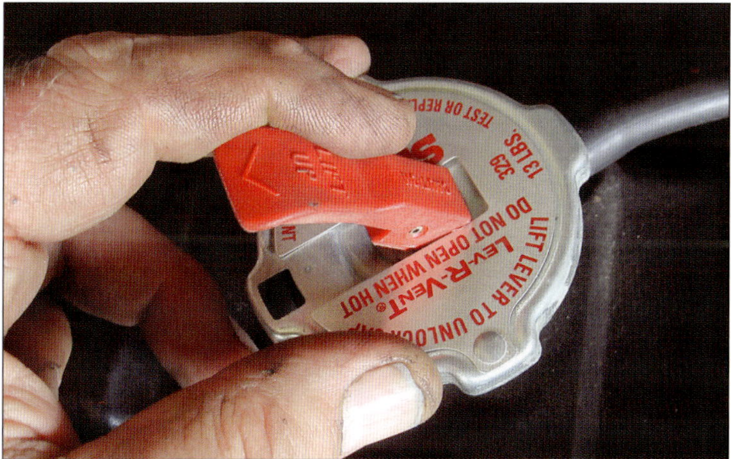

2 Now, drain the coolant from the radiator. First, remove the radiator cap to allow the coolant to flow out more quickly and steadily. If the cap is left on, the draining coolant creates a suction that slows the coolant flow.

3 Place the largest drain pan under the radiator petcock and rotate it counterclockwise until it is fully seated. Before disconnecting the hoses, be sure that all of the coolant has drained.

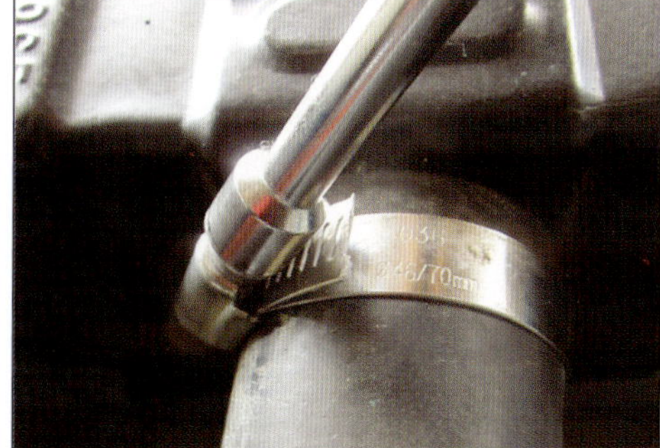

4 Remove the upper radiator hose. It is common to find aftermarket worm-type clamps on the radiator and heater hoses. They can be removed with a nut driver (shown) or a flat-blade screwdriver. If a nut driver is available, it is a better choice because it won't slip.

5 Disconnect the smaller-diameter heater hoses. One is on the water pump, and the other is attached to the heater control valve at the rear of the engine on the passenger's side.

6 Old hoses may adhere to their fittings. It's easy to damage the fittings if you pull too aggressively. This special hooked tool breaks the adhesion around the fitting so that the hose can be pulled off more easily.

Draining Coolant and Disconnecting Hoses *continued*

7 *If you don't have the special hooked tool, gently grip the hose with pliers and rotate the hose, which will often break the adhesion. Don't grip too tightly. If you do, the fitting can be damaged.*

8 *As a last resort, the hose can be carefully slit with a sharp utility knife and peeled away from the fitting.*

Removing the Fan and Shroud

1 *If possible, remove the fan and shroud together. First, remove the four bolts that attach the fan to the water-pump hub. If the fan moves as you try to loosen the bolts, try tapping on the wrench with a soft-face hammer, which usually breaks the bolts loose.*

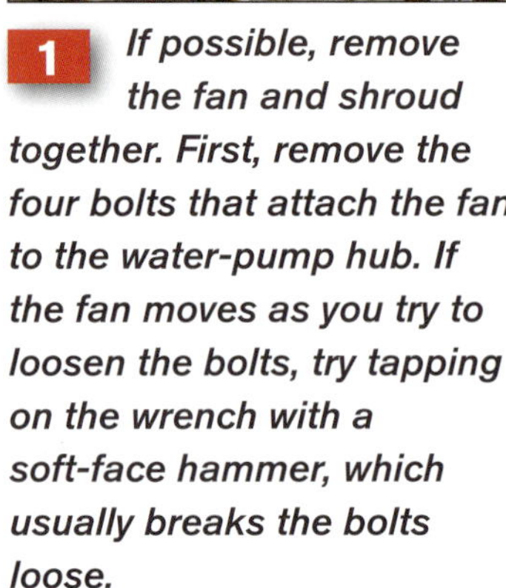

2 *Remove the fan shroud attachment bolts. On most models, they thread in vertically from the top.*

3 *Some early models use horizontal bolts to secure the shroud. These models usually have a bolt at the top center of the shroud that is accessible from inside the shroud. It's easy to miss. If you try to remove the shroud without removing the bolt, the damage shown here is the result.*

Removing the Fan and Shroud *continued*

4 *Most models do not have bolts at the bottom of the shroud. Just lift the shroud off the alignment tabs.*

5 *Gently work the fan off the water-pump hub and remove the fan and shroud at the same time. Do all of this slowly and carefully because it's easy to damage the radiator, which is made of thin copper. With the fan removed, the water-pump pulley can usually be removed, which also releases the belt tension and allows the belt(s) to be removed.*

6 *Place a drain pan underneath the lower radiator hose and disconnect the hose from the radiator. Be ready for coolant to splash everywhere. It usually does.*

Removing the Radiator and Transmission Lines

1 *If the car has an automatic transmission, use the appropriately sized flare-nut wrench to disconnect the transmission-cooler lines. It's wise to buy a full set of flare-nut wrenches because other sizes will be needed as the engine is further disassembled.*

2 *The automatic-transmission cooler lines (arrows) are attached to the bottom or side of the radiator tank. Sometimes, a backup wrench is needed to hold the fitting on the tank to avoid damaging the tank or twisting the line. Keep a drain pan underneath and plug the lines to prevent further leakage.*

3 *The transmission lines are often clipped to the side of the engine. Disengage the clips so that the lines don't get bent when the engine is removed. It may be easier to unclip the lines from below. If that is the case, wait until the car is raised later in the procedure.*

4 *Lift out the radiator carefully. Some early models have bolts that secure the radiator, but most often, the radiator just sits on two rubber isolators like this. Make sure that they're in good shape and, if necessary, replace them.*

Removing Accessories and the Distributor

1 *Remove the crankshaft pulley bolts and remove the pulley, disengaging any remaining belts. Keep the center bolt in place for now.*

2 *Remove the four bolts that secure the A/C compressor to the mounting brackets at the front and rear. Then, lift out the compressor from the brackets and tie it out of the way with the hoses still attached. Take care not to damage the hoses. The A6 compressor (shown here) is heavy, so be careful.*

3 *Now, remove the two alternator bolts and lift away the alternator. The bolt that is under the socket is the adjustment bolt, and the one on the bottom is the pivot bolt. Be aware that there is often a spacer on the pivot bolt that will need to be returned to its original position.*

4 *Over the years, Buick used various methods to mount the power-steering pump. This big aluminum piece is secured to the engine with three bolts. After removal, the bracket can be separated from the pump (if desired).*

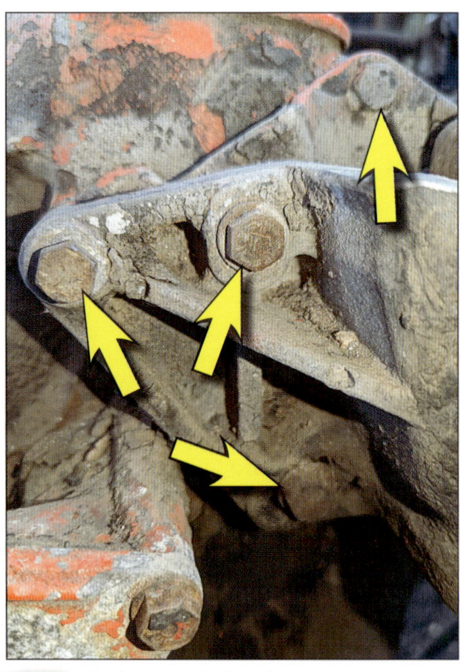

5 *Later models use a more conventional mounting system for the power-steering pump. Remove these four bolts at the front.*

6 On some later models, a nut is hidden behind the pump. The head size is 9/16 inch. Regardless of the bracketry used, it's easiest to tie the pump out of the way with the lines still attached. Be sure to orient it upright because the pump reservoir holds a significant volume of fluid.

9 Then, the wire retainer lifts off, which provides access to the wires.

7 Locate the distributor at the front of the engine and remove the distributor cap. It is secured with spring-loaded fasteners. Press a flat-blade screwdriver firmly down onto each fastener and rotate it counterclockwise 90 degrees. The 1974-and-earlier models have two fasteners, and the 1975-and-later models have four fasteners.

10 Remove each wire by twisting and pulling at the boot.

8 Sometimes, the distributor cap can be moved off the distributor and out of the way far enough to remove the distributor. If that is not the case, remove the wires from the cap first. On 1975-and-later models, a wire retainer must be removed by prying open two clips.

11 On 1975-and-later models, remove this wiring connector. Then, remove the distributor cap.

Removing Accessories and the Distributor *continued*

12 The distributor is secured to the engine with a bolt/clamp. While it can usually be removed with a 1/2-inch wrench or socket, a special tool with a cranked end (shown) makes the job easier.

13 The distributor housing should rotate freely. It can be pulled up and out of the engine with moderate effort. If the distributor housing does not rotate freely, some force can be applied. Some housings have a square-shaped portion near the bottom that accepts an open-end wrench for more aggressive rotation.

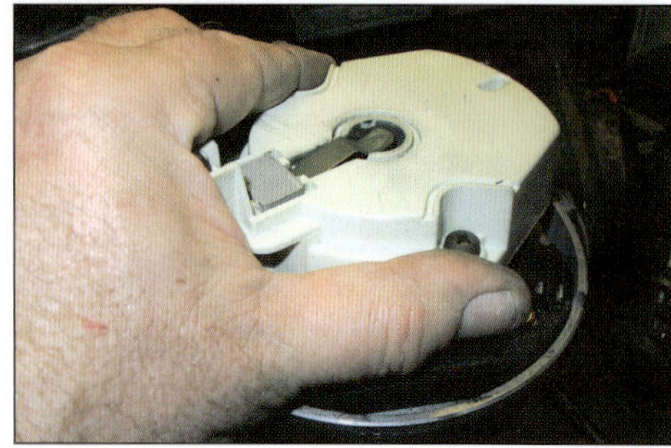

14 While pulling up on the distributor, turn the rotor clockwise. Since the distributor drive gear is bevel cut, rotating the distributor assists in its removal.

15 Raise the front of the vehicle and support it safely on jack stands.

Draining the Remaining Fluids

1 Position a drain pan underneath the drain plug at the bottom of the oil pan. Then, unscrew the drain plug and allow the oil to fully drain. Screw the plug back in place to prevent perpetual dripping.

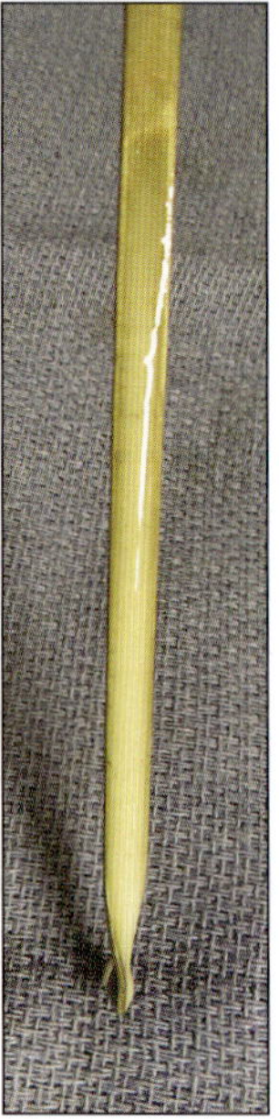

2 The condition of the oil may indicate problems within the engine. Milky oil (such as this) generally indicates a blown head gasket or a cracked cylinder head.

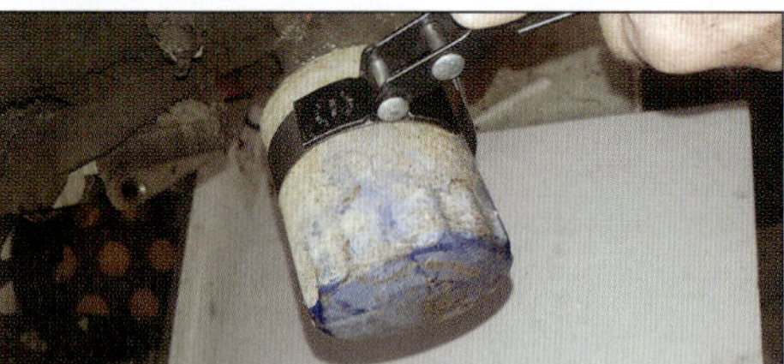

3 Use an oil-filter wrench to unscrew the oil filter, which is located at the right front of the engine. Place a drain pan underneath, as the oil will drain.

4 The left and right sides of the engine block have a coolant drain plug. If the plugs are not too difficult to remove, it's wise to remove them because additional coolant will drain. Otherwise, that additional coolant will spill when the engine is removed.

Disconnecting the Engine

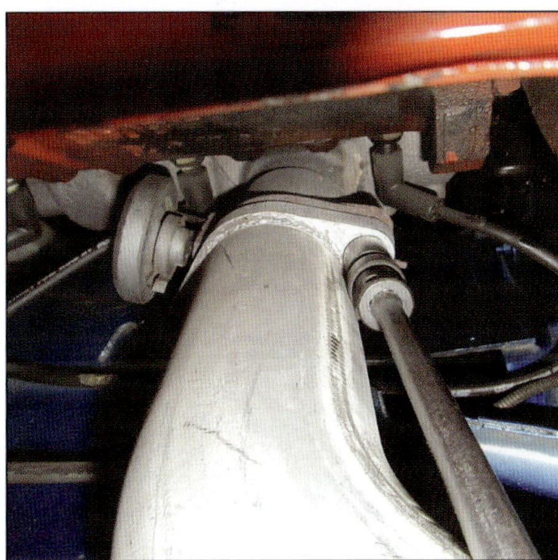

1 *Disconnect the exhaust pipes from the exhaust manifolds on the engine. These bolts are often rusted in place. In most cases, it helps to apply penetrating oil to the threads. Let it soak for at least 30 minutes.*

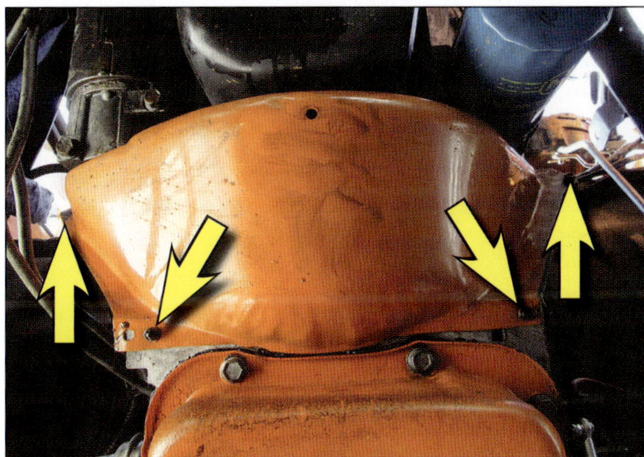

2 *Remove the four torque converter cover bolts.*

3 *Disconnect the wires from the solenoid on top of the starter. If they're difficult to access, it may be easier to unbolt the starter and reposition it for better access to the wires.*

4 *Remove the two mounting bolts at the front of the starter and lower the starter out of the way. Support the starter securely while removing the bolts. The starter may be heavier than you expect.*

5 *Remove the rubber hose(s) from the fuel pump. This pump has one hose secured by a worm-type clamp. For now, leave the steel tube attached to the pump.*

6 *Remove the bolts that attach the flexplate to the torque converter. If steady force on the wrench causes the engine to turn, strike the wrench sharply with a mallet while holding the wrench in place at the bolt end.*

Disconnecting the Engine *continued*

7 *Rotate the engine to access all of the converter bolts. This can be done using a pry bar or a large screwdriver on the flexplate ring-gear teeth.*

8 *After removing the last converter bolt, mark the relationship between the converter and flexplate.*

9 *Slide the converter back, away from the flexplate to be sure that it doesn't interfere with engine removal.*

10 *Support the front of the transmission so that it doesn't fall when the engine is removed. Here, a chain is being used. Other options include using a jack under the transmission pan or securing the top of the transmission bellhousing from under the hood. If you use a jack, the vehicle will need to remain stationary after engine removal.*

11 *Remove the six bolts that attach the engine to the transmission. Use a flexible socket and a 3-foot-long extension. In some cases, it may be easier to access the upper bolts from above the engine compartment.*

Removing the Engine

1 Remove the engine-mount through bolts. There are two of them (one on each side of the engine). A long punch and hammer can be used to drive the bolts out far enough to remove by hand.

2 Bolt a heavy-duty chain to the engine. The usual method is to remove one bolt from the front and rear of the cylinder head or intake manifold on opposite sides. Install longer, high-strength bolts in their place through the chain ends, using thick washers. Engine-lifting plates and load levelers are better alternatives, but they increase the cost.

3 After the chain has been securely attached to the engine, attach the engine-hoist hook as close to the engine's center of gravity as possible. Lift the engine slowly and carefully. It's best to have a friend on hand who can make sure that the engine does not contact anything during removal and that you haven't missed anything.

4 After the engine has been lifted safely out of the car, lower it to a safe working height and take photos while it's still fully assembled. These photos are important during reassembly. Don't place any part of your body under the engine when it's supported by only the hoist.

5 Purchase or rent a quality engine stand.

6 Remove the flexplate from the rear of the engine. An impact tool (shown) makes the job easier.

Removing the Engine *continued*

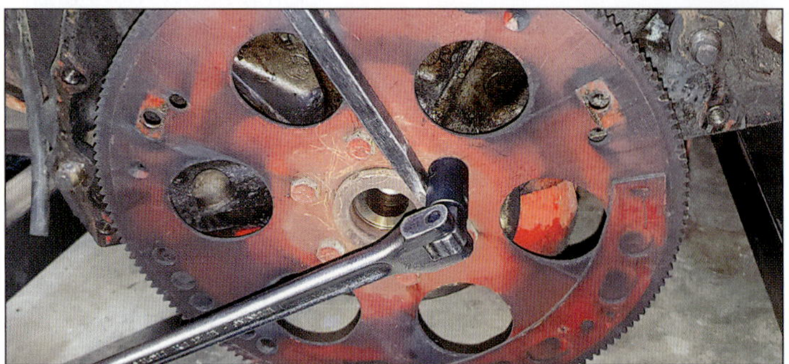

7 If your budget does not include impact tools, use a pry bar and a long breaker bar. Wedge the pry bar between the socket and the boss on the crankshaft.

8 Carefully maneuver the engine to the base of the engine stand. Loosen the large bolts/nuts and position the arms to align with the upper and lower transmission-mounting-bolt holes. Install high-strength bolts to attach the engine to the stand.

9 Carefully adjust the height of the engine using the hoist. Then, join the two components of the stand together, locking them with the supplied pin. Slowly lower the hoist until the full weight of the engine is on the stand. Then, remove the chains.

Removing External Components

1 Remove the spark-plug wires. If they are still attached to the distributor cap, leave them there and label the spark-plug end of the wires with the associated cylinder number. This allows you to match up the lengths of the new wires. Check the condition of the wires. These are obviously worn out and possibly causing a misfire.

2 The spark plug on the left shows carbon fouling from a rich mixture. Seven of the plugs show this fouling, which is most likely a carburetor problem or it could be the result of spark plugs with a heat range that is too low. The plug on the right shows oil fouling, as oil must be finding its way into that cylinder.

3 Remove the PCV valve. The valve should rattle when shaken. A stuck PCV valve can cause rough running, noise, oil leaks, and excessive oil consumption.

Removing External Components *continued*

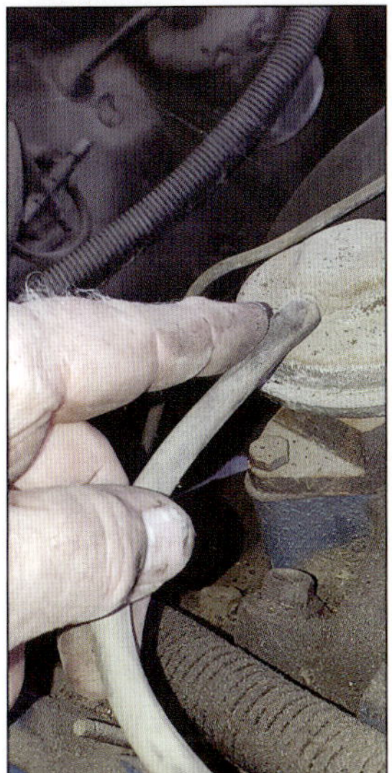

4 On later models with an exhaust gas recirculation (EGR) valve, remove the vacuum hose and then unbolt the EGR valve from the intake manifold. The EGR valve is an important emissions device. Be sure that it is clean and functioning smoothly. A malfunctioning EGR valve will cause the engine to run poorly.

5 Beginning in the late 1970s, most factory carburetors had a heat tube that circulated intake manifold heat directly to the choke coil housing on the carburetor. Disconnect the heat tube with a flare-nut wrench.

6 Use a flare-nut wrench as well as a backup wrench when disconnecting the fuel line from the carburetor. Disconnect the fuel line before unbolting the carburetor from the intake manifold.

7 On stock Quadrajet 4-barrel carburetors, the two front mounting bolts are at the top of the carburetor.

8 The two rear carburetor mounting bolts are at the base of the carburetor.

9 A variety of vacuum hoses and check valves are found on later models. Take note of how they're installed. Take photos because it's easy to forget how they're connected by the time that you're ready to reassemble the engine.

Removing External Components *continued*

10 As the hoses are removed, note their condition. All hoses will be replaced, but corrosion such as this on the inside of the coolant hoses indicates that there is worse corrosion in the cooling-system components, particularly the aluminum ones.

11 Now, remove the vacuum valves, fittings, and other items that are threaded into the intake manifold. They're more difficult to remove after the intake manifold has been removed from the engine. This is the coolant temperature sensor. Replace it with a new one during reassembly.

12 Replace the heater control valve (on the passenger-side rear of the intake manifold) during an overhaul. It's a common failure item and is difficult to replace when the engine is installed.

13 If the heater control valve is difficult to remove due to corrosion, apply penetrating oil to the threads and allow it to soak in.

14 Use a hammer to tap near the threads to help the penetrating oil seep into them.

15 Old, severely corroded valves require special removal methods. You may get lucky with a pipe wrench.

16 *This valve was so badly stuck that I had to cut it off the intake manifold (just above the nut portion).*

17 *After trimming off the top of the valve, I removed the remainder with a six-point deep socket.*

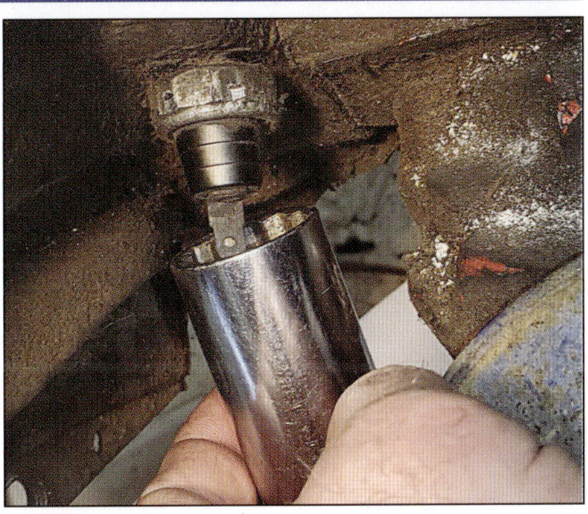

18 *A special socket was designed to remove the oil-pressure sending unit, but sometimes a standard deep socket will work. If all else fails, use a pair of locking pliers. Install a new sending unit during reassembly.*

19 *Each exhaust manifold is secured with seven bolts. They are frequently frozen in place from rust and heat cycling. Soak them thoroughly with penetrating oil, tap the bolts with a hammer, and let them set overnight. Try to unscrew them by hand only (no impact tools). If they still won't budge, try heating them with a torch.*

20 *After the exhaust manifolds have been removed, the heat shields are revealed. Unbolt them and note their orientation so that they can be reinstalled the same way.*

21 *Remove the five bolts that secure each valve cover. Lift off the covers. If needed, gently tap the covers to break the gasket seal.*

22 *Note that some valve-cover bolts have risers on the heads. These are for mounting the factory spark-plug wire separators. A deep socket or a box-end wrench is needed to remove these.*

Removing External Components *continued*

23 The engine mounts are on the sides of the engine. Remove the bolts that secure them. There are two bolts for each mount. Inspect the mounts for deterioration of the rubber. During an overhaul, engine mounts are routinely replaced.

24 Disconnect the coolant-bypass hose from the thermostat housing. Then, remove the two thermostat-housing bolts.

25 Remove the thermostat housing. Then, remove the thermostat, noting the way that it was installed.

26 Always replace the thermostat during an overhaul and inspect it for signs of failure. If it's stuck closed or is not opening fully, it's a sign that the engine has overheated. If it has overheated, it has likely blown the head gaskets, warped the heads, and possibly cracked the cylinder heads.

27 No matter how careful you are, one or more fasteners will likely break during disassembly. See chapter 2 for information about removing broken fasteners. This bolt extractor grips the unbroken portion of the bolt shank. Use lots of penetrating oil and let it soak. Heating the bolt with a torch can also help.

Removing the Intake Manifold

1 Remove the 12 bolts that attach the intake manifold. If the intake manifold sticks to the heads, pry gently, but do not pry at a gasket surface. Some of the bolts have studs at the top. Note their location so that they can be put back in the same places during reassembly.

Removing the Intake Manifold *continued*

2 The intake-manifold bolts are sometimes hidden beneath other components. In this case, the intake-manifold bolt also secures the throttle dashpot. If the intake manifold does not come loose with mild persuasion, make sure that a bolt hasn't been missed.

3 The stock iron intake manifold is quite heavy. Get a good grip on it and lift it straight up.

4 Most engines have a tin valley tray that also serves as the intake-manifold gasket. It should lift out easily.

Disassembling the Valvetrain

1 You don't want to see this during disassembly. The end cap from this rocker-arm shaft popped off at some point, which caused zero oil pressure to the rocker arms and valves.

2 Remove the rocker-arm-shaft bolts, loosening each one two turns at a time. This prevents distortion of the rocker-arm shafts, which are under load from the valve springs.

Disassembling the Valvetrain *continued*

3 Pull the pushrods straight out. Store them in order so they can be returned to their original locations.

4 Leave the rocker-arm shafts assembled for now. Mark each shaft as to its orientation on the engine. The "RF" stands for "right front."

5 On an engine that's not too gunky, the lifters can be removed easily. Use a pick-type tool to pull up gently on the wire clip. If they stick, apply penetrating oil.

6 Be sure to store the lifters so they can be returned to their original locations. For conventional flat lifters, this is critical if the original camshaft and lifters will be reused. Mixing up the lifters during reassembly can lead to accelerated wear. Even if you plan to install a new cam and lifters, keeping the lifters in order can be helpful during diagnosis.

7 If the lifters do not easily lift out of their bores, a special tool such as this can be used to pull them out. This tool is a slide hammer that creates upward force.

8 When every other method has failed, clamp the lifter in the reduced-diameter area and gently rotate back and forth while pulling up. This is an extreme method that will loosen the caked crud and possibly allow the lifter to pull through. If it doesn't work, leave it in place and let the machine shop deal with it. The lifter foot may be mushroomed.

Removing the Fuel Pump, Water Pump, and Timing Cover

1 *Unbolt and remove the fuel pump from the front driver's side of the engine. It's secured by two bolts.*

2 *Slide the water-pump drive pulley off over the mounting studs.*

3 *Remove the bolt from the center of the harmonic balancer. An impact gun works the best for this task, but it can also be removed with a socket and a breaker bar after securing the crankshaft so that it can't rotate.*

4 *Now, pull off the balancer. Sometimes, it can be removed by rocking it back and forth by hand. However, a bolt-type puller is often necessary. Use a large screwdriver between the puller bolts to lock the crankshaft in place while tightening the puller draw bolt.*

5 *Remove the 11 bolts that secure the water pump. The larger bolts also secure the timing cover. The bolts are commonly corroded in place. Soak them with penetrating oil.*

6 *As the timing cover/ water-pump bolts are removed, coolant will likely pour out. Be prepared for it.*

Removing the Fuel Pump, Water Pump, and Timing Cover *continued*

7 If the water pump does not pull off easily, tap it with a mallet to break the gasket seal. Hold the pump as it is tapped so that the pump does not fall.

8 Remove the nine remaining timing-cover bolts. The bottom four bolts secure the oil pan to the front cover. They are accessed from the bottom of the engine.

9 This view from beneath shows the four lower timing-cover bolts. When removing them, be sure that the socket is square against the oil-pan flange. The bolts are angled slightly, so it's easy to get the wrong angle on the bolt heads.

10 It's common to find that the timing cover is stuck in place from years of corrosion. Cut the oil-pan gasket loose with a utility knife. Tap around the cover with a soft-face mallet and rock it back and forth. If necessary, pry gently at various points around the cover with a plastic prying tool.

11 With the timing cover removed, this rope-type oil-seal assembly is revealed. Note the way that it's assembled (there are two metal pieces) and its orientation on the engine.

Removing the Cylinder Heads and Oil Pan

1 Each cylinder head is secured by 10 bolts. Loosen each bolt with a socket and breaker bar and feel for any differences in the break-away torque as the bolts are loosened. Loose bolts may indicate a warped cylinder head. Use care when removing the heads from the engine. They are heavy!

2 Turn the engine upside down and remove the oil pan. Most likely, some coolant and/or oil will drip out when the engine is flipped, so be prepared. The oil pan is secured by 18 bolts.

3 The oil pan may need some persuasion to be removed. If that is the case, use a soft-face mallet to tap around the pan. If that doesn't work, some light prying may do the trick. Again, pry just a little bit, moving around the perimeter of the pan.

4 Remove the two bolts that secure the oil-pickup tube and screen. Note how small the tube is. I recommend upgrading to a larger-diameter tube, which is discussed in chapter 6.

5 Inspect the condition of the pickup screen. This one is pretty gunked up. When the screen is heavily plugged, the relief valve (top) will allow oil to bypass the screen. This can lead to large-size chunks of gunk being pulled into the engine.

6 Remove the windage tray. It is secured by three bolts.

CYLINDER HEAD
AND VALVETRAIN OVERHAUL

A traditional valve job includes resurfacing the valve seats and faces as well as inspecting and measuring the valves and guides to determine if there's excessive wear. The valve springs are inspected and measured for pressure at installed height and open height. Then, the cylinder head is reassembled with new valve-stem seals, and the spring height is set at the manufacturer's specification. A complete rebuild of the cylinder heads should also include new springs and all-new valve guides that are correctly sized to the valve stems.

If this is your first time rebuilding an engine, it's probably best to leave the cylinder head reconditioning work to an engine machine shop. The machine shop will have the equipment and expertise to do this job correctly. The prices are usually reasonable compared to what you would otherwise spend when purchasing the required tools.

If you're willing to spend some money on tools, consider doing the disassembly, cleaning, and visual inspections. This may save you some money at the machine shop, and

you'll get to learn about cylinder heads in the process.

Keep in mind that reconditioned cylinder heads are commonly available on an exchange basis. Prices usually aren't much higher compared to the cost of having existing heads rebuilt. This is where doing the inspections yourself can save you some money. If serious problems are found with the heads, it may be less expensive to exchange them than to rebuild them.

Special Considerations for Buick V-8 Engines

Buick V-8 rocker arms are shaft mounted, which improves valvetrain stability versus the typical stud-mounted rocker arms that were used in Chevrolet and Pontiac engines. However, there are a few special considerations when servicing Buick valvetrains:

1. Valvetrain geometry must be checked carefully (as discussed in chapter 7). Valve-stem height can change after the valve seats and guides are reground. The

machine shop should check for correct valve-stem height as a part of a normal valve job. Nevertheless, be sure to discuss this matter with the machine shop. Correcting this issue normally requires disassembling the cylinder heads again, so get the height right the first time.

2. Stud-mounted rocker arms permit small corrections in valvetrain geometry by moving the rocker arms up and down on their studs. On Buick V-8 engines, the rocker arms have a fixed height, which makes it critical to precisely select the correct-length pushrods (also discussed in chapter 7) to maintain the correct geometry and proper lifter preload.

3. Rocker arms are of two different designs, depending on the year and model. The 1969-and-earlier models use cast-aluminum rocker arms, and later models use stamped-steel rockers. Additionally, rocker arms vary slightly in ratio. The specifications at the end of this book list the variations.

Disassembly

If you plan to disassemble the cylinder head yourself, carefully label and organize the parts. This will help with your inspections and will also help the machinist who will do the actual machine work. Bringing in a box full of dirty parts is unlikely to save you any money compared to bringing in the fully assembled heads.

Disassembling the Cylinder Heads

1 On 1967–1969 models with cast-aluminum rocker arms, note the orientation of the components on the shafts prior to disassembly. Here are two spring-steel waved washers (arrow) pressing up against the end cap. It's important to return these to their original locations.

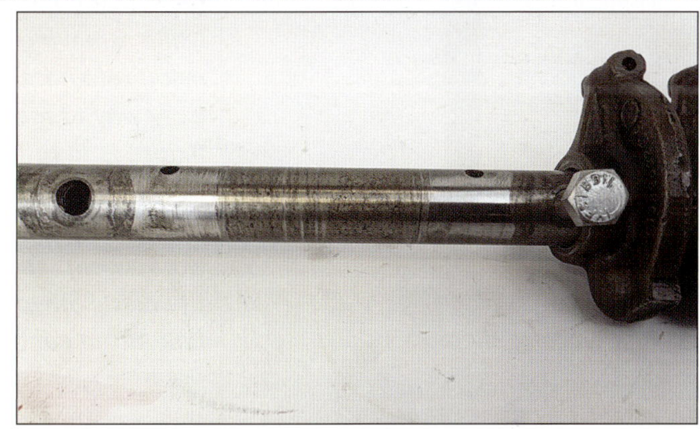

2 Remove the bolts and spacers. Then, push the rocker on one end down a few inches and secure it in place. This allows easier access to the end cap.

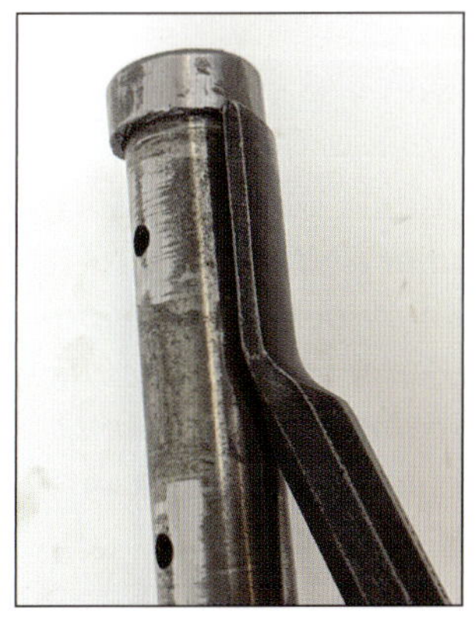

3 Remove one of the rocker-shaft caps by gently tapping with a hammer and a punch. Here, I'm using a blunt punch with a contour that matches the shaft. Work around the cap to prevent it from becoming cocked on the shaft.

4 If a cap is stubborn, heat it with a propane torch. Do this in a well-ventilated area because oil and deposits within the shaft will generate smoke. Use fire-safe gloves to avoid burning your hands.

6 The cap on the opposite end can be removed by gently tapping on it from the inside with a long dowel, rod, or pipe. Secure the shaft in a vise, using padding to prevent the shaft from being scratched.

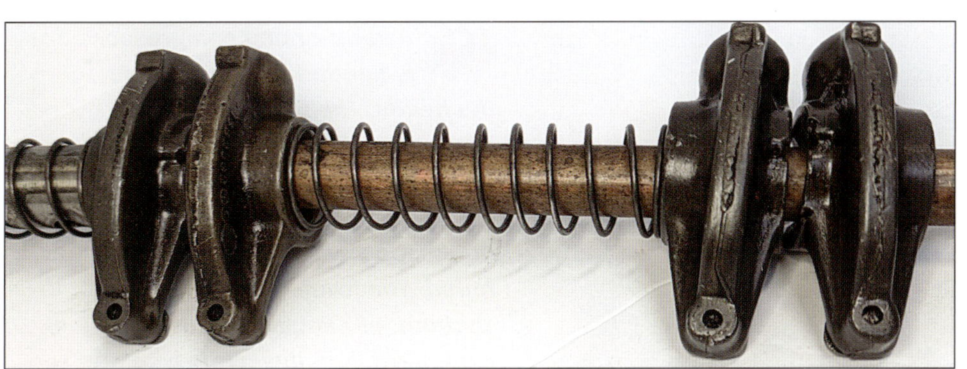

5 Once a cap has been removed, slide off the rocker arms, springs, and spacers directly onto a dowel or a similar item. I'm using a copper pipe. This maintains the correct order of components, which allows you to make more meaningful inspections.

Disassembling the Cylinder Heads *continued*

7 For 1970-and-later models, make a fixture to support the rocker-arm shafts while removing the nylon retainers. An easy way to make a fixture is to drill a hole lengthwise in a piece of wood (a 2x4 works well). Then, cut the piece of wood in half at the center of the hole.

8 Place each rocker-arm shaft on top of the two grooved pieces of wood that were made in the previous step. Then, cut off the tops of the nylon retainers with a hammer and a wood chisel or a different sharp tool.

9 Slide the rocker arms off the shafts. Keep them in order by sliding them directly onto a dowel or a similar item. Keeping the rockers organized assists with diagnosis. It will help to know which pushrod, lifter, and camshaft lobe is associated with a badly worn or damaged rocker arm.

10 Use a hammer and a punch to drive the remainder of the retainers into the rocker-arm shafts. Tiny bits of retainer will remain inside the shaft, held in place by accumulated gunk. A thorough cleaning is important.

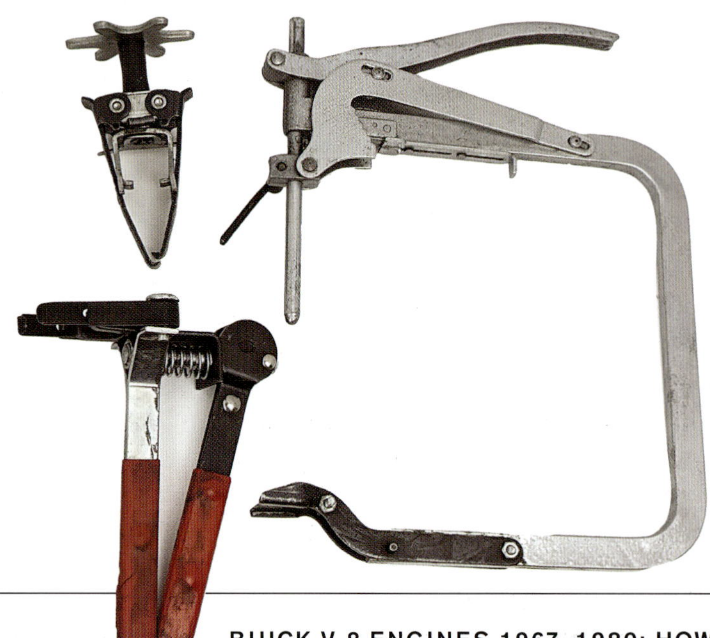

11 A valve-spring compressor is needed to disassemble the heads. The C-type compressor (right) is the fastest but most expensive choice. The screw-type compressor (upper left) is slower but cheaper and more commonly found. The lever-type compressor (bottom left) is quicker but more expensive than the screw-type compressor.

12 Compress the valve spring fully. Then, carefully remove the two keepers, which are sometimes called valve locks. A small magnet is helpful. Be careful when using the valve-spring compressor because they can slip and cause the valve to suddenly release, which can result in injury. After removing the keepers, slowly release the spring tension.

13 The keepers may stick in place. If they do, place the cylinder head on a bench and put a small block of wood under the valve head. Using a 9/16-inch deep socket and a hammer, hit the retainer. This should jar the keeper loose from the retainer. If you hit the retainer hard enough, the keeper might come loose, releasing the retainer. If this doesn't work, reinstall the compressor. The keepers should come out easily now.

14 Remove the valve spring and retainer.

15 Grasp the head of each valve and carefully pull it from the cylinder head. The keeper groove at the top of the valve stem will often cut into the seal during removal. It's okay if the seal is damaged because the seals will be replaced with new ones.

16 If the valve doesn't pull out easily through the valve guide, there's probably a burr at the top of the valve stem. Use a fine-toothed file to remove the burr. Rotate the valve stem as you do this.

17 If shims are underneath the valve springs, note their locations so they can be returned to their original locations. Shims are used to achieve the correct valve-spring installed height. After the valves and seats are ground, an additional shim (or a thicker one) may be required.

Disassembling the Cylinder Heads *continued*

18 *Intake valves can be differentiated from exhaust valves due to their size difference. An intake valve (left) is significantly larger than the exhaust valve (right).*

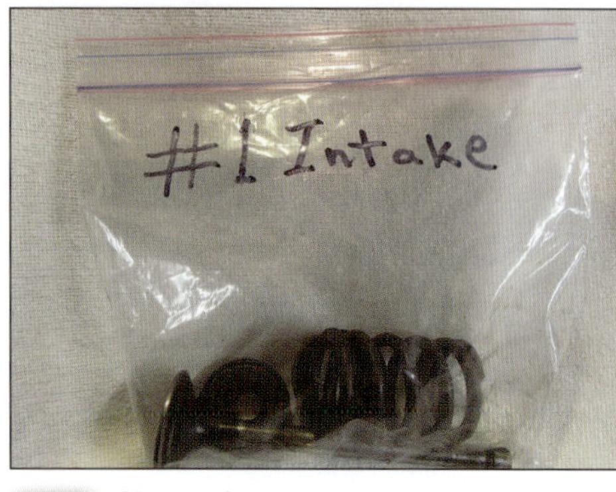

19 *Keep the components for each valve together in a labeled plastic bag.*

20 *Mark the head of each valve with a permanent marker. Make sure that the valve head is clean before doing this.*

21 *Remove the valve seal from the top of the valve guide. The special tool that is shown makes this easier, but the seal can usually be pried off with a screwdriver or removed with a pair of pliers if you're careful.*

Cleaning

If a machine shop will be rebuilding the heads, skip the heavy cleaning work. The machine shop will have much better cleaning equipment, and the cleaning is usually inexpensive when it is priced as a part of the machine work.

If a solvent tank isn't available, use engine degreaser or a spray solvent. A foaming degreaser such as this is very effective. After it soaks into the grease, hose it off. Use gloves and eye protection when using these caustic solvents.

Cylinder heads and their components usually have two types of deposits on them after long service: greasy, oily deposits and carbon deposits. Remove the greasy, oily deposits first. Do this in a solvent tank, where the heads can soak and the deposits can be brushed away.

A fine wire wheel on a bench grinder or rotary tool can help to remove heavy carbon accumulation. Avoid using such tools on gasket surfaces because they must remain smooth for proper gasket seating.

Spots of carbon and gasket pieces can be removed from surfaces with a razor-blade scraper.

Mild abrasive pads on a rotary tool can be used to remove stubborn gasket material and dry deposits.

Most of the deposits on valvetrain components can be removed by using a solvent, and using a brush on a rotary tool can make the combustion chambers spotless. Doing this will reveal any cracks.

This same method is helpful for removing deposits within the ports.

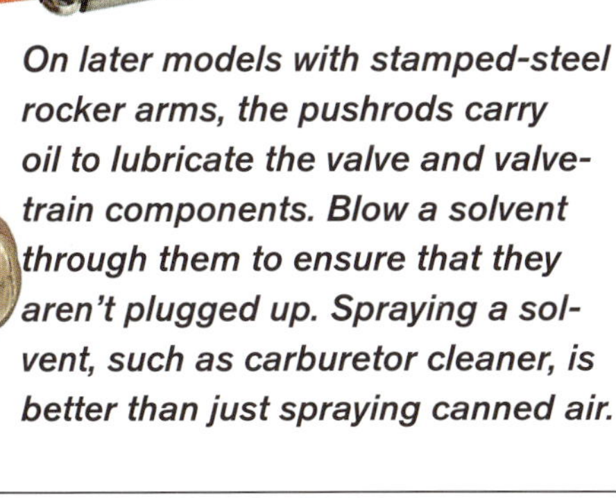

Thoroughly clean the rocker-arm shafts and rocker arms. Pay particular attention to the inside of the rocker shafts, which are a common location for carbon and sludge to accumulate. A bottle brush makes this job easier.

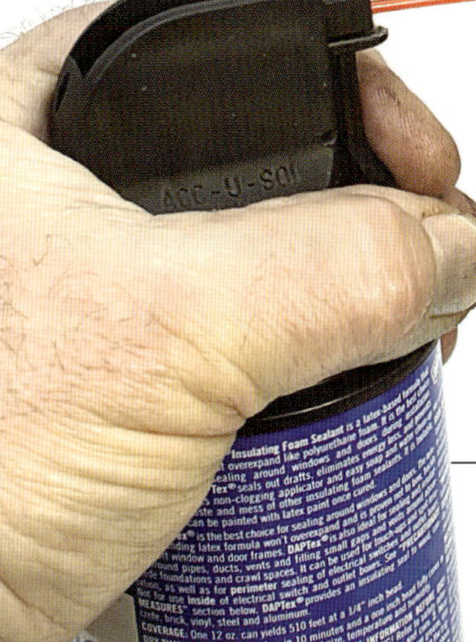

On later models with stamped-steel rocker arms, the pushrods carry oil to lubricate the valve and valvetrain components. Blow a solvent through them to ensure that they aren't plugged up. Spraying a solvent, such as carburetor cleaner, is better than just spraying canned air.

Upgrading Earlier Engines to the Later-Style Valvetrain

Beginning in 1970, Buick changed from cast-aluminum rocker arms to the stamped-steel type. The later rocker arms are lubricated through the pushrods, whereas the earlier rocker arms are lubricated through the cylinder heads and rocker-arm shafts. If you are working with a 1967, 1968, or 1969 model, consider switching to the later-style rockers/shafts, especially if there is excessive valvetrain wear in the engine.

Upgrading requires the replacement of the rocker arms and rocker shafts. Also, pushrod ends and lifter caps must be the type that have drilled lubrication holes. Note that there is limited avail-ability of lifters without lube holes, which is another reason to make the upgrade. An additional requirement for the upgrade is to block off the top-end lubrication holes in the engine block (see chapter 6) ■

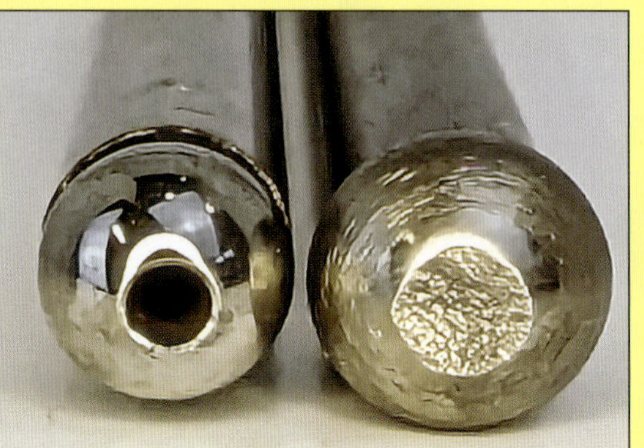

Later-style push-rods have holes in the ends to accommodate the through-the-pushrod oiling. On the right is an earlier-style push-rod without a hole. New pushrods with holes are relatively inexpensive. Do not try to drill holes in old pushrods!

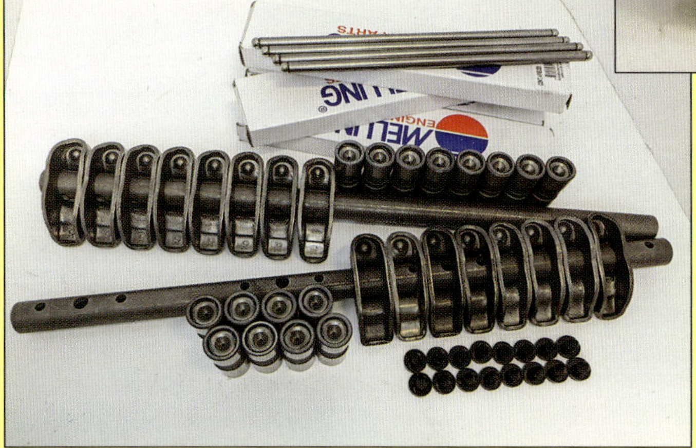

These components are needed to make the upgrade to later-style rocker arms: the rocker arms themselves, rocker-arm shafts, pushrods, and lifters.

The later-style lifters also have oiling holes (as shown on the right). Lifters are normally replaced during an overhaul, so there's no additional cost for this part of the upgrade.

Replacement Steel Rocker Arms

If you use new steel rocker arms, pay attention to the markings. Most replacement rocker arms will be marked with "R" and "L." The rocker-arm marking is used to identify which side of a rocker-arm "pair" it should be installed on.

At a quick glance, the new rocker arms look identical, but look very carefully at the cupped area where the pushrod contacts the rocker arm. There may be a small offset to one side or the other.

The purpose of having offset pushrod cups in the rocker arms is to be sure that the pushrods will be centered in the holes in the cylinder heads. If the rocker arms do not have the correct offset or are installed incorrectly, there may be contact between the pushrod and the cylinder head. This leads to excessive wear and/or engine damage.

Many Buick engines came from the factory with no offset on the rocker arms. Such rocker arms have no marking. It's okay to reuse these rocker arms as long as there is no contact between the pushrods and cylinder head after installation. ■

Replacement Steel Rocker Arms *continued*

This is the pushrod-cup area of a rocker arm. Note the slight left offset to the pushrod cup. This means that it is a right-side rocker arm (thus the "R" marking).

Replacement rocker arms usually have offset pushrod cups. They are marked to denote the side of a rocker-arm pair on which they should be installed.

The purpose of the pushrod-cup offset is to ensure that the pushrod is centered in its hole in the cylinder head (as shown).

This pair of rocker arms has been installed. They are separated by a mounting pedestal/bolt. The rocker on the right should be marked "R," and the rocker on the left should be marked "L." Factory rocker arms are usually not marked because the pushrod cup is centered (not offset).

If the pushrod is making contact with the cylinder head (as shown), the rocker arms are probably installed incorrectly. If this issue is not corrected, the pushrods will wear down and contaminate the new engine with metallic debris.

Inspection

With the components clean, do a thorough inspection to determine what parts need to be purchased and if there are major problems that would make an overhaul prohibitively expensive. In these cases, exchanging them for remanufactured heads is an attractive option.

The heads must be replaced in pairs. Even heads with the same part number can have subtle differences, such as a slightly different combustion-chamber volume due to previous machine work. This can lead to an imbalance in the compression ratio among cylinders.

Inspecting the Cylinder Heads

1 Inspect the heads thoroughly. Look for cracks in the combustion chambers, particularly if the engine was consuming coolant. If one combustion chamber is cleaner than the others, coolant was probably leaking into that cylinder from a blown head gasket or a crack in the head. Cracks can usually be seen. However, if you are in doubt, have a machine shop check the heads.

2 If the engine was severely overheated, the heads are most likely warped. This can be checked (usually by a machine shop) with a precision straightedge. Gaps beneath the straightedge greater than 0.003 inch across any length of 6 inches or 0.006 inch total means that both heads need to be resurfaced (and usually the intake-gasket surface as well). This ensures that the intake manifold will fit correctly.

3 Look for scored areas on the rocker-arm shafts where the rocker arms ride. This area should be smooth and shiny. Scoring is associated with insufficient lubrication, oil contamination, overheating, or mechanical issues in the valvetrain. If the wear grooves are deep enough to catch a fingernail, the shaft must be replaced.

4 Inspect each rocker arm where it contacts the shaft. Scoring indicates oil starvation or contamination. Discoloration indicates overheating. If any of these conditions are present, replace the rocker arms with new ones. A normal wear pattern (smooth, shiny, and relatively small) is shown on the left. The rocker arm on the right shows heavy scoring and galling. It must be replaced.

Inspecting the Cylinder Heads *continued*

5 On early aluminum rocker arms, look for the same signs of wear as on steel rocker arms. This rocker arm shows only minor wear and can be reused.

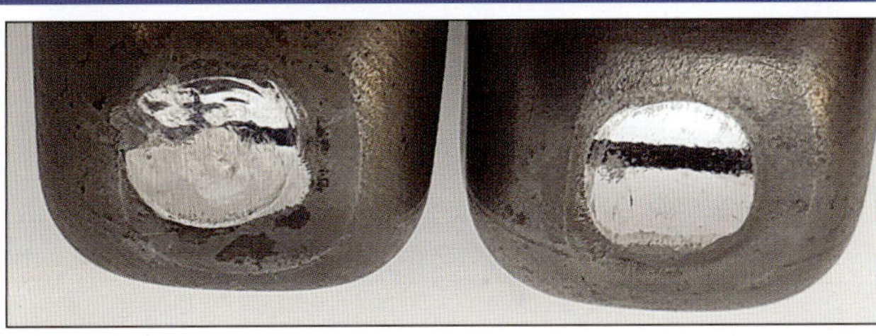

6 Inspect the surfaces where each rocker arm contacts the pushrod and valve-stem tips. Smooth and shiny is normal. If there's scoring and/or uneven surfaces, replace the rocker arms. If you're trying to save a few dollars, it's okay to reuse rocker arms with a normal wear pattern (right). If there is scoring or impact damage (left), the rocker arms must be replaced.

7 Sometimes wear is more subtle, such as the wear ridge on the tip of this early-style aluminum rocker arm. A scribe tool is pointing to the ridge.

8 On early models with aluminum rocker arms, slide each rocker arm onto its associated spot on the shaft. Then, try to rotate it back and forth. It should be difficult to detect any movement at all. Any significant movement is reason to replace the rocker arm and/or shaft. Worn valvetrain components in our engine provides one of many good reasons to upgrade to later-style steel rocker arms.

9 Inspect the pushrod ends for excessive wear. A round, smooth, and shiny area should be seen at each end that's smaller at the lifter end than at the rocker-arm end. The pushrod end on the left has normal wear. The pushrod on the right has a damaged end and must be replaced.

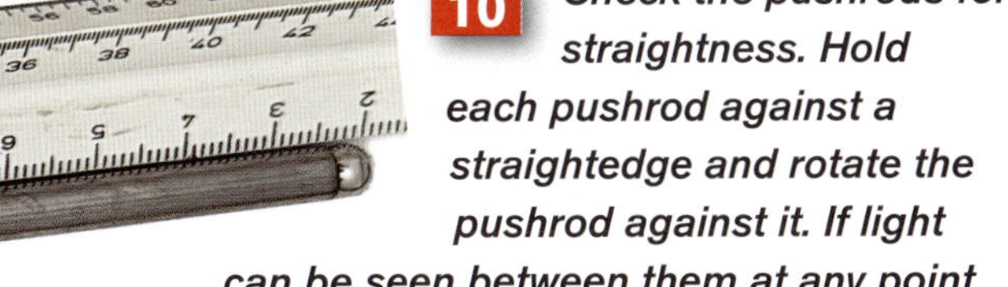

10 Check the pushrods for straightness. Hold each pushrod against a straightedge and rotate the pushrod against it. If light can be seen between them at any point while rotating the pushrod, replace it. It's best to replace pushrods as a set.

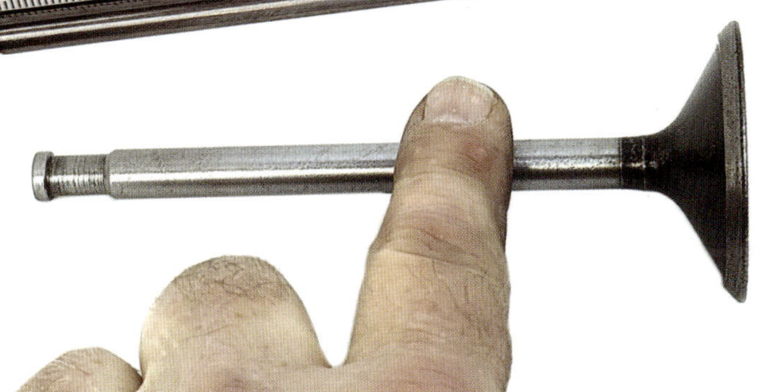

11 Check the valves for straightness. A valve can become bent through contact with a piston head. Even the slightest bend will cause the valve to not seat correctly. Roll each valve across a flat surface and look for a wobble. In addition, check the head of each piston for signs of contact with a valve. A valve that has struck a piston must be replaced.

Inspecting the Cylinder Heads *continued*

12 *Valves must fit in their guides without any significant side play. Install each valve into its associated guide and pull it out about 3/8 inch off its seat. Move the valve head side to side. You should not be able to detect any significant side-to-side movement.*

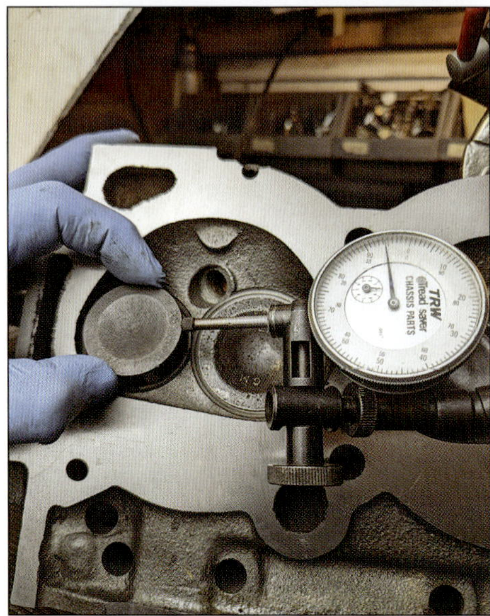

13 *To precisely measure the valve stem-to-guide clearance, mount a dial indicator with the probe perpendicular to the valve stem (as shown). Move the valve left to right. Divide the total amount that the indicator fluctuates by 2 to obtain the stem-to-guide clearance. See the appendix for the specification on your engine.*

14 *If the valve stem-to-guide clearance is excessive, the valve guides need to be reconditioned or replaced. Sometimes, the valves also need to be replaced to get the clearance correct. Valve-guide reconditioning and replacement must be done by a machine shop because special equipment is required. Here, a guide is being cut to the correct length.*

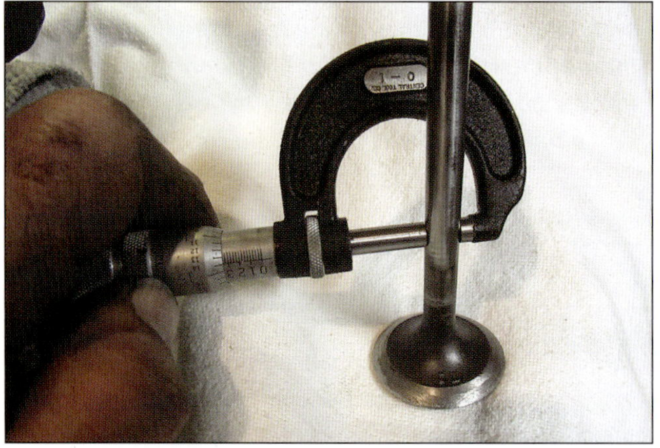

15 *Measure the valve stems, particularly at the wear areas, which will appear shiny. Compare the measurements to the specifications in the appendix. Replace the valves if they are excessively worn.*

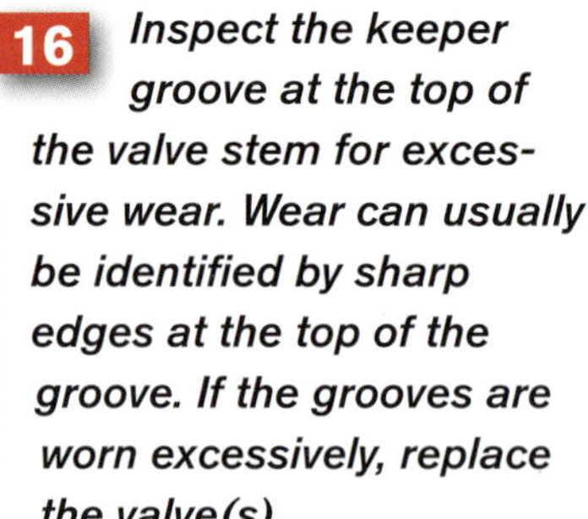

16 *Inspect the keeper groove at the top of the valve stem for excessive wear. Wear can usually be identified by sharp edges at the top of the groove. If the grooves are worn excessively, replace the valve(s).*

17 *Inspect the face of each valve at the point where it contacts the seat. Look for wear and signs of erosion. This valve had been overheated, and erosion of the face is evident. Although the corresponding seat was not damaged, the damage that is shown caused low compression in the associated cylinder. Damage this severe requires replacement of the valve.*

18 *If erosion from the valve overheating is not identified and corrected early, it causes a valve to become "burnt." Damage such as this will result in almost no compression in the cylinder. It's usually an exhaust valve that gets burnt.*

19 *Check the tip of each valve for evidence of wear. Minor wear can be corrected by machining. If the wear is excessive, find the problem in the valvetrain that led to the wear. The severe wear on this valve tip indicates serious problems in the valvetrain.*

20 *Carefully inspect the valve seats for signs of pitting, cracks, and wear. Minor wear and pitting will be removed during a "valve job" at the machine shop.*

21 *Valves and guides that are not severely worn can be reconditioned by an automotive machine shop. During this process, the seats and guides will be ground to precise angles (usually 45 degrees on the seat and 44 degrees on the valve). Grinding also ensures that the worn seats and faces will be made concentric so they will fit together perfectly.*

22 *Valves must always have a margin, which means that there should not be a sharp edge around the face. The margin should be at least 1/32 inch on the exhaust and 1/64 inch on the intake.*

23 *It's best to replace the valve springs during an overhaul. However, if you're on a tight budget, you can try reusing the old ones. Inspect the springs carefully and replace any that have nicks or scratches. If one or more springs are shorter than the others, replace all of the springs. Keep in mind that valve springs are critical parts that can be worn or damaged in ways that you cannot see.*

Inspecting the Cylinder Heads *continued*

24 Check the "free" length of each valve spring. If one or more springs are shorter than the others, replace all of the springs. The appendix provides the free-length specifications.

25 The ability of a spring to stand up straight without leaning one way or another is called squareness. On a flat surface, rotate the spring while holding it gently against a precision 45-degree angle. If the spring leans more than 1/16th inch in any direction, replace it.

26 A special tool is needed to check valve-spring pressure at the installed height and the open height. The appendix has specifications for stock rebuilds, but if you're upgrading your camshaft, use the specifications provided by the camshaft manufacturer.

Assembly

The shop that is performing the machine work on the cylinder heads will usually do the assembly. This is highly recommended, as the inexperienced are likely to make mistakes.

Assembling the Cylinder Heads

1 Before final assembly, check the installed height of the valve springs. With the valve installed in the guide, assemble the retainer and keepers on the end of the valve. Hold the retainer up tightly and measure between the valve-spring seat on the cylinder head and the retainer. Compare the reading to the specification in the appendix.

2 A more precise method to check the installed height of the valve springs is to use a special micrometer-type tool, such as the one that is shown here. Considering the greater precision and the time that it will save, it may be a good investment.

Assembling the Cylinder Heads *continued*

3 If the installed height is excessive, use a shim under the spring to get it right. Shims are available in various thicknesses and are often necessary when the original valves and seats are reused. If new valves or seats are used, there may be too little installed height. In that case, the valve/seat needs to be ground farther or the spring seat on the head needs to be machined down.

4 The valve-stem height is critical to ensure proper valvetrain geometry. A special tool, such as the one that is shown, allows for a precise measurement. This measurement should be carried out by a machine shop. The correction is to grind the valve-stem tip to make the valve shorter or grind the valve face and/or seat to make the valve protrude farther.

5 Apply assembly lube to the valve stem. Then, slide the valve stem into the valve guide. Work the valve-stem seal over the stem. Sharp edges on the keeper grooves can cut the seal, so tape may need to be wound around the keeper grooves (as shown) to protect the seal. Stock Buick valve stems do not usually have sharp edges.

6 Tap each valve seal into place over the top of the valve guide. Special tools are made for this purpose, but a socket that's slightly larger than the valve guide can be used.

7 Install the valve spring and retainer.

Assembling the Cylinder Heads *continued*

8 Compress the spring and install the valve keepers. It's often difficult to get the keepers to stay in place. Put some grease on each keeper to make this task easier.

9 With the heads reassembled, turn each head upside down and pour water into the combustion chamber. Check for leakage into the intake and exhaust ports. There should be a perfect seal with no leakage. If not, there is a leak between a valve and its seat.

10 Valves that are not sealing properly can sometimes be corrected by lapping. With the spring removed, the valve is held by a suction-cup tool and rotated back and forth against its seat with a special abrasive compound between the valve and the seat.

11 The process of lapping will reveal problems with the valve seal. It should leave an even ring on the valve and the seat that is roughly centered on the valve. If it does not do so, there is a problem with the valve job.

12 On 1967–1969 models, double-check that the rocker-arm shafts are clean inside and out. Then, reassemble them, returning the rocker arms and springs to their original locations. Place a small dab of assembly lube into the shaft bore on each rocker.

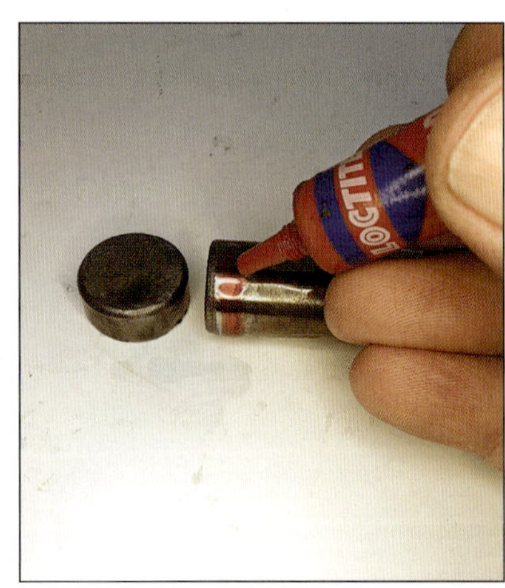

13 When installing the rocker-shaft caps used on 1967–1969 models, use red Loctite. It acts as a lubricant during reassembly and also ensures that the cap will be secure.

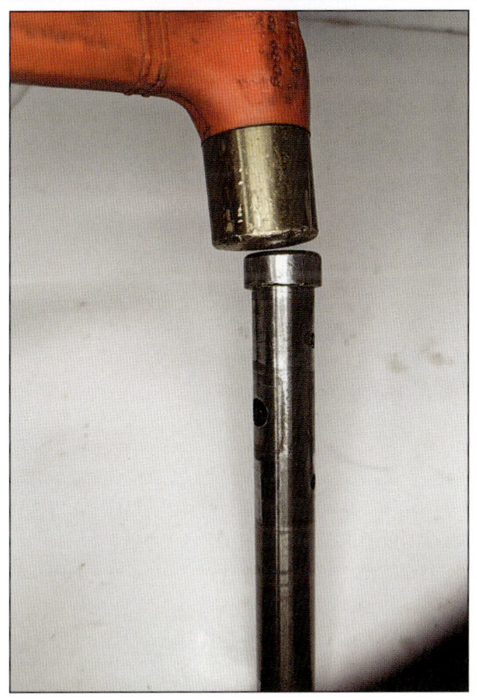

14 To seat the 1967–1969 caps, the best practice is to use a hydraulic press. If you don't have access to a press, use a hammer. Install both caps and place one end on a hard surface while tapping the caps into place. Flip over the shaft and tap on the other side. Here, I'm using a brass hammer to prevent denting the cap.

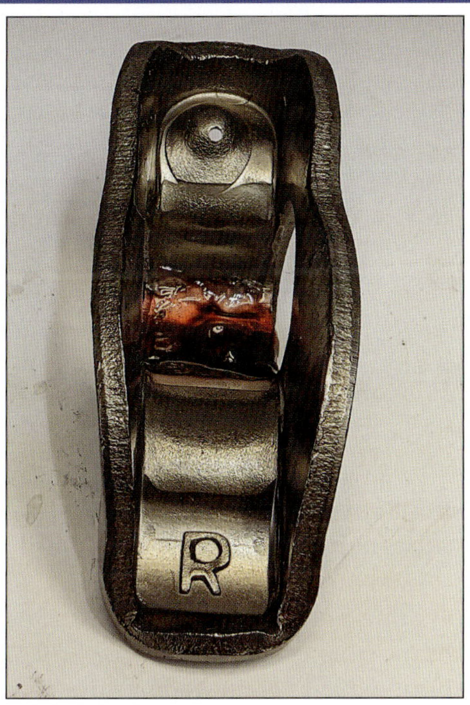

15 If you are using the original rocker arms on 1970-and-later models, lubricate the contact surfaces on the rocker arms. Then, return them to their original locations on the shafts.

16 Install a new nylon retainer by tapping it into place with a hammer and a suitably sized driver. Retainer ribs tend to shear off during assembly, creating little bits of nylon that resemble fingernail clippings. If this happens, clean all debris from the rockers and shafts.

17 TA Performance offers a superior retainer with ribs that resist shearing during reassembly.

18 For further insurance against rib shearing, soak the retainers in near-boiling water for about 30 minutes prior to installation. This temporarily softens the nylon material, making it more pliable.

ENGINE BLOCK OVERHAUL

The cylinder block contains the crankshaft, camshaft, pistons, connecting rods, and the timing chain and sprockets. The block and its components need to be disassembled, cleaned, and inspected. The machine shop can handle this, but I recommend for DIYers to perform the disassembly, basic inspection, and wear measurements. These are things that can be performed at home without many special tools. In addition, they help you understand any issues with the engine so that you can have an informed discussion with the machine shop about the reconditioning work that will be done.

Machining operations need to be done by an automotive machine shop. Do your research to find a shop with a good reputation that has worked on Buick engines of this era before. Ask other Buick owners and club members. A perceived bargain regarding machine work can be a false economy if the engine does not go together correctly or fails prematurely.

Reassembly can be done at home and is a way to save some additional money during an overhaul. If you're careful and take your time, you should be able to do as good of a job as the machine shop.

Disassembly

It's time to disassemble the engine. The following headings cover all of the components.

Timing Chain and Sprockets

First, remove the timing chain and sprockets. These components are often stuck in place from years of varnish buildup, so some persuading is usually needed.

Removing the Timing Chain and Sprockets

1 On big-block engines, remove the two bolts from the camshaft sprocket.

2 On small-block engines, remove the bolt at the center of the camshaft. If the shaft rotates, reinstall the vibration-damper bolt and hold it with a wrench as the camshaft bolt is being loosened.

Removing the Timing Chain and Sprockets *continued*

3 Small-block engines have a distributor drive gear and a fuel-pump eccentric that are attached to the end of the camshaft. Pull them off and inspect the gear and eccentric for wear. On big-block engines, the eccentric and gear are part of the camshaft.

4 Pull off the camshaft sprocket, rocking it back and forth. Lower the camshaft far enough to disengage the chain from the lower sprocket. Then, remove the camshaft sprocket and chain.

5 The crankshaft sprocket is often tight on the crankshaft and will need to be pulled loose. Here, a three-jaw puller is being used. This can sometimes be done with two small pry bars.

6 After the gear is loose, carefully work it off the end of the crankshaft by hand. Be aware that there is a Woodruff key that is pressed into the crankshaft for gear alignment. Remove this before sending the crankshaft to the machine shop.

Pistons and Connecting Rods

Check for a wear ridge at the top of each cylinder. If there's enough of a ridge to catch a fingernail, it means that it will catch the piston rings when the pistons are pushed out the top of the bore. A ridge reamer is necessary to remove the ridge.

Ridge reamers can damage the cylinder bore if they are not used correctly, so I recommend that wear ridges should be removed by the machine shop before the pistons are removed. If only a few cylinders have a significant wear ridge, the crankshaft can sometimes be removed with the corresponding pistons pushed all the way to the top of the bores.

Adequate connecting-rod side clearance ensures that the connecting rods remain square to the crankshaft and perfectly centered in the cylinder bore. Excessive side clearance indicates wear on the side surfaces of the connecting rods at the "big-end" bore and/or wear at the ends of the connecting-rod journals on the crankshaft.

Excessive side clearance is usually associated with excessive wear at the thrust surfaces of the number-3 main bearing. Wear in these areas (rod sides, rod journal ends, and the thrust bearing) often indicates that the crankshaft is receiving excessive forward pressure. This can be the result of a torque converter being improperly installed.

On manual-transmission vehicles, pressure applied to the clutch pedal over many years of use will cause some wear. If a high-pressure (racing-type) clutch is used, the wear will be accelerated.

Loosen each connecting-rod cap nut three-quarters of a turn, which allows the cap to be pulled loose from the connecting rods. Rotate the crankshaft until the number-1 piston is near the bottom of its bore, which allows easy access to the connecting-rod nuts.

A bearing insert is in each connecting-rod cap. If it falls out during removal, be sure to keep it with its associated cap. Knowing where each bearing came from can help with bearing failure diagnosis.

Once the connecting-rod caps are removed, press firmly on the connecting rod to push the piston into the cylinder bore. Position a hand at the other end of the cylinder bore to catch the piston when it comes out of the cylinder. If the piston gets stuck at the top of the bore, it's because the top piston ring is encountering the wear ridge at the top of the cylinder.

Use moderate pressure to try to overcome the resistance, but if the piston is stuck, just leave it there for now. The crankshaft may be able to be removed with the piston in place. If so, remove the piston from the bottom. If not, a machine shop can ream away the ridge to allow the piston to be removed from the top.

Repeat this procedure for the remaining piston/connecting-rod assemblies. After removal, install each bearing cap back on its associated connecting rod and install the nuts finger-tight. This will keep all of the associated parts together to aid in failure analysis. Now, remove the piston rings from the pistons.

Removing the Pistons and Connecting Rods

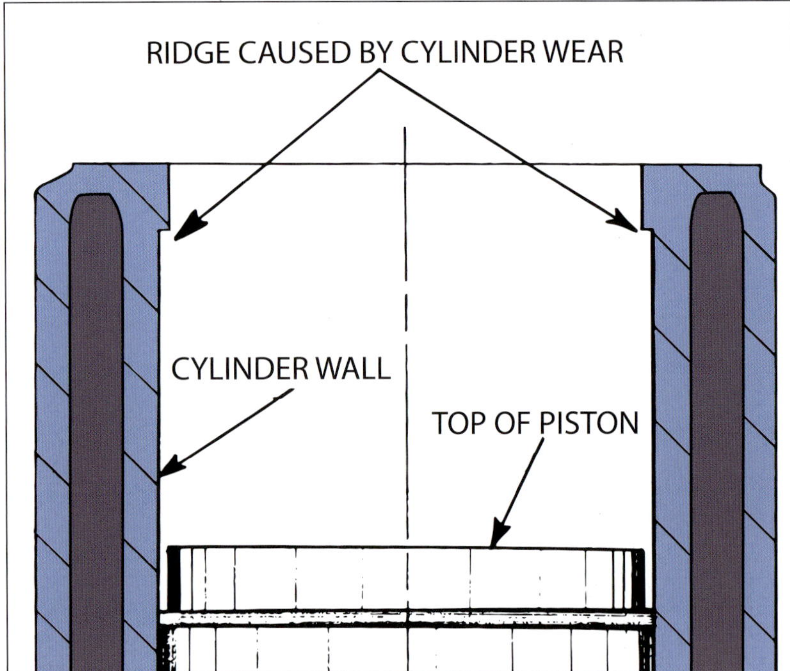

1 *Piston rings do not travel to the very top of the cylinder bore during engine operation, so a wear ridge forms over time. This ridge can catch the top piston ring, preventing piston removal. If that happens, don't force the piston through because it might cause a piston ring land to break.*

2 *Using feeler gauges, check the connecting-rod side clearance at each pair of connecting rods (four total points of checking). Firmly push both rods outward on the crankshaft journal and measure the gap between them with feeler gauges. The combined thickness of feeler gauges that will insert with a slight drag is the side clearance. Compare this to the specifications in the appendix.*

Removing the Pistons and Connecting Rods *continued*

3 Check for marks where each connecting rod and cap meet. Aftermarket rods, such as the one shown here, are usually marked clearly.

4 OEM rods and caps are usually not well marked. Mark them with number-stamping dies or a hammer and punch (shown). The number of dots indicates the cylinder number. This is the number-5 cylinder connecting rod.

5 Remove each connecting-rod cap. A 12-point 9/16-inch wrench or socket is required.

6 If the cap is stubborn, screw the nuts back on a few turns. Then, tap the nuts with a soft-face hammer, moving back and forth. This should separate the rod from the cap. Don't worry about dislodging the bolt from the rod because the rods will be reconditioned as a part of the overhaul.

7 Pull the cap off the connecting rod bolts carefully. Wiggle it back and forth while lifting.

8 Place rubber covers over the ends of the connecting-rod bolts. This protects the cylinder walls as each rod is removed. If special covers, such as these, are not available, short lengths of 3/8-inch-inner-diameter rubber hose works as well.

Removing the Pistons and Connecting Rods *continued*

9 *Gently push against the bottom of the connecting rod while keeping a hand in place beneath the piston. A hammer handle is a good way to apply pressure against the bottom of the connecting rod as it moves out of easy reach.*

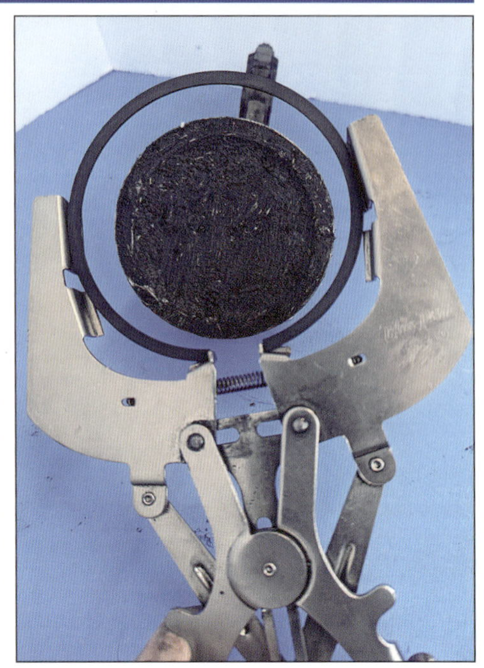

10 *Remove the two compression rings, starting with the top ring. A special tool is required to do this without breaking the rings, which are cast iron and brittle.*

11 *The oil-control ring is a three-piece design that can be removed by hand. Lift out and rotate each of the thin steel rails at the top and bottom. Use a feeler gauge to protect the piston against scratching.*

12 *The oil-ring expander can be easily removed at this point. Even though the rings need to be replaced, keep each ring set together and numbered as to which cylinder it came from. This may help with diagnosis.*

Crankshaft

Check the crankshaft endplay. It is important to check because it indicates the level of wear on the thrust bearing faces (and possibly the thrust faces on the crankshaft). If endplay is excessive, determine the reason why.

The main bearing caps should have cast-in numbers that indicate their orientation on the block. The numbers (1 through 5) begin at the front of the block.

Remove the bolts from the main bearing caps. They are very tight, so a large breaker bar is needed. Pull each cap off the block. The machined recesses in the block are an interference fit with the machined surfaces on the sides of the caps. The caps are tight to the block by design.

If you are short on space, store the crankshaft on its end against a wall (indoors) with the rear of the crankshaft down. Tie the top of the crankshaft securely to an anchor point on the wall. If it is stored in a garage with a concrete floor, place a piece of wood between the floor and the bottom of the crankshaft.

Removing the Crankshaft

1 *Before removing the crankshaft, check the endplay. Mount a dial indicator at the front of the engine with the probe directly in line with the crankshaft. Use a large screwdriver to gently pry the crankshaft to the rear, zero the dial indicator, and then pry the crankshaft forward. Be careful where you pry so that you do not to cause damage. The total gauge reading is the endplay.*

3 *If the markings on the bearing caps are not clear, use a punch and hammer to mark them. It's critical that the caps are returned to their original locations with the correct end facing forward. I recommend taking photos prior to disassembly.*

2 *If you don't have a dial indicator, pry the crankshaft forward (as shown). Then, measure the gap between the crankshaft and the front surface of the number-3 (thrust) bearing.*

4 *Unscrew the main bearing cap bolts. Start loosening at the center cap and work your way out to the end caps.*

5 *The main bearing caps fit tightly, so leverage is usually needed to remove them. Here, I'm using a pair of large punches. Pull the punches together and lift up while gently rocking the cap back and forth. Be careful not to rock the caps excessively. Use punches that will not travel all the way into the bolt holes in the block.*

Removing the Crankshaft *continued*

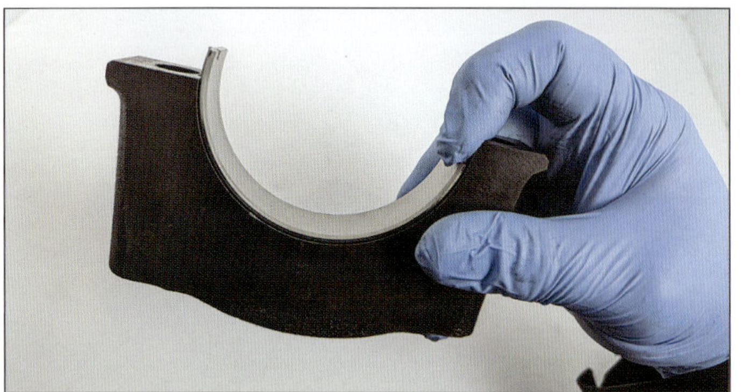

6 *Remove the bearing inserts by pressing on the side opposite of the bearing tang. The bearing will slide out the other side. Sometimes the inserts are tight, particularly on the thrust bearings. It may be necessary to use a plastic tool to help them along. During removal, mark each bearing as to its location on the engine.*

7 *The center bearing (the number-3 bearing) is a thrust-type of bearing that controls the front-to-rear movement of the crankshaft. Inspect it for wear on the vertical surfaces that contact the crankshaft. Excessive wear should be diagnosed. Thrust-bearing wear is most commonly found on manual-transmission vehicles due to the forward load that is transmitted by clutch actuation.*

8 *Most likely, your engine has a rope-type seal or a two-piece, lip-type seal. Take note of the type of seal that was used. The superior lip-type seals are now available for all Buick engines. I'll be upgrading from the rope-type seal that is shown here.*

9 *Lift the crankshaft up and out of the block. It's heavy, so be careful. If it's not lifted straight up, it will become stuck and you won't be able to lift it any higher. If this happens, lower the crankshaft and try again. A bit of light rocking may be necessary to find the sweet spot where the crankshaft will lift up easily.*

Camshaft

Now, remove the camshaft. Keep the camshaft perfectly flat during removal. If you do not do so, the lobes of the camshaft will scratch the camshaft bearings. The bearings will be replaced as part of the overhaul, but now is the time to practice so that the new bearings will not be harmed during reassembly.

Sometimes, the center of the camshaft can be supported from underneath. It will often need a heavy wire to support it through the opening in the valley area of the block.

Removing the Camshaft

1 *Carefully remove the camshaft from the block, keeping it as level as possible throughout the process.*

2 *Support the camshaft in the center with a coat-hanger wire, which will help the camshaft stay straight during removal. As the camshaft is removed, rotate it while pulling gently.*

Oil and Coolant Plugs

Remove the oil gallery plugs. There are two main oil galleries that run the length of the block and have plugs at each end (four plugs total). The rear plugs are threaded in place and can be removed with a 1/4-inch-drive tool. They are usually very tight.

Use penetrating oil and tap them with a hammer to make sure that the lube penetrates into the threads. A 1/4-inch breaker bar will not usually provide enough leverage. Use a quality 1/4-inch to 3/8-inch reducing adapter with a 3/8-inch breaker bar.

If the plugs do not unscrew, it may be necessary to heat the area with an acetylene torch. If you don't have a torch and the experience to use it safely, it's best to leave the job to a machine shop.

To remove the front plugs, insert a long rod, screwdriver, or similar tool into the hole at the rear of the block. The tool must be long enough to travel the entire length of the block. Tap on the rod until the plug is dislodged. Then, do the same for the other plug.

Removing the Oil and Coolant Plugs

1 *All of the plugs need to be removed. Here, I'm removing one of the two threaded plugs at the rear of the block. They are 1/4-inch square drive, so a 1/4-inch-drive tool fits.*

Removing the Oil and Coolant Plugs *continued*

2 *After the rear plugs have been removed, insert a long rod (arrow) and use it to drive out the front plugs.*

3 *A total of six core plugs, or freeze plugs, are in the block (three on each side). Remove them by knocking them into the block with a hammer and a large punch or a similar tool.*

4 *The core plug can now be removed by extracting it from the block with locking pliers.*

Lubrication System Modifications

Buick engines are very durable, but the lubrication system is a known problem, particularly on earlier big-blocks. A primary area of concern is the "suction" side of the system (from the oil pickup in the pan to the oil-pump inlet). The 1970-and-earlier big-blocks have 1/2-inch-diameter passages in the engine block and a 1/2-inch-diameter pickup tube. This does not provide sufficient oil flow, especially when considering the large 3.25-inch main bearing journal diameter on the big-block. To ensure long engine life, any rebuild of a 1970-or-earlier big-block should include an upgrade to a 5/8-inch-diameter pickup tube and an enlargement of the suction-side oil passages to 5/8 inch.

The first passage to enlarge is the horizontal hole that starts at the front of the block. It is just above the oil-pan rail on the passenger's side and runs to the base of the oil-pickup tube. Starting with the short 5/8-inch bit, slowly and carefully drill as straight as possible, following the existing hole. Use plenty of lubrication, stop frequently to clean out the shavings, and look inside to confirm that you are not going off center.

If the drill gets off center, straighten the hole by applying some pressure in the opposite direction. It doesn't have to be perfect, but try to make the hole as straight as possible. When the short bit bottoms out, switch to the long bit and keep drill-ing. The long bit should reach the end of the hole just before the drill bottoms against the block.

Now, drill out the short passage from the oil-pickup mounting point to intersect with the horizontal hole that you just drilled. This hole is drilled at an angle.

Early big-block engines also have relatively small oil passages in the front cover. It's important that adequate oil volume can pass through the cover on its way into and out of the oil pump. Replacing the front cover during an overhaul is always wise. New covers have the later-style large oil passages.

The small-block oiling system is basically a scaled-down version of the big-block engine, so small-blocks can be subject to the same lubrication

Tapping Main Oil Galleries for Threaded Plugs

The stock main oil-gallery plugs at the front of the engine don't usually come loose during service, but the damage to the engine if one pops out can be catastrophic. There's not much cost or work involved in tapping these holes for threaded plugs. There's peace of mind in having threaded plugs, knowing they can never pop loose.

It is necessary to thread the holes for 3/8-inch pipe plugs, but don't use just any plugs. TA Performance sells a kit (part number 1519) that uses a shallow machined plug for the passenger's side. It is used to prevent obstructing an intersecting oil-feed passage just behind the plug opening.

Using a 37/64-inch drill bit, drill the holes in the block a bit deeper than they are currently—but not all the way through. The purpose is to make the tap easier to turn. Start with the driver-side hole, which uses the thick plug. Square up the tap in the hole. Then, rotate it about a half turn (180 degrees) at a time. Back it out half turn and then advance another half turn.

Use a 5/8-inch, 12-point socket and ratchet to turn the tap. Keep the tap well-oiled and continue to check it for straightness. Remember that a large hole is being tapped into cast iron, so it won't be easy. A 1/2-inch-drive ratchet or a breaker bar is needed when the going gets tough. When a few threads have been made, remove the tap and check the fit of the plug. Continue this process until the plug can be tightened flush with the block.

Next, do the same with the passenger-side gallery. It's very important to not tap too deep because the main feed to the passenger-side lifter gallery is directly behind the plug. If you tap the plug too deep, the feed will be obstructed. Once you are close, check the plug depth every quarter turn or so to make sure that the plug doesn't go any deeper than flush with the block.

When the holes have been properly tapped, remove the plugs so that the oil passages in the block can be properly cleaned. ◼

Stock oil gallery plugs are pressed into the block. The block area around each plug is staked in four places to keep it from popping out. This is effective for normal service, but if the oil pressure spikes, it's possible for one to pop out.

To install threaded plugs, open the passages with a 37/64-inch drill bit. Then, tap the holes with a 3/8-inch national pipe thread (NPT) tap. Do this with care. Follow the instructions in the "Tapping Main Oil Galleries for Threaded Plugs" sidebar.

issues as the big-block. It is wise to upgrade to a 5/8-inch oil-pickup tube and to enlarge the suction-side passages to 1/2 inch.

When drilling out these passages, be aware that the deep "skirt" below the main bearings on the 350 makes the short hole trickier to drill. There is the potential for block damage if the drilling is not done precisely. I suggest getting help from a machine shop if you plan to drill out this hole on a 350 engine.

Whether you are rebuilding a small-block or a big-block engine, it is likely to find misalignment of the main bearing lubrication holes. This is easily corrected by chamfering the oil holes in the block.

Another significant problem area for all of Buick V-8 engines is that

The suction side of the lubrication system on 1970-and-earlier big-block engines is inadequate, even for a stock engine. Enlarge the suction passages in the block from the stock 1/2 inch to 5/8 inch. Two 5/8-inch drill bits are needed for this job: one 6 inches long and one 12 inches long.

The 1/2-inch pickup tube (left) is found on early big-block engines. It does not allow adequate flow for even stock big-block rebuilds. The 5/8-inch pickup (right) is a great upgrade and is recommended for all rebuilds.

To open up the suction passages in the block, do some careful drilling. The hole from the front of the block to the base of the pickup tube is 10¾ inches long. Take your time and carefully monitor your progress. Follow the existing hole and make corrections if you get off course.

The 1/2-inch hole below the oil-pickup tube also needs to be opened up. This hole is drilled at an angle, which should be followed as closely as possible. On this block, the angle of the hole was about 60 degrees.

Once both holes are drilled, clean up the intersection point with the drill and a carbide ball bit. Make the transition as smooth as possible.

For the final step, use a carbide bit to smooth out the corner where oil will flow up into the front cover. The faint outline of the front-cover passage can be used as a guide.

The oil suction passage in the early big-block front cover is only 1/2 inch, which is shown by this 1/2-inch drill bit.

Fix the misalignment by using a drill and a 45-degree chamfering tool. After using the chamfering tool, smooth out the opening with a 45-degree abrasive stone.

Here is the same drill bit in the suction hole of a later-style timing cover with a 5/8-inch passage. Note how the opening around the hole is larger, not just the oil hole itself. New aftermarket covers are all the larger size.

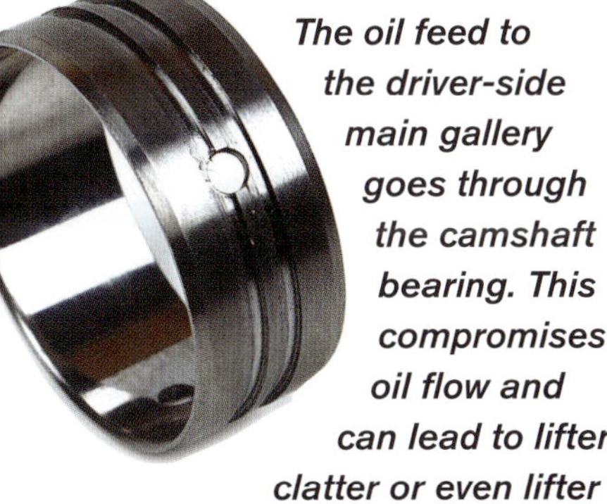

The oil feed to the driver-side main gallery goes through the camshaft bearing. This compromises oil flow and can lead to lifter clatter or even lifter failure. TA Performance manufactures special camshaft bearings that direct the oil flow underneath the camshaft bearing to ensure lifter lubrication.

It's common to find that the main bearing oil holes do not align properly with their associated oil holes in the block. This is particularly true for big-block engines.

I'm converting to through-the-pushrod oiling, so I need to plug the oil holes on the cylinder decks (the surfaces where the cylinder heads mount). The holes are located at the upper left corners. Tap each hole with a 1/8-inch NPT tap. Then, install a 1/8-inch pipe plug. Make sure the plug is below the deck surface so that it does not interfere with the head gasket.

the pressurized oil for the driver-side lifter gallery passes through the front camshaft bearing. This flow is inadequate, especially as the camshaft bearing wears over time. A grooved front camshaft bearing should be used in all rebuilds.

If you are switching a 1967–1969 engine to through-the-pushrod oiling, plug the holes in the upper left corner of each deck surface on the block. These holes previously fed oil to the rocker-arm shafts and are no longer needed. If the holes are not plugged, there may be oil leaks.

If you are rebuilding a 455 (regardless of year), there is one of these same holes on the driver-side deck surface. I recommend to plug that hole in the same way.

Lubrication Modifications for High-Performance Engines

The previous text addresses common lubrication system upgrades for stock and mild performance engines. It's important to note that other lubrication-system upgrades may be necessary when building a race engine or a serious performance engine. These modifications include enlarging the main oil-feed passage and main bearing bulkhead passages.

These upgrades are beyond the scope of this rebuild book and should only be done after consulting with Buick engine experts about your specific engine build. Jim Weise of Tri-Shield Performance wrote an excellent article on diyauto.com about these and other lubrication-system modifications.

Cleaning

Cleaning engine parts is the worst part of an overhaul. All of the dirt, grease, and carbon deposits must be removed. If the parts are not cleaned, it is impossible to determine their condition. Cleaning the engine block itself is the most challenging task. Begin by removing the plugs in the block. This exposes internal passages that need special attention.

With all of the plugs removed, find a place outdoors with good drainage and begin cleaning the block. This requires an effective cleaning solvent, wire brushes, heavy-duty gloves, and eye protection. Remove all of the gunk and grime so that a thorough inspection can be performed. Stubborn, baked-on deposits can be left if the machine shop is doing the final cleaning, which is highly recommended.

After the block has been scrubbed with solvent, spray it down with water to remove the deposits and solvent residue. Dry it immediately because cast iron rusts quickly. Use compressed air to blow off the moisture. After drying the block, spray a light coat of WD-40 onto it to disperse the remaining moisture and protect the block from rusting. At this point, the block is clean enough that the machine shop can finish the job.

Use brushes and spray solvent to remove deposits from the oil holes in the block. Begin with the smaller holes before cleaning the main oil galleries because debris that is removed from the smaller oiling holes ultimately ends up in the oil galleries.

The internal parts require a more thorough cleaning because there can be no deposits on parts that require precision measurements. Clean the drilled holes in the crankshaft with solvent and a rifle-type brush that fits snugly in the passageways. These passageways transmit oil to the main and connecting-rod bearings, so any deposits remaining will be immediately sent into the new bearings and cause damage.

The pistons and connecting-rod assemblies are usually the most difficult items to thoroughly clean. The pistons are made of aluminum, so wire brushes can scratch and erode the material. The steel connecting rods can be cleaned more aggressively. Scrapers and wire brushes may be needed to remove the deposits from the piston heads. This must be done very carefully, testing a small area first to be sure that the aluminum will not be damaged.

Cleaning Engine Parts

1 *These are common engine-cleaning chemicals. Engine degreaser (left) must be rinsed off after use. It is the most harsh of these three cleaners and is usually used for large components, such as the engine block and cylinder heads. Spray solvent (center) can be used on small parts. The green cleaner is environmentally friendly and also does a good job on grease. It should also be rinsed off, as it is water soluble.*

Cleaning Engine Parts *continued*

2 Cleaning the block perfectly is not necessary because the machine shop has special equipment to perform the final cleaning. This is basically an oven that heats the block to a high temperature, which causes deposits to dry up and fall off.

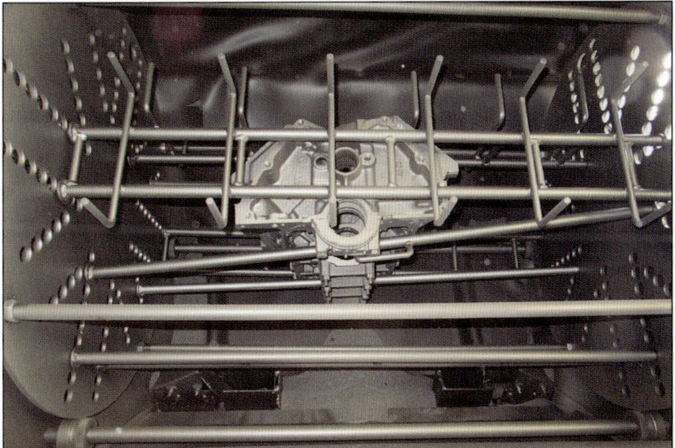

3 This machine is a media blaster, which takes cleaning to the next level. Media blasting is not a necessary step for a basic overhaul, but it ensures that all dried deposits are removed. The block comes out of the blaster looking new. The downside of this process is that the abrasive particles can become lodged in oil galleries and elsewhere in the block. Use great care when performing the final cleaning of the block.

4 When the block comes back from the machine shop, there's more work to complete. Make sure that there is no machining or cleaning debris in the oil galleries and other nooks and crannies of the block. For this job, a spray solvent and brushes are required.

5 The main bearings are fed through the holes at the center of each main bearing. Clean them with a brush and solvent.

6 The main feed travels from the oil-sending-unit mounting point to the camshaft bearing. Clean it thoroughly.

Cleaning Engine Parts *continued*

7 *Scrub the main oil galleries, which are common areas for gunk to accumulate. A very long brush is needed to do this properly.*

8 *Clean any remaining gunk from the lifter bores.*

9 *Use taps and spray solvent to clean all of the threaded holes in the block, particularly those for the main bearing caps and the cylinder heads. There is usually a bunch of gunk in these holes. If they're not completely clean, it can affect the torque readings during reassembly.*

10 *Clean each critical bolt with a die. Once the bolts and threaded holes are cleaned, the bolts thread easily into their holes by hand.*

11 *Clean the passages in the crankshaft thoroughly. Arguably, this is the most important cleaning operation because any remaining debris will go directly into the main and connecting-rod bearings. Brush thoroughly and spray plenty of solvent through each hole. If the crankshaft journals have been machined, there's an excellent chance that there are metal particles in these passages.*

12 *The most effective way to clean individual parts is to use a solvent tank. Let the parts soak and then brush away the grease and deposits.*

13 *Most of us are not lucky enough to own a solvent tank. So, use an oil drain pan, spray solvent, and brushes.*

14 *Using solvents and scrubbing does not always remove the most stubborn deposits and bits of gasket material, so scraping tools are also necessary. Here, I'm using a razor blade to remove deposits from the main-bearing-cap contact area on the block. These areas (as well as the main bearing caps) must be spotless.*

15 *A fine wire wheel on a bench grinder can be used on steel parts and sometimes even on aluminum piston heads. Use a light touch and don't use a wire wheel on the sides of the piston.*

Inspections that You Can Do

Now that the engine has been disassembled, inspect the following areas for damage to determine the causes of failure and what parts are suitable to reuse.

Block

Inspecting the block carefully and completely is imperative because problems are not always obvious. Cracks in an engine block usually appear between the main bearing saddles, between the core plugs, or at the bottom of the cylinders. They can be difficult to see, so it's best to have the machine shop inspect the block. If the condition of the block is questionable, it may be worth having the block Magnafluxed. A Magnaflux check will reveal cracks that are not otherwise visible.

Inspect each cylinder bore carefully, looking for cracks and scoring. Measure the bore diameters at the point of maximum wear (usually just below the wear ridge, perpendicular to the crankshaft). In addition, measure perpendicular to the point of maximum wear and note the difference between the two measurements, which is the out-of-round dimension. Cylinders should not be out of round by more than 0.001 inch.

Measure the cylinder at the point of minimum wear (at the bottom of the bore) and subtract this measurement from the maximum-wear dimension. The difference between the two measurements is the cylinder taper. Taper should not exceed the specification that is listed in the appendix. Excess taper causes the piston rings to expand and contract slightly but rapidly as the piston moves up and down. This causes the rings to lose tension prematurely.

If the block is seriously worn and/or damaged, consider starting with another used block in better condition. Extensive machine work can be expensive, and a used block can often be found at a reasonable price. Of course, if the block is numbers-matching to a valuable car, do what you can to preserve the original block.

Inspecting the Cylinder Block

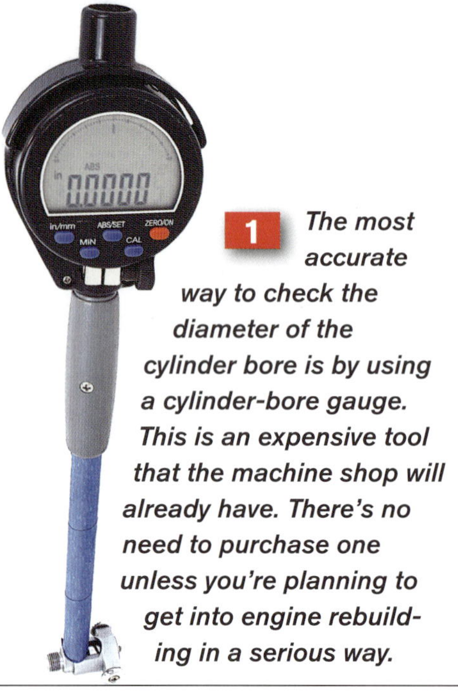

1 *The most accurate way to check the diameter of the cylinder bore is by using a cylinder-bore gauge. This is an expensive tool that the machine shop will already have. There's no need to purchase one unless you're planning to get into engine rebuilding in a serious way.*

2 *In a home garage, use a large micrometer and telescoping gauges (sometimes called "snap gauges") to check the cylinder-bore diameters. Telescoping gauges are tricky to use because you must find the maximum diameter, which is usually just below the wear ridge with the gauge perpendicular to the crankshaft.*

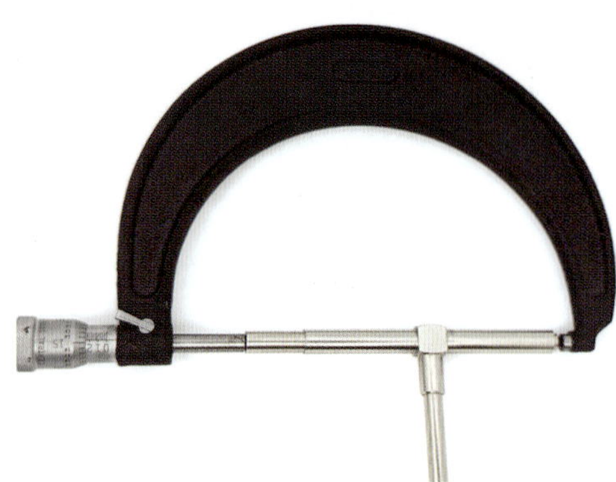

3 *Measure the telescoping gauge with a micrometer to determine the cylinder bore's diameter.*

Crankshaft

Ideally, the crankshaft bearing journals should be shiny with no scratches. This is seldom the case. Over its life, the crankshaft is subjected to dry starts and oil contamination, which leave scratches. Unless the engine had a problem with low oil pressure or metallic debris in the oil, the scratches are usually light and not of much concern.

If there is no serious scratching on the crankshaft journals, proceed to measuring them with a micrometer. Check each journal in multiple places to determine if it is out of round or if there is journal taper.

Now, check the main bearing oil clearance. As previously mentioned, snap gauges are finicky, so several practice tries will most likely be needed. Measure the snap gauge on each try until the results are consistent.

The oil clearance will almost certainly be excessive when compared with the specification in the appendix. However, new bearings will be installed, which will tighten up the clearances.

Inspect the rear-main-seal contact surface carefully to determine if there is any scratching, roughness, or a wear groove from contact with the oil seal. This area is critical and a common point of leakage. There's nothing worse than starting up a new engine and finding a drip at the rear of the engine. To fix it, raise the engine and remove the oil pan in the vehicle. Spend a little extra time to be sure to get it right the first time.

If there is any reason to suspect a bent crankshaft, check for crankshaft runout. A bent crankshaft will also leave uneven wear patterns on the main bearings. Buick crankshafts rarely bend under normal operating conditions, but it sometimes happens during an engine seizure.

Inspecting the Crankshaft

1 *Visually inspect the bearing journals on the crankshaft. Light scratching, which is shown here, can be polished away by the machine shop. Deeper scratches require grinding the crankshaft undersize and using oversize bearings.*

Inspecting the Crankshaft *continued*

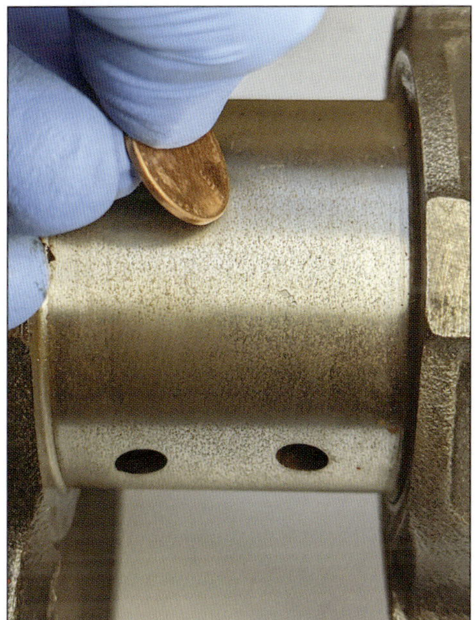

2 *Run a fingernail over any scratches on the journals. If your fingernail gets caught on them, the crankshaft will likely require grinding. An old mechanic's trick is to rub a penny across the bearing surface. If copper is left on the surface, it means that the scratches are deep and sharp. Again, the crankshaft will likely require grinding.*

5 *Measure the main bearing bores on the engine block with the bearing inserts installed and the caps torqued to the correct specification. Subtract the journal diameter from the bore measurement to determine the bearing clearance. During reassembly, check this clearance again using Plastigauge.*

3 *Measure the diameter of the five main journals on the crankshaft and compare the readings to the specifications in the appendix. Since the crankshaft journals are large in diameter, calipers cannot be used.*

6 *The crankshaft has three different ways of controlling oil leaks at the rear seal. On the left is a larger-diameter section called an oil slinger, which sheds most of the oil using centrifugal force. To the right of the slinger is a knurled surface that drives oil away from the seal as the crankshaft rotates. The pointer identifies where the seal contacts the crankshaft. A wear groove in this location will likely result in an oil leak.*

4 *There are four connecting-rod journals with two connecting rods attached to each journal. Measure both sides of each journal. The very center of the journal is a point where there should be no wear. With an accurate pair of calipers, you may be able to use them to obtain a measurement, but the calipers will not be as accurate as a micrometer.*

7 *To check the crankshaft runout, put the crankshaft in place with only the upper main bearings installed. Set up a dial indicator over the number-3 (center) main bearing. Rotate the crankshaft. There should not be any variation in the dial indicator reading. If it's more than 0.0005 inch, there is likely a problem.*

Camshaft

Inspect the camshaft lobes and journals. After cleaning, they should appear shiny with no scratching. The tops of the cam lobes are the most critical points for inspection. An area down the center of each lobe should appear where the lifter is in contact. If it's not centered, there's a problem with camshaft alignment—possibly the cam plug was installed too deep.

Look for scratching, pitting, and chipping at the lobes. A bad cam lobe will usually have deep scoring and appear dull rather than shiny. The lobes should be uniform in appearance.

Measure each camshaft lobe across the top of the lobe and then measure at the base diameter (often called the base circle). The difference between these two measurements is the camshaft-lobe lift. Keep in mind that the intake and exhaust lobes often have different lift specifications, so it's common to find eight lobes that are one height while the other eight are a different height.

Inspecting the Camshaft

1 Visually inspect the camshaft for wear and damage. This lobe shows excessive wear. Note the rough surface at the top of the lobe and the chunk that is missing on the left side. Worn or damaged camshafts must be replaced along with the lifters.

2 Measure each camshaft lobe at the smallest diameter, which is also called the base circle.

3 Measure each camshaft lobe at its maximum height. The difference between these two diameters is the camshaft-lobe lift. Most importantly, the lift should be equal among all of the lobes. Any significant variance indicates camshaft-lobe wear.

4 If you are reusing the original camshaft, clean out the oil hole that travels from the front camshaft bearing to the forward end of the camshaft. This hole provides lubrication to the timing components. The hole is shown in a big-block camshaft. Small-blocks have the lube hole behind the timing gear.

Lifters

Buick engines were equipped with conventional, flat lifters, which require careful inspection. The most important areas to inspect are the foot and sides. If problems are shown on the lifters, there is usually damage to the camshaft as well. You want to see a circular wear pattern on the lifter feet. If you do not see it, the camshaft lobe may have worn flat.

Camshaft lobes are ground at a slight angle and are designed to impart spin to the lifters. If a cam lobe wears to the point that it is flat, it can cause the lifters to stop spinning. Other possible causes of a lifter not rotating are a valve adjustment that is too tight or the lifter that is fitting too tightly in its bore.

The hydraulic components within each lifter often get plugged up. To remove the internal components, remove the clip and tap the top of the lifter on a bench to remove the internal components.

Inspecting the Lifters

1 *Check each lifter foot for signs of wear. They should be shiny with an even, circular wear pattern. If there are wear grooves across the foot of a lifter, it means that the lifter was not rotating properly in its bore.*

2 *The sides of the lifters should be relatively smooth with no scratching or galling. Note the circular wear pattern toward the bottom. This indicates that the lifter has been rotating within its bore, which is normal.*

4 *This close-up photo shows a worn lifter foot. Do you see the light showing through in the middle? That means that the lifter foot is slightly concave. However, it should be convex, with light showing through at the outer areas and making contact in the middle.*

3 *The lifter feet appear to be flat, but they are actually slightly convex. This prevents scuffing and allows the lifter to rotate during operation.*

Place one lifter foot against the side of another lifter and try to rock the foot against the side. If the lifter foot is flat or concave, replace all of the lifters and the camshaft.

5 *If a lifter fits too tightly, it might be necessary to hone the lifter bore a bit. The idea is to remove only the glazed deposits that are restricting the lifter's movement. Do not remove metal and carefully clean the area when you are done.*

6 *It's best to replace the lifters at the time of overhaul. If you want to take them apart to inspect and clean them, push down on the pushrod seat with a pushrod and remove this clip.*

7 *These are the parts that are inside each lifter. Keep the parts from each lifter in a separate plastic bag. It's easy to lose them or mix them up.*

Pistons

Piston wear and damage can be obvious or subtle. A piston may have a hole in the head or a broken skirt. A serious problem would have already been known because the engine would have been running horribly. Less-obvious problems are wear in the ring grooves or excess clearance in the bore. These problems would have been indicated by knocking sounds, excessive oil consumption, or a drop in compression.

Visually inspect the piston for any signs of cracks, scuffing, deep scratching, or galling. Unlike scratching, galling is a wider stripe of roughness caused by seizure. Pistons that have been seized must be replaced because they were most likely overheated. Make sure that the oil-return holes in the lower groove are not plugged.

Observe the wear pattern on the piston skirts. The wear pattern should be centered. If the wear pattern is not centered, it's a sign that the connecting rod may be bent. The machine shop will have equipment that can test rods for straightness. Make sure that the piston is tight on the pin and that the pin is tight on the connecting rod. The connecting rod should move smoothly through its arc with no binding or noticeable looseness.

Most piston pins are locked to the connecting rod with a press fit. Because of this, they cannot be removed from the rods without a hydraulic press. This is a job for a machine shop.

Measure the piston diameter. Subtract it from the bore diameter that was measured earlier. This provides the piston-to-bore clearance. Compare this to the specification in the appendix.

The pistons should have already been cleaned with solvent and brushes, but carbon in the ring grooves will remain. This buildup can lead to inaccurate measurements of the ring-groove side clearance. Clean the ring grooves until there are no signs of carbon remaining.

With the ring grooves now clean, place a ring into each ring groove and try to slip a feeler gauge between the ring and the groove. When a feeler gauge fits in with light resistance, that is the ring side clearance, which should be within the limits that are listed in the appendix. Keep in mind that new rings will tighten the gap a bit.

Inspecting the Pistons

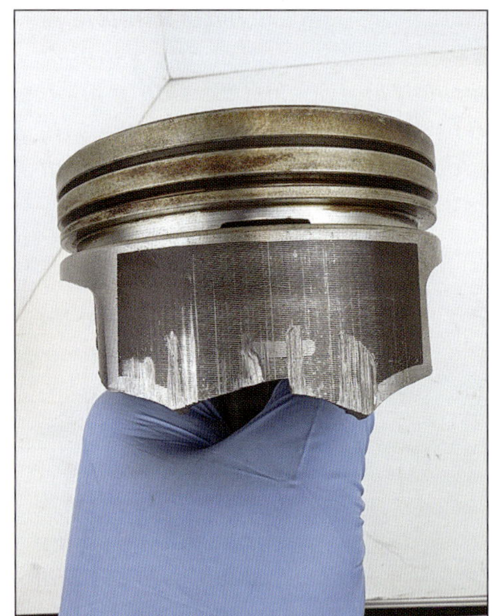

1 Inspect each piston for signs of obvious damage. This piston shows mechanical damage (the skirt is broken). Whenever there is damage like this, other damage is likely to be found in the engine.

2 Damaged or broken piston heads (left) can be the result of foreign objects in the cylinder. Foreign objects in the cylinder usually damage the cylinder walls as well.

Eyebrow-shaped dents in the piston head are the result of contact with a valve, which likely means that there is a problem in the valvetrain. Severe detonation can cause the piston head to melt (right).

3 Try to rotate each piston against its connecting rod. There should not be any detectable movement. If there is any movement, the connecting-rod pin is probably loose within the piston due to wear or damage. Let the machine shop know.

Inspecting the Pistons *continued*

4 *Using a large micrometer, measure the piston perpendicular to the piston pin from just below the pin area down to the bottom of the skirt.*

5 *To clean the compression-ring grooves, break an old piston ring and use the sharp edge to scrape out the carbon. Special ring-groove cleaning tools are available but usually aren't necessary. Be careful to not scratch the ring grooves.*

Bearings

If the bearings exhibit anything other than normal wear, determine the cause of failure before reassembling the engine. Common causes of bearing failure are lubrication issues, dirt, excessive loading, corrosion, and metallic particles from problems elsewhere in the engine.

Issues with bearing lubrication aren't always solely the result of low oil pressure. When an engine is badly overheated, the oil becomes less viscous and cannot protect the bearings properly. Loading an engine excessively at low engine speed can contribute to lubrication issues.

Misalignment of the oil holes in the block due to improper bearing installation can lead to insufficient oil delivery to the bearing surface. In the most severe cases of lubrication failure, the bearings will overheat so much that the steel backing of the bearing will turn blue.

Inspecting the Bearings

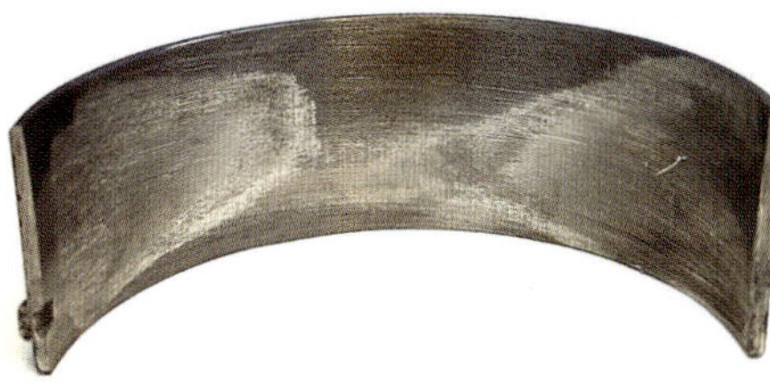

1 *This connecting-rod bearing has its overlay wiped out. This indicates excessive wear.*

2 *This main bearing shows the result of engine overloading, or "lugging."*

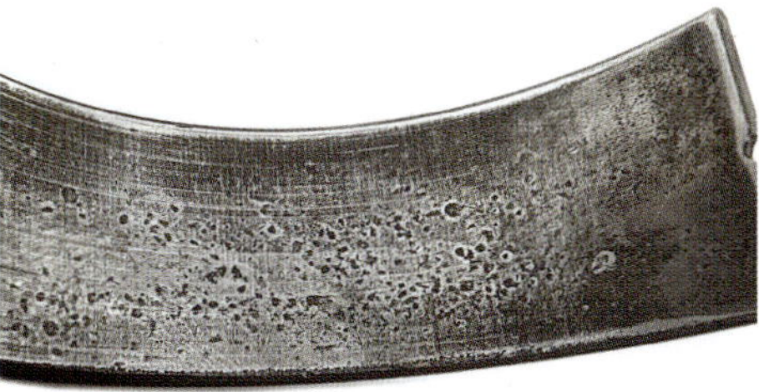

3 *This bearing shows corrosion that was most likely caused by acidic contamination in the oil. This kind of damage can also be caused by an engine sitting for long periods of time without being operated, or it can be caused by coolant contamination.*

4 *The scratches on this bearing are the result of sharp debris circulating in the oiling system.*

Oil Pump

Normally, the oil pump should be replaced at the time of an overhaul, but it is useful to inspect it as a part of diagnosing engine problems.

Inspecting the Oil Pump

1 *To disassemble the oil pump, remove the six bolts. The bolt at the oil-filter mounting point is easy to miss.*

2 *Inspect the oil-pump gears. These gears are worn, and one of them has a chunk missing. Gears are inexpensive and should be replaced routinely during an overhaul.*

3 *Inspect the pump-gear pocket. This one has light scoring. The gear pocket is part of the front-cover assembly, so it is necessary to replace the front cover if the gear pocket is excessively worn. Replace the cover for any pre-1971 big-block because replacement covers have enlarged oil passages.*

4 *Inspect the oil-pump cover for wear. This is the most common area to find excessive wear, and this engine definitely has a wear problem.*

5 *Worn covers can be repaired by installing a specially designed machined plate between the cover and the housing. This creates a new wear surface for the pump. The only potential downside is that it makes the pump assembly slightly longer.*

Inspecting the Oil Pump *continued*

6 *Unscrew the cap and then remove the oil-pressure-regulator valve and spring. Clean all of the parts thoroughly.*

7 *Check and clean the intake screen at the oil filter–mounting location.*

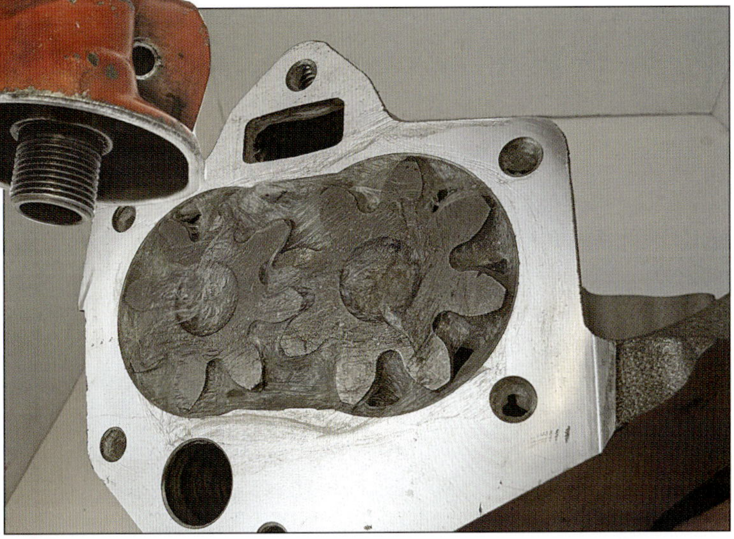

8 *When reassembling the oil pump, pack it with petroleum jelly. This will allow the pump to prime quickly when the engine is started.*

Machine Shop Inspections

Machine shops have special equipment to check a block for cracks. Have the block checked if the engine has been severely overheated, the block has been frozen, or there was a phantom leak and the cause was never identified. Magnafluxing is the most common method to check for cracks.

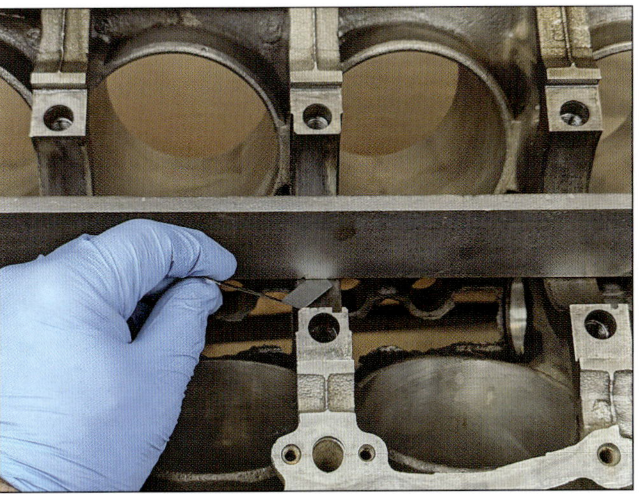

Use a precision straight-edge to check the main bearing–bore alignment. With the bearing inserts removed, a 0.001-inch feeler gauge should not be able to be inserted at any point. If the bores are out of alignment, they should be align-honed. It is a good idea to do an align-hone whenever an engine is rebuilt.

The Magnaflux machine magnetizes the block (or a portion of the block). Then, metal filings are applied to the magnetized area. If there is a crack, the filings will outline the crack. More advanced Magnafluxing equipment uses fluorescent filings that are viewed under a black light. The fluorescent glow allows the filings to be seen more easily so that smaller cracks are more easily identified.

Engine blocks are subjected to thousands of heating and cooling cycles, which can cause distortion over time. If the engine is overheated, the distortion will be greater. Machine shops have precision straightedge tools to check the block deck for straightness as well as the alignment of the main bearing bores.

Use a precision straightedge and feeler gauges to check flatness of the cylinder-head deck surface. The thickness of feeler gauges that can be inserted at any point indicates the warpage, which should not exceed 0.006 inch overall or 0.003 inch within any 6 inches.

Machining Operations

Machine shops conduct the following procedures.

Cylinder Boring

If the cylinder measurements are within their specified tolerances, the cylinders can generally be honed and the original pistons can be reused (assuming that they are in serviceable condition). If the cylinder measurements are not within the specified tolerances, the cylinders need to be bored oversize for the use of new oversize pistons. The most common oversizes are 0.030 and 0.060 inch. Based on the amount of wear in the bores, the machine shop can make recommendations regarding the best size of oversize pistons to use.

Cylinder Honing

Whether or not the cylinders are bored larger, they need to be honed so that the new piston rings will seat correctly. Honing is best carried out by a machine shop because it's important that the correct surface finish is provided for proper piston-ring seating. Different ring types require different surface roughness factors.

If the surface of the cylinder walls is too rough, it can damage the piston rings. If it isn't rough enough, the rings will not seat correctly. The correct finish depends on the type of honing stones that are used, the pressure applied to them, and the rotational speed of the hone as it's lifted up and down in the cylinder bore.

Align-Honing

Over time, an engine block can become slightly distorted for a number of reasons, primarily the thousands of heating and cooling cycles to which it is subjected during its life. Align-honing corrects any misalignment of the main bearing bores that could cause uneven wear of the main bearings.

Block Deck Resurfacing

Block distortion can cause warping of the surfaces where the cylinder heads attach (commonly called the deck). Deck warpage can cause the head gaskets to not seat correctly. Resurfacing the deck will restore a perfectly flat surface and ensure that the head gaskets will not fail prematurely.

During the resurfacing process, it's essential that the block is set up on the resurfacing machine perfectly.

Even a variance of a few thousandths of an inch from the front to the rear or from the left to the right is problematic and can lead to misalignment of the intake manifold or uneven compression. This is one reason to pick a reputable machine shop.

Crankshaft Polishing and Grinding

Light scratches on crankshaft journals can be removed by polishing with a fine emery cloth. Machine shops have special equipment that can quickly polish each journal. This is normally done at a reasonable price and is a much better option than trying to polish the crankshaft by hand at home.

Deep scratches and damage are dealt with by grinding the journals to a smaller standard diameter, or "undersize." This must be accompanied by oversize bearings to provide the correct oil clearance. If only the connecting-rod journals are damaged, they can be ground separately so that they would only need oversize bearings for the connecting rods.

Main bearing journals can also be ground separately from the connecting-rod journals. When a crankshaft has been ground, the machine shop will usually mark it to be sure that the correct oversize bearings are used. A common marking is "10/10," which means that the main journals and rod journals were ground 0.010 undersize.

Connecting Rod Reconditioning

At the machine shop, the connecting rods and pistons will be separated, and the connecting rods will be checked for bending and twisting. The pin bore will be inspected, and the bearing bore will be checked for out-of-roundness. New connecting-rod bolts will be installed, and the rod bearing bore will be honed to ensure that it is perfectly round. After the rods are reconditioned, the machine shop will usually reassemble the pistons to the rods.

Camshaft Bearing Replacement

Camshaft bearings must be pressed into the engine block using a special tool. Even with the special tool, properly aligning the bearings and oiling holes requires practice. Camshaft bearings have different diameters (the bearings at the rear of the block have a smaller diameter than those at the front). Each bearing requires a specific arbor to drive the bearing into place.

Here's what the cylinder bores should look like after honing. The scratches from the hone should be light and intersect at about a 45-degree angle. The slightly rough surface aids in ring seating and carries oil across the ring and bore surface for cooling during break-in.

Even if the engine does not require an overbore, it needs to be honed to ensure that the new piston rings seat correctly. I recommend that the machine shop should handle this job.

Align-honing is a requirement if an engine has been severely overheated, seized, or shows uneven main bearing wear. Many machine shops align-hone cylinder blocks as a routine part of any engine overhaul.

Camshaft bearings are routinely replaced at the time of an overhaul, and this bearing definitely needs it. Replacing camshaft bearings is a precise operation that requires special equipment. A machine shop can handle this. Be sure to use a double-groove front bearing to ensure proper lubrication to the driver-side main gallery.

Reassembly

Now that all of the machine work is done and the block and components have been cleaned, begin the reassembly process.

Engine Block Plugs

The reassembly process begins by installing new front and rear oil-gallery plugs. Apply thread sealant to the rear plugs and tighten them securely. If you are using stock-type front gallery plugs, apply a bit of red Loctite prior to installation, drive them into place with a small socket, and be sure to stake the area around the plug with a chisel. If the block has threaded plugs in the front, install them now. If the TA Performance plug kit is used, the Teflon coating provides a good seal, so there's no need to add any sealant.

Spread non-hardening sealant onto the outside circumference of the camshaft plug. Then, drive it into place at the back of the engine block using a large socket and a hammer. Drive the plug in until it is flush with the surface of the engine block. Do not drive the plug in too deep. If the plug is installed too deep, it may not

Brass core plugs resist corrosion better than steel plugs, but it can be more difficult to get them to seal properly. Regardless of what type of plug is used, place a bit of sealant around the outer edges when you install them.

Special tools are available to install core plugs, but they can be driven into place with a hammer, a large socket, and an extension.

allow the camshaft to be installed to the correct depth.

Buick engines have six core plugs: three on each side of the block. Although the factory plugs were steel, I recommend replacing them with brass plugs to prevent rust that could cause the plug to fail. However, brass plugs are more likely to have trouble sealing correctly, so use plenty of sealant and make sure that the plugs are square in their bores.

Camshaft

Lubricate the camshaft with thick assembly lube and carefully install it into the block. Be extremely careful to avoid scratching the new bearings. Thread a long bolt into the end of the camshaft to use as a handle as

Hopefully, camshaft manipulation was practiced during the removal process. Be even more careful during the installation of the camshaft. New camshaft bearings have less clearance, so installation of the camshaft is even more difficult than the removal. If there is a lot of resistance during the installation of the camshaft, it's possible that the camshaft bearings were installed incorrectly.

the camshaft is slowly and carefully moved rearward. The camshaft must be kept completely level.

When the camshaft can be seen through the window in the center of the engine-block valley area, fish a coat hanger wire beneath it to support it from that point. The camshaft can also be supported from below by reaching between the main webs. If there is any resistance as the camshaft is installed, move it backward slightly, rotate it a bit, and try again.

Crankshaft

Prior to the final crankshaft installation, check the crankshaft-bearing oil clearance using Plastigauge. First, turn the engine block upside down and install the upper main bearing halves into their saddles on the block. Be sure that the saddles and undersides of the bearing shells are completely clean. Remember that the thrust bearing is installed on the center (number-3) bearing saddle.

Make sure that the main bearing journals on the crankshaft are completely clean. Then, install the crankshaft onto the new bearings. Make sure that the crankshaft is completely level as it is lowered slowly into place.

Cut off a piece of Plastigauge that's slightly shorter than the width of the number-1 main bearing. Lay it carefully into place parallel to the crankshaft.

Install the main bearing caps and torque the bolts to their specifications. Be sure to not move the crankshaft in the process. Remove the main bearing caps and observe the Plastigauge, which should have been compressed when the main bearing caps were tightened. The amount that the Plastigauge is compressed indicates the oil clearance.

Use the scale on the Plastigauge envelope to read the oil clearance by comparing the width of the Plastigauge to each of the bars on the envelope. The bar that most closely approximates the width of the Plastigauge indicates the oil clearance. Note that the Plastigauge envelope has both standard and metric measurements, so be sure to use the correct side of the envelope.

If the Plastigauge measurements are not within specification, the bearing insert(s) may not be seating correctly. They may be the wrong bearing sizes or an error may have been made during the machining process. Remove the crankshaft and upper bearing halves, clean and inspect them thoroughly, and double-check that they are the correct bearing sizes.

Repeat the check. If the clearance is still not correct, contact the machine shop for advice. Do not proceed until the clearance is correct. Otherwise, the new engine will likely be damaged.

Install the lower half of the rear oil seal. This is a critical step because a poor seal here will result in a leak that's very difficult to fix after the engine has been installed into the car. There are two types of seals that are available for these engines: a rope type and a lip type. I recommend using the lip-type seal because it's a simpler installation that is generally easier for the DIYer to accomplish.

If a lip-type seal is used, insert one of the halves into the groove in the block with the lip facing toward the front of the engine. Make sure that the groove is completely clean because dirt can lead to leaks.

Position one end of the seal so that it is protruding about 1/4-inch above the block surface. The idea here is to offset the seal parting lines so that they are not aligned with the edges of the main cap and block. This can help reduce the possibility of leaks. Wipe some engine oil on the seal lip. Avoid getting oil on the ends of the seal.

Rope-type seals are more difficult to install. However, some say that they seal very well when they are installed correctly. As I mentioned earlier, I prefer the lip-type seal. Anyway, to install a rope-type seal, lay one of the rope pieces on a bench and roll a large socket across it until it has been flattened enough to fit into the seal groove on the block.

Press the seal into the seal groove. Then, roll the large socket across the

Potential Issues During Camshaft Installation

Camshaft installation requires patience and finesse. In addition, you should never assume that everything will be correct. Camshaft bearings are sometimes installed incorrectly at the machine shop. It's also possible for something to be wrong with the camshaft.

During one engine build, I was installing a camshaft that wouldn't go all the way in. I spent a great deal of time trying to figure out what was wrong. I finally realized that the camshaft lobes protruded slightly above the rear camshaft journal! The camshaft lobes had been measured for lift, which was correct, but somehow the crankshaft grinding machine was set to grind the lobes on a larger base-circle diameter, which made the lobes too big overall.

I contacted the camshaft manufacturer, and it said this was a one-off problem. I continue to purchase camshafts from this manufacturer and have never seen a problem like this again. In fact, I have never heard of this happening to anyone else. Nevertheless, this experience taught me to never assume that a part is correct out of the box. Always confirm the dimensions of machined components. ■

seal until it is flattened and fully seats in the groove. Using a sharp razor blade, trim the seal flush with the block surface on each side. There should not be any bits of rope hanging off and the rope ends should not appear uneven—in other words, make a clean cut.

After the upper bearings are installed in their saddles and lubricated, reinstall the crankshaft, making sure to not disturb the rear seal in the process. Be sure that the crankshaft bearing surfaces are adequately covered with assembly lube.

Prepare the rear main bearing cap for installation. First, make sure that the mating surface of the cap and the block are completely clean. Wipe the surfaces with brake cleaner or acetone to be sure that they're completely clean. Install the other seal half into the cap.

If a lip-type seal is used, offset the seal about 1/4 inch on the side opposite of what was done on the other half in the block. If a rope-type seal is used, roll it into place in the cap and trim the edges as was done on the other half of the seal.

Install the lower main bearing into the caps. Remember that the center (number-3) bearing is the thrust bearing. Lubricate the bearings, install the main bearing caps, and torque the bolts to specification.

On 350 engines, the rear main bearing cap is recessed into the engine-block skirt and requires side seals to prevent leakage. Install the seals immediately after cap installation, making sure that the ends of the seals bottom against the engine-block surface. It's helpful to soak the seals in light oil for about two minutes immediately prior to installation, which promotes seal swelling and a tight seal. Don't be concerned if the seals protrude slightly above the oil pan rail surface—this is normal. If necessary, they can be trimmed at the time of oil pan installation.

Rotate the crankshaft by hand. The thick assembly lube provides initial resistance, but once the crankshaft is rotating, it should turn easily with no spots of resistance.

Again, check the crankshaft endplay as was done during disassembly. With new thrust bearings installed, the endplay should now be within the specification that is listed in the appendix.

Installing the Crankshaft

1 *Install the upper main bearings on the saddles in the engine block. Make sure that each tab aligns with the groove in the block.*

2 *Place a piece of Plastigauge on the main bearing journal. Make sure that it's as straight as possible along the journal.*

Installing the Crankshaft *continued*

3 The Plastigauge flattens when the bearing-cap bolts are tightened. The width of the Plastigauge should be uniform across its length. If it's significantly wider on one end or the other, there may be a problem. Remove the bearing inserts, clean the cap and the saddle, clean both sides of the inserts, and recheck the clearance.

4 A rope-type seal (top) was installed at the factory. The lip-type seal (bottom) is easier to install and is recommended for most rebuilds. Lip seals are usually not included in rebuild gasket kits and need to be purchased separately.

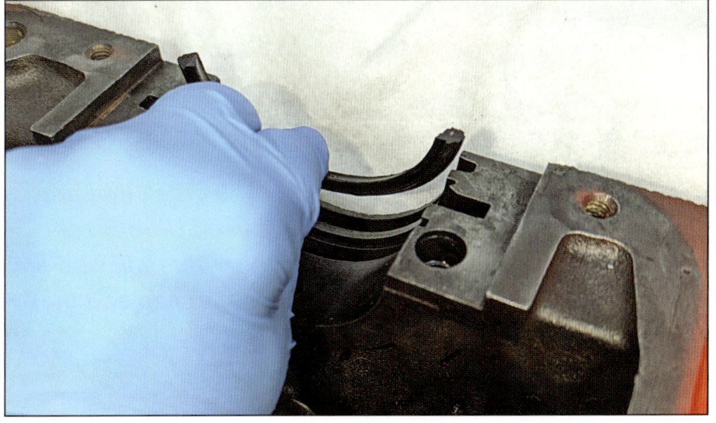

5 Insert the lip-type seal into the groove in the block. Make sure that the lip faces forward.

6 When installing a lip-type seal, let one end of the upper-seal half protrude above the block surface approximately 1/4 inch. Let the seal half that is in the cap protrude an equivalent amount on the opposite side. You want to prevent the parting lines of the seal halves from aligning with the parting lines of the cap and block, which can lead to an oil leak.

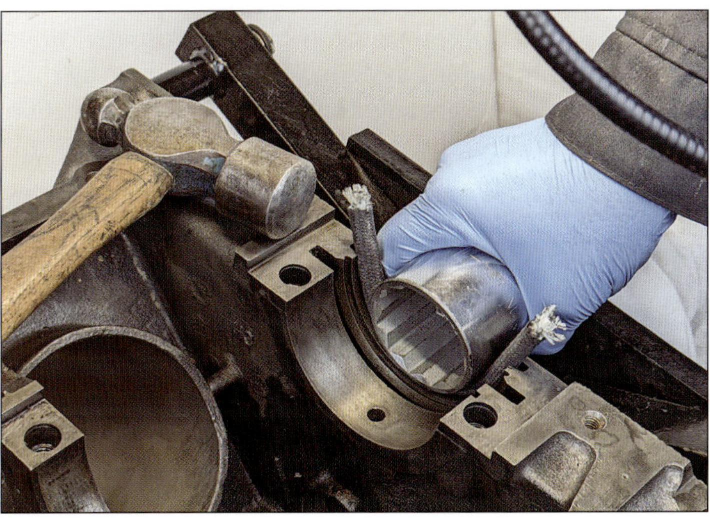

7 If you are installing a rope-type seal, use a large socket to roll the seal half into place in the seal groove. Tap on the socket with a hammer to seat the seal in the groove.

Installing the Crankshaft *continued*

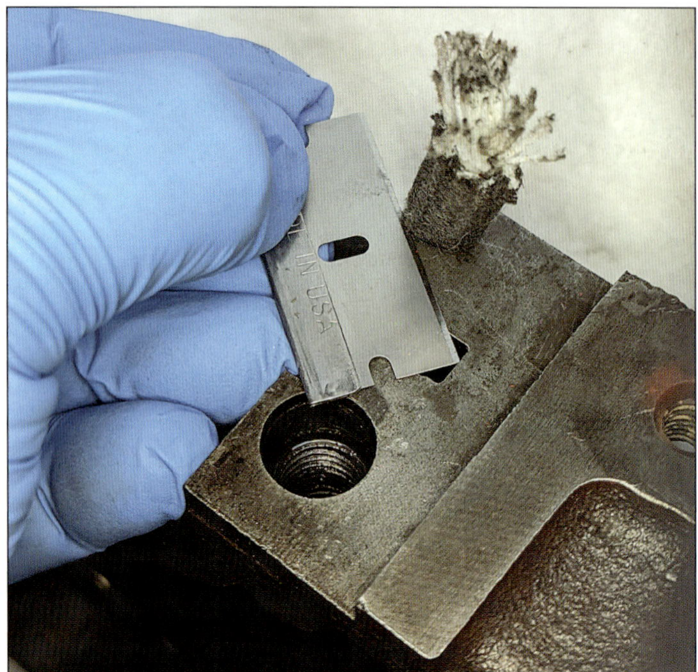

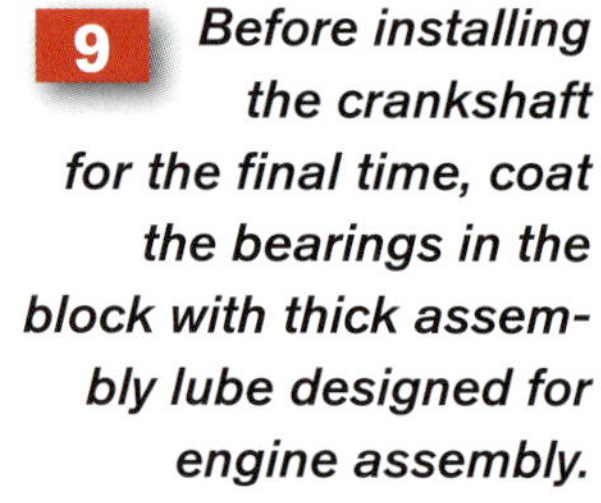

8 *When trimming a rope-type seal, nothing should protrude above the block or cap surface, and the cut needs to be absolutely clean. Use a brand-new razor blade and a slight sawing motion.*

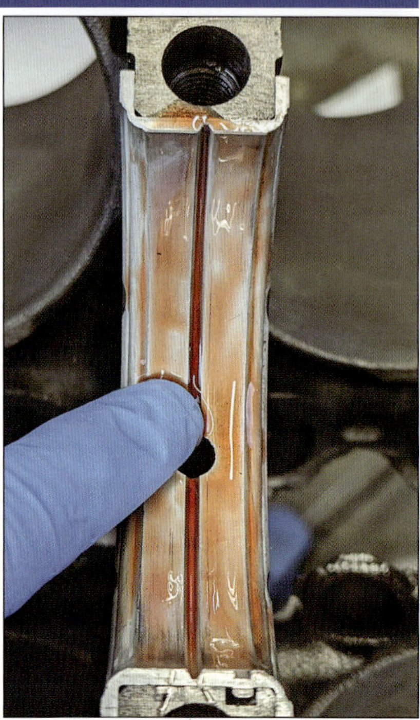

9 *Before installing the crankshaft for the final time, coat the bearings in the block with thick assembly lube designed for engine assembly.*

10 *Apply a very light coat of sealant to the areas that are shown in yellow. During assembly, I used Ultra Black room-temperature-vulcanizing (RTV) silicone. This will seal any oil that tries to sneak between the main bearing cap and the block.*

Piston Rings

The first step to install the piston rings is to check the ring end gap of the compression rings. This is done to make sure that the correct rings have been chosen and that the machine work has yielded the correct bore size. First, insert a compression ring into the number-1 cylinder and square it in the bore. This is commonly done with an overturned piston.

Using feeler gauges, determine the piston ring end gap and compare it to the specification (see the appendix). If the gap is too small, the ring ends must be filed down until the gap is correct. A gap that is too small can cause the rings to contact each other in operation and damage the cylinder walls and piston.

If the gap is larger than the specified gap on a stock engine, it won't cause an issue unless it exceeds approximately 0.040 inch. On a high-performance or racing engine, where every tiny bit of compression is desired, match the gap to the specification provided by the ring manufacturer for the type of usage that is intended.

Repeat the end-gap check for each of the two compression rings in each cylinder. The top and bottom compression rings are usually different designs. Do not mix up the rings among the cylinders because there could be slight differences in the bore sizes.

Install the oil-ring expander in the lower groove and then install the side rails. Do not use the piston-ring-expander tool on the oil-ring side rails. Unlike the cast-iron compression rings, the oil-ring side rails can be twisted lightly during installation. Place one end of a side rail in the lower rail (below the expander) and hold it there. Next, carefully wind the expander into place. Do the same for the upper side rail.

Note that the side rails are all the same, so they don't have to be installed with a particular orientation (up or down). With the side rails in place, make sure that both colored ends of the expander can still be seen. If not, remove the side rails, reposition the expander, and reinstall the side rails. With the oil-ring assembly properly assembled, position the gaps of the side rails so that they are each 90 degrees offset from the ends of the expander and 180 degrees opposite of each other.

Next, install the lower compression ring. The piston-ring package should identify which ring is for the upper groove and which ring is for the lower groove. Also, there will be a dot on each ring, which must face up. Repeat this process for the upper compression ring.

Position the compression-ring gaps so that the lower ring is aligned with the colored ends of the oil-ring expander. The upper ring should be 180 degrees opposite of the lower ring.

Installing the Piston Rings

1 *Square the piston ring in the bore by pressing against it with an overturned piston. Installing an old compression ring in the second groove ensures that the piston won't be cocked in the bore.*

2 *Measure the piston-ring end gap with feeler gauges. The correct gauge is the one that slides through the gap with light resistance.*

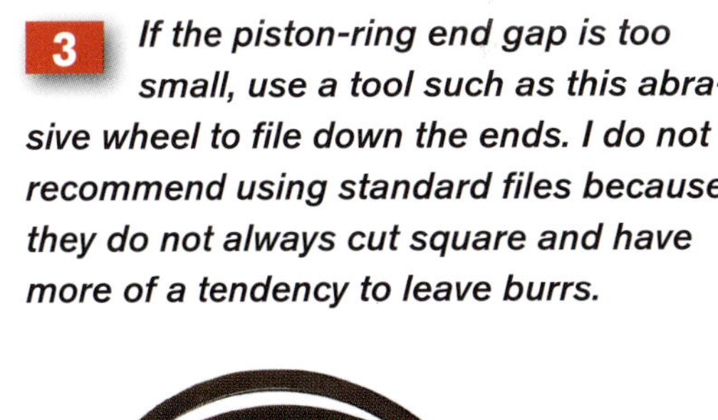

3 *If the piston-ring end gap is too small, use a tool such as this abrasive wheel to file down the ends. I do not recommend using standard files because they do not always cut square and have more of a tendency to leave burrs.*

4 *Keep the compression rings for each piston together and mark the number of the cylinder to which they belong.*

Installing the Piston Rings *continued*

5 *When installing the oil-ring expander, the ends should butt up against each other (arrow). Make sure that the ends of the ring do not overlap each other.*

6 *Hold one end of the side rail while winding the other end into place. Install the lower rail first. Use a feeler gauge to avoid scratching the piston during this process.*

7 *Use the piston-ring expander tool to open the ring just enough for it to fit over the piston and into the lower ring groove.*

Pistons

Coat the inside of the number-1 cylinder with engine oil. Do not use assembly lube because it could delay piston-ring seating, which requires the friction from direct contact with the cylinder walls during break-in. Rotate the crankshaft until the journal for the number-1 cylinder is positioned opposite the cylinder (bottom of the piston stroke).

Remove the bearing cap from the number-1 connecting rod and install a bearing insert into the connecting rod, aligning the tab with the notch in the connecting rod. Place short sections of rubber hose over the connecting-rod bolts to protect the crankshaft as the piston is installed in the bore. Do not lubricate the bearing at this point.

Apply oil to the piston rings and position the piston so that the notch faces forward. Install the piston in a piston-ring-compressor tool with the bottom of the piston skirt protruding from the bottom of the tool. Tighten the tool to compress the rings and slide the bottom of the piston skirt into the cylinder bore. Align the bottom of the tool with the block deck. It is critical that there is no gap between the tool and the block deck.

Gently tap the piston into the cylinder bore. Each tap should move the piston just a little bit at a time. If there is any resistance, it's probably because the ring compressor is not tight enough or a piston ring has popped out between the tool and the block. Remove the piston and try again. It's common for oil-ring side rails to pop out during installation, and they are very easily bent.

After the piston has cleared the compressor tool, continue to tap the top of the piston while carefully guiding the connecting-rod bearing onto the crankshaft journal. When the bearing is tight on the journal, install a piece of Plastigauge on the journal and install the connecting-rod bearing and cap over the bolts, making sure to align the markings on the rod and cap.

Install the connecting-rod nuts and tighten them to specification. Remove the bearing cap and check the connecting-rod oil clearance by comparing the width of the crushed Plastigauge with the envelope. Compare this measurement to the specification in the appendix. If the measurement is not within specification, the incorrect bearing was used or there is a problem with the machine work. Once the oil clearance has been checked, scrape off the Plastigauge with a piece of plastic, such as a credit card.

After determining that the connecting-rod-bearing oil clearance is correct, push up on the connecting rod. This is most easily done by pushing on the rod bolts. Push up far enough to allow lubrication of the upper bearing half. Use thick lubricant that is designed for engine bearing assembly.

Rotate the crankshaft so that the crankshaft journal presses against the connecting-rod bearing. Place a bearing insert into the connecting-rod cap and install the cap and nuts, aligning the markings on the cap and rod to be sure that the cap isn't installed backward. Torque the nuts to the specification listed in the appendix. Follow this procedure for the next seven cylinders.

Installing the Pistons

1 *When installing the pistons, note that the notch on the top must face the front of the engine.*

2 *Use a hammer handle to gently drive the piston into its bore. Go slowly because it's easy to damage a piston ring if it pops out of the ring compressor.*

3 *Align the timing marks as shown. The mark on the camshaft sprocket should face straight down, and the mark on the crankshaft sprocket should face straight up.*

Timing Chain and Sprockets

Reinstall the Woodruff key at the front of the crankshaft. Align the groove of the crankshaft sprocket with the Woodruff key and press on the crankshaft sprocket. Tap lightly on the sprocket to get it to move but don't pound on it. If the gear does not go into place easily, there's probably a burr on the Woodruff key or crankshaft that needs to be filed off.

Use the following procedure to install the timing chain and sprockets:

1. Rotate the crankshaft until the mark on the crankshaft sprocket faces straight up.
2. Temporarily place the camshaft sprocket on the end of the camshaft. On big-block engines, loosely install the sprocket bolts. Rotate the camshaft until the timing mark on the camshaft sprocket faces straight down.
3. Remove the camshaft sprocket and drape the timing chain over the sprocket with the timing mark still facing down.
4. Lower the sprocket and chain as an assembly, looping it under the crankshaft sprocket.
5. Pull the chain tight and press the camshaft sprocket over the end of the camshaft. If the mounting bolt holes are not perfectly aligned, rotate the camshaft slightly to obtain perfect alignment.
6. On small-block models, the chain may be too tight to install the camshaft sprocket. The crankshaft sprocket may need to be moved out slightly. Reinstall the chain and move both sprockets into place at the same time.
7. Press the camshaft sprocket over the camshaft. On big-block models, install the bolts.
8. Once the camshaft sprocket is in place, check the alignment of the marks, which should point exactly toward each other.

On small-block engines, install the fuel-pump eccentric and camshaft gear. Then, install and tighten the bolt to the torque specification listed in the appendix.

FINAL ASSEMBLY

This chapter shows you how to assemble the components that you've so carefully overhauled. All parts should be prepared for assembly, all bolt holes should be clean, and a new and complete engine gasket set should be used. Inspect the gaskets that you purchased to be sure that they are correct for the engine and that all of the correct gaskets are included. If any gasket is incorrect or missing, purchase the necessary gaskets.

These gaskets and seals are needed for assembly:

- Valve-cover gaskets
- Cylinder-head gaskets
- Intake-manifold gasket/valley pan
- Thermostat cover gasket
- Exhaust-manifold gaskets
- Front engine-cover gasket
- Water-pump gasket
- Oil-pump-cover gasket
- Distributor O-ring seal
- Fuel-pump gasket
- Front crankshaft oil seal
- Oil-pickup-tube gasket
- Oil-pan gasket set

Strongly consider replacing the following components at the time of an overhaul:

- Front cover, especially if the oil pump pocket is worn
- Oil-pump gears and pressure-relief-valve spring
- Cylinder-head bolts (particularly if the engine was overheated)
- Water pump (strongly recommended)
- Thermostat (essential)
- Fuel pump
- Distributor (new or rebuilt)
- Oil-pressure sending unit (strongly recommended)
- Coolant-temperature sending unit (strongly recommended)

Assemble the rest of the engine in the following order:

- Oil pump (covered in chapter 6)
- Oil-gallery plugs
- Oil-pressure sending unit
- Oil dipstick tube
- Engine front cover
- Water pump (immediately after front cover)
- Oil-pickup tube
- Windage tray
- Oil pan
- Vibration damper
- Fuel pump
- Cylinder heads
- Valvetrain
- Intake manifold

- Thermostat and housing
- Distributor
- Valve covers
- Engine mounts
- Exhaust manifolds

Oil Pump Cover and Oil Filter Adapter

The oil pump cover is sealed with a thin paper gasket. Do not apply sealant because the gasket surfaces are smooth and flat (replace oil pump parts if they are not smooth and flat). Oil pump disassembly and inspection are covered in chapter 6. Install the six mounting bolts and tighten them to the specification that is listed in the appendix.

Oil Gallery Plugs and Sending Unit

Inspect the block thoroughly to ensure that all coolant and oil plugs are in place on the block. For a quick review, there are four main gallery plugs on the engine (two at each end and just above the camshaft tunnel). It's best to tap for threaded plugs in the front (as covered in chapter 6). On big-block engines being converted to through-the-pushrod oiling, thread and plug the oil passages on the block deck surface (also covered in chapter 6).

The oil-pressure sending unit is threaded into a hole on the right front lower part of the engine block. Use a new sending unit because old sending units cannot always be relied upon. Place some thread sealer on the threads to avoid an oil leak. Some say not to use sealant on the sending units because they ground electrically through the threaded fitting. In practice, the tapered pipe threads will force metal-to-metal contact at the top of the threads when the sending unit is tightened securely.

Sealing Tips

Modern engine designs use machined gasket surfaces and high-tech gaskets. Unfortunately, that's not the case with Buick engines that were designed more than half of a century ago. At the time that these engines were produced, cork, paper, and rubber were the primary materials that were available. Stamped sheet-metal covers, which are prone to warpage and leakage, were common.

When assembling the engine, great care must be taken to ensure that there will be no leaks. Inspect all sheet-metal gasket surfaces for bending and warpage.

Although factory service manuals do not recommend some of the techniques that are included in this book, keep in mind that some of the sealers I recommend were either not available or not thoroughly tested when these engines were manufactured. For example, the quality of room-temperature-vulcanizing (RTV) silicone has improved dramatically since the 1970s.

I recommend using a light coat of RTV for many gasket installations, even in situations where it might not be absolutely necessary to achieve a good gasket seal. This is done to protect against potential issues related to imperfections in metal gasket surfaces that may have scratches or dents that are not easily seen.

In some cases, I call out sealants by brand. This does

RTV sealant is great for filling scratches or uneven surfaces.

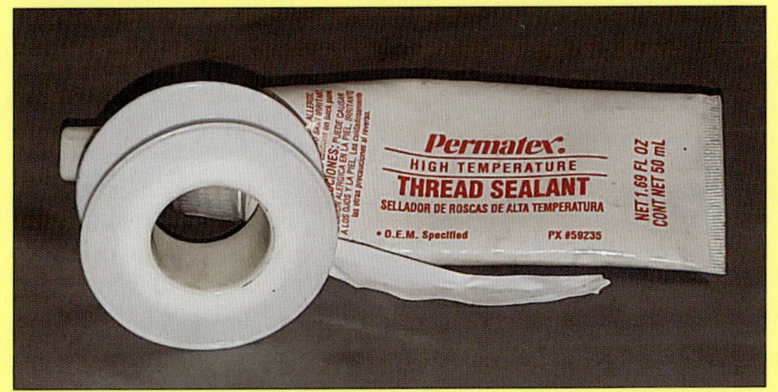

Teflon thread sealant (either in tape or liquid form) is used to prevent leaks at threaded fittings, such as on sending units and oil-gallery plugs.

Gasgacinch gasket sealer and belt dressing (or an equivalent) holds gaskets tightly in place, preventing them from moving or deforming during component assembly.

not represent any kind of brand endorsement. These sealant brands are common to the industry and I have experience using them. Alternatives are available. Use what you know and trust. For example, some people use weatherstripping adhesive to attach gaskets to surfaces instead of Gasgacinch. Weatherstripping adhesive will work. I just think that weatherstripping adhesive is more difficult to work with and more difficult to remove during disassembly.

Don't be influenced by purists who may say, "The factory didn't use those sealants, so you don't need them." When your engine was originally built at the factory, all of the parts were brand new with perfectly flat gasket surfaces, and they were assembled by people who were well practiced in the techniques that are necessary to make a leak-free engine. Even so, leaks were common from the factory. ■

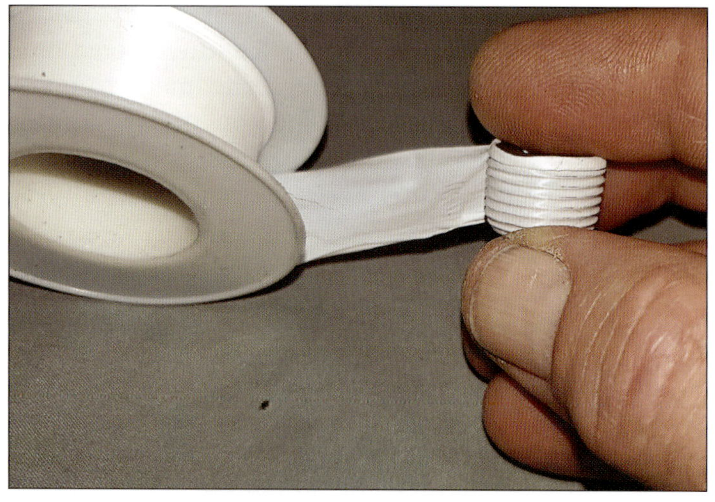

Place thread sealant on the threads of the oil-pressure sending unit. Then, install and tighten it securely. A special socket that is designed to fit over the end of the unit and fully engage the unique contours of the sending unit is shown. The socket is not always required. A standard deep socket usually works as long as the sending unit is not over-tightened.

Oil Dipstick Tube

The oil dipstick tube is a press fit. Thoroughly clean the tube and the hole in the engine block to ensure that varnish does not interfere with the installation. Place a bit of RTV sealer around the tube. Then, tap it into place with a soft-face hammer. The RTV not only seals but also lubricates as the tube is knocked into place.

Engine Front Cover and Water Pump

Thoroughly clean and inspect the front cover. The aluminum cover is susceptible to corrosion, particularly in the areas around the water pump and coolant passages. The bolts in these areas are often corroded as well. Replace them if corrosion is significant.

Before installing the cover, make sure that the distributor will engage the oil-pump driveshaft completely. This is especially important if a new front cover or oil-pump gears are being installed.

There are four threaded holes in the cover that must be in good condition because they are for the upper and lower water-pump bolts. If the threads are stripped, they can be HeliCoiled.

Most factory front covers were designed for rope-type front seals and have a machined bore on the inside of the cover. I recommend replacing the original rope-type seal with a modern lip-type seal, which is available from TA Performance. Rope-type seals are more difficult to install and are more prone to leakage. Replacement front covers have the seal bore on the outside and must use a lip-type seal.

After the seal has been installed, attach the front cover to the engine block. Double-check the valve timing marks on the camshaft and crankshaft gears to be sure that they're perfectly aligned.

Install the oil slinger. It "slings" oil away from the front seal, keeping the seal cooler and from being

Prior to installing the front cover, put the distributor in place in the front cover and check to ensure that it engages properly with the oil-pump driveshaft. Proper engagement is shown. No part of the drive slot in the pump driveshaft is visible.

Part of the oil-pump-driveshaft slot is shown here, which means that the distributor is not fully engaged. Occasionally, you will find a problem with aftermarket covers, especially the cheap ones. Other possible causes are a distributor or an oil-pump drive-shaft that's too short.

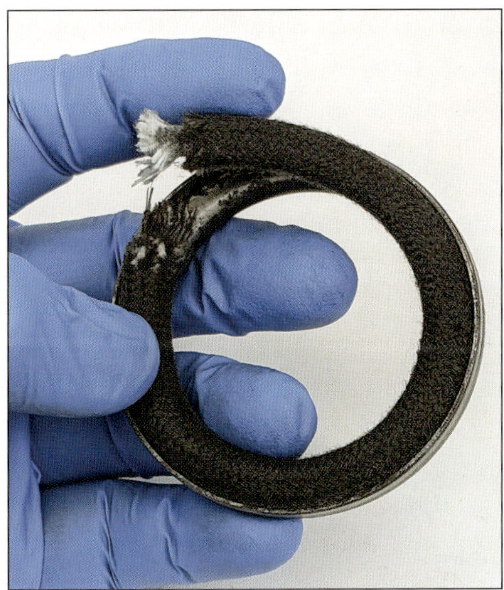

I don't recommend using the stock rope-type front seal. It's better to use the lip-type seal, which is avail-able from TA Performance. However, the rope-type seal is included with most gasket sets, so budget-minded engine builders may use it. Wipe the rope-type seal with oil and wrap it into the retainer. You may need to trim it.

On later-style covers, the seal is pressed in from the front. If you don't have a seal driver (shown), use a large socket that's slightly smaller in diameter than the outside diameter of the seal.

Install the retainer into the front cover. It should fit tightly. Press the vibration-damper hub into the front cover and rotate it back and forth. When the damper is removed, there should be no gap at the ends of the seal.

A common mistake for engine build-ers is to forget to install this oil slinger and then find it on the bench after the engine has been installed into the car. This is your official reminder.

overwhelmed by oil during engine operation. Don't forget to install this part, but if it happens to still be on the bench after the engine has been installed in the car, don't panic. The seal will generally still do its job—probably for a long time. Just don't expect it to remain supple and leak-free after 200,000 miles!

Make sure that every bit of gasket material is removed from the block and the front cover. Then, attach the front-cover gasket to the engine. This can be done with Gasgacinch, which will make sure the gasket remains in place during the installation of the cover and water pump. With the gasket firmly in place, place a very thin coat of RTV sealant on the front cover.

Now, place the front cover on the engine, guiding it over the align-ment pins. Install the five lower bolts (three on the passenger's side and two

Secure the front-cover gasket to the engine block with Gasgacinch, which will hold it in place while the cover is being installed. There are two dowel pins in the block that help with alignment.

Several bolts thread into water passages or the crankcase. Place some sealant on the bolts to ensure a good seal.

When installing the oil-pickup tube, be sure to use the gasket, which is normally included in the gasket kit. If there is any space where air can be drawn into the suction side of the oiling system, there will likely be no oil pressure.

on the driver's side). Leave the bolts finger-tight for now. Proceed immediately to water-pump installation.

I always recommend installing a new water pump. The last thing that you want to do is overheat the new engine, which will be running warmer than ever during break-in. Nevertheless, I know there are a few who want to save a few bucks by not replacing this critical item. If it is not replaced, make absolutely sure that there is no looseness in the shaft, that the impeller is tight to the shaft, and that there are no signs of leaking out the weep hole underneath the pump.

Attach the water-pump gasket to the front cover using Gasgacinch. Then, place a very thin coat of RTV on the water pump. Place the water pump against the front cover, guiding it over the alignment pins on the

front cover. Install the four large bolts at the left and right side of the pump. The bolts on the left thread into coolant passages and the crankcase, so it's important to apply sealant to the threads to prevent coolant leaks.

Now, tighten the larger bolts, which are the lower cover-to-engine bolts and the water pump-to-engine bolts. After the large bolts are installed, install the seven small bolts that attach the water pump to the front cover. The two large bolts around the left coolant passage are exposed to coolant and require thread sealant. Tighten all bolts to the torque specified in the appendix.

Oil-Pickup Tube, Windage Tray, and Pan

The oil-pickup tube is secured by two bolts and sealed to the block with a gasket. The windage tray is

secured by three bolts. Torque the bolts to the specifications listed in the appendix.

The oil-pan-gasket sealing surfaces must be free of any gasket material. The oil pan itself cannot have bends or dents at the gasket sealing surfaces. Deformation at the bolt holes from the previous overtightening of the bolts can be removed with a hammer, socket extension, and appropriately sized socket.

With the engine upside-down, install the oil pan gaskets and seals as follows:

1. On big-block engines, install the rear-end seal on the rear main bearing cap.
2. On all engines, apply a thin bead of RTV sealant at the points where the front cover and gasket meet.
3. On small-block engines, apply thin beads of RTV at the points where the rear seal retainer and block meet.
4. On all engines, apply Gasgacinch to the oil-pan rails on the block. Then, install the gaskets on the

The oil windage tray is secured by three bolts.

Apply a small bead of RTV sealant to the corners where the block and front cover meet.

block, interlocking them at the front and rear. Apply a small dab of RTV sealant to the points where the gaskets interlock.

5. On all engines, carefully set the oil pan in place and install all of the bolts finger-tight. Snug up the bolts gradually until all are at the torque that is listed in the appendix.

Note the corroded area on the oil-pan mating surface of this block. Small imperfections such as this can be sealed with RTV.

Oil-pan-gasket rails are commonly deformed, particularly at the bolt-hole areas. Check for uneven surfaces on the rails with a straightedge. Dents at holes can be removed by using an appropriately sized socket and extension as a driver. Do this on a solid, flat surface, such as concrete.

Vibration Damper and Hub

Inspect the hub for signs of a wear ridge from contact with the front seal. This is a common issue, and repair sleeves are available to repair the seal surface. The repair sleeve slides over the end of the hub, creating a new seal surface.

The vibration damper consists of two steel components that are bonded together with rubber. The outer ring can become loose from the hub, resulting in a knocking noise. It can also cause inaccuracy of the timing marks on the damper.

The vibration damper usually presses easily into place, but it may require some persuasion with a soft-face hammer. If gentle tapping isn't enough, check to be sure that there are no burrs on the crankshaft and that the Woodruff key is properly installed. Install the crankshaft bolt and tighten it to the torque that is listed in the appendix. The crankshaft needs to be held in place as this is done. Using a pry bar wedged into

On big-block engines, the rear seal and oil-pan rail interlock. Apply a dab of RTV to ensure a good seal.

the flexplate bolts is a good way to do this.

Fuel Pump

The fuel pump should be replaced routinely during an overhaul unless it was replaced very recently and was working properly. Even if the old pump was working well, it may not have been operating at full efficiency and may have even been one of the reasons that the engine was running poorly.

Apply Gasgacinch to the fuel-pump gasket and put it in place on the fuel pump. Apply a light coat of RTV sealant on the top surface of the gasket. Spread grease across the top of the fuel-pump arm, put the pump in place on the engine, install the bolts, and tighten them to the torque that is listed in the appendix. If the fuel-pump bolts do not easily align, the fuel-pump eccentric may be pressing against the arm. Rotate the crankshaft until the bolts thread easily in place.

Cylinder Heads

Make sure that the cylinder-head gasket surfaces on the block and cylinder head are completely clean of any bits of gasket material or oil. Wipe down the gasket surfaces with acetone prior to gasket installation to ensure ultimate cleanliness. The head gaskets are a common failure item, so don't rush through this part of the job.

Position the cylinder-head gasket over the dowels on the block. Make sure that all of the passages in the gasket line up correctly with the holes in the block. Lift the cylinder head onto the block, aligning the dowels with the dowel holes in the head. Be very careful not to allow the edges of the cylinder head to nick the gasket. It may be necessary to rock the cylinder head back and forth until it seats solidly on the head gasket.

Unlike engines from other manufacturers, Buick engines have blind cylinder-head bolt holes, so there's no reason to put any sealant on the cylinder head bolts. Put a small amount of oil on each bolt and thread it into place. Don't use too much oil. If you do, it will fill the bolt holes and cause the bolts to hydro-lock and not torque down correctly. If the bolts do not thread

Apply grease to the fuel-pump arm when it is installed. This will prevent friction with the fuel-pump eccentric until oil gets to it. If the pump does not sit flush against the block, rotate the crankshaft until it does.

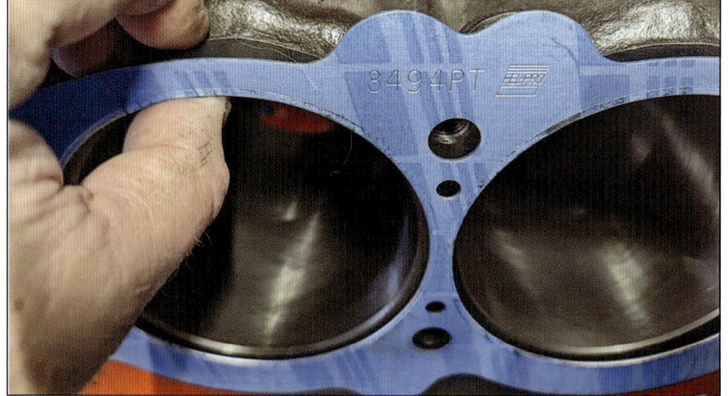

Position the cylinder-head gasket on the block over the dowel pins near the lower edge. Usually, there's lettering stamped into the gasket and/or stripes printed onto one surface. These indicate the surface that faces up. If you are using a standard-composition gasket, no sealant is required. The head and block surfaces must be completely clean.

Tighten the cylinder-head bolts in the sequence that is shown. Do not apply full torque to the bolts all at once, as the clamping force on the gasket must be applied evenly. Go through the sequence in three stages, increasing torque each time until the final torque is reached.

in easily by hand, there's a problem. Look down into the bolt holes to see if there's a problem with the alignment of the gasket or between the cylinder head and block. If the issue cannot be corrected with the head in place, remove the head and inspect carefully.

Once the bolts are threaded down against the head by hand, use a socket and breaker bar to gradually tighten the bolts about half of a turn at a time in the sequence shown. When the bolts start getting tight, use a torque wrench to tighten the bolts in the sequence shown to the torque rating that is listed in the appendix.

Valvetrain

Do not prime the lifters with oil at this time. Check the lifter preload first. The lifters will be primed later in this procedure.

Install a lifter into each lifter bore to ensure that it slides easily up and down and that the fitment is the same among all bores. The lifter should not move side to side when it is in the bore. If all is good, install all 16 lifters, applying assembly lube on the foot of each lifter.

Place a dab of assembly lube on the end of a pushrod. Then, install it through the hole in the cylinder head with the end seating in the cupped area in the center of the lifter. Repeat this process for the other 15 pushrods.

The rocker-arm shafts should have already been assembled (see chapter 5). It's important that rocker-arm assembly is done correctly.

Wipe some assembly lube onto the spots on each rocker arm that contact the pushrod and valve tip. Then, install the shafts onto the cylinder heads. The pushrods will be at varying heights, preventing the shaft from seating across all pedestals. Install the bolts and spacers, make sure that each rocker arm is in place on the pushrod and valve tip, and then tighten each bolt a half turn. Continue tightening the bolts a half turn at a time (working from the inside out) until all of the bolts are snug. It's important to tighten the bolts gradually to avoid cock-

ing and damaging the shafts. Once the shaft is seated, tighten the bolts to the torque that is listed in the appendix.

Check the lifter preload. This is important, even if you're using the same engine block, cylinder heads, pushrods, and rocker arms. The machining of the cylinder heads or block deck or even a different gasket thickness will change the preload.

Set the number-1 piston to TDC on the compression stroke. If the crankshaft has not been rotated since installing the front cover, the marks should still be aligned. In this position, the intake and exhaust lifters for the number-1 cylinder should both be positioned on the base circle of the camshaft. You'll know this because the lifters will be at the lowest point of their travel. In this position, check the preload at the number-2 and number-7 intake lifters and the number-8 and number-4 exhaust lifters.

To check lifter preload, use wire-type feeler gauges, such as those that are used for checking spark-plug gaps. Position the feeler gauge between the lifter plunger and the retaining clip at the top of the lifter. The clearance should be 0.020 to 0.060 inch. Check the preload for the remaining lifters, rotating the crankshaft a half turn (180 degrees) clockwise between each adjustment. Follow the chart provided.

Lifter Preload Checking Sequence		
	Intake Number	Exhaust Number
TDC number-1 cylinder, check	2, 7	8, 4
Rotate 90 degrees, check	1, 8	6, 3
Rotate 90 degrees, check	3, 4	7, 5
Rotate 90 degrees, check	6, 5	1, 2

If the preload is not as specified, correct it by selecting pushrods of the correct length. Pushrods are available in varying lengths for common variations. Custom pushrods can also be made to the exact length required. To determine the pushrod length that is needed, use a pushrod-length checking tool.

After checking the preload and making any corrections necessary, place the crankshaft back to the number-1 TDC position. This position is needed for installing the distributor.

Remove the lifters and lubricate them for final installation. Coat the foot of each lifter with the thick assembly lube that is designed for the break-in of conventional lifters. The lube should contain a high-pressure, anti-scuff additive. Do not put assembly lube on the sides of the lifters, as conventional lifters need to spin in their bores at start-up, otherwise the camshaft and lifters can be damaged.

When tightening the rocker-shaft bolts, work from the inside out, turning each bolt only a half turn at a time. Check periodically to make sure that the pushrods remain seated in the lifters and rocker arms.

Align the ignition timing marks and be certain that they are at TDC on the number-1 cylinder. This can be confirmed by looking at the positions of the number-1 cylinder lifters. They should both be at the bottom of their travel.

It's important that the lifter preload is within the appropriate range. Not enough preload can allow clearance to develop, which leads to lifter clatter and potential damage. Too much preload can lead to lifter "pump-up" at higher RPM, which can hang the valves open, possibly even causing them to contact the piston heads.

If the preload is not within the acceptable range, select pushrods that will correct the issue. Use an adjustable pushrod to obtain the correct preload. Then, measure the adjustable pushrod to determine what pushrod length is needed.

Lubricate the lifter feet with thick assembly lube that's designed for camshafts and lifters. Lubrication is critical, as severe damage can occur if the wrong lubricant is used. Place the lube on the feet only. Lubricate the sides of the lifters with a light film of engine oil.

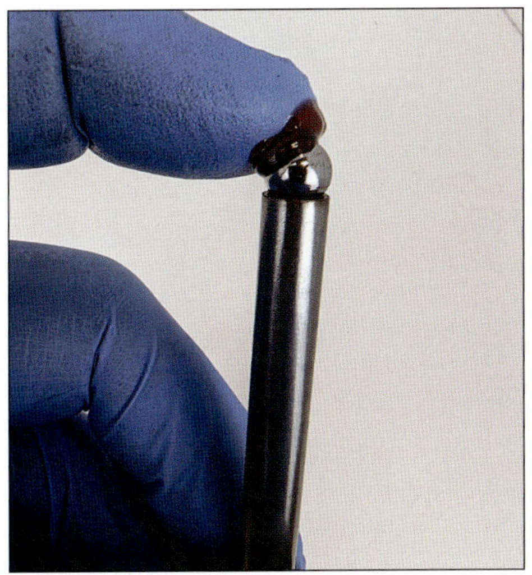

Lubricate both ends of the pushrods with thick assembly lube.

A light coat of oil on the sides of the lifters is all that's needed.

Put a bit of assembly lube on the top and bottom of each pushrod. Then, install the pushrods. Now, install the rocker-arm shaft assemblies.

Intake Manifold

Installing the intake manifold involves several operations that must be carefully coordinated so that the entire installation can be completed before the RTV "sets." Before beginning the procedure, check all clearances and have all components and tools ready to make sure that things go smoothly during the actual installation process.

The intake manifold is one of the most common sources of leaks—particularly vacuum leaks at the port areas. Any issues with machining of the cylinder heads or the intake manifold can lead to misalignment of the parts. It's a good idea to do a dry run, where the intake is fitted in place and checked for any misalignment.

Be clean and meticulous when installing the intake manifold. Clean the gasket mating surfaces thoroughly and clean the threads of the bolt holes with a tap. Also run a die over the bolts. Remember that if a mistake is made when installing the intake manifold, there could be a vacuum, oil, or coolant leak—or maybe all three.

Buick V-8 engines came from the factory with steel intake-manifold gaskets that have an integral valley tray. This design provides a baffle that prevents oil from being drawn into the intake system through the PCV valve, which is located at the rear of the intake manifold. This design also helps keep hot oil off the bottom of the intake manifold, allowing the manifold to operate slightly cooler and keep the intake air slightly cooler and more dense.

Test-Fitting

Set the intake manifold in place and check its fitment on the block and heads. The manifold should fit flush against the cylinder head.

Measure the gap between the manifold and the engine block as well as the thickness of the manifold end seals. If the gap is 75 percent of the seal thickness, plan to use the manifold end seals (included in

Check the alignment of the cylinder head–to–intake manifold mating surfaces. Here, there is proper alignment with no gaps (the gasket is normally installed for this check but is left out for clarity of the photo). Slight misalignment can be corrected using paper gaskets. Major misalignment must be corrected with machining.

Measure the gap between the intake manifold and the engine block. Here, I'm using a stack of feeler gauges.

gasket sets) to seal the gap. If the gap is smaller than 75 percent of the seal thickness, plan to use a thick bead of RTV in place of the seals. If the gap is larger than 75 percent of gasket thickness, plan to put a bead of RTV on top of the end seal to ensure proper sealing.

Valley Tray Gasket

If you use a steel gasket assembly with a valley tray, apply a thin coat of RTV sealant at the four water ports at the front and rear of the cylinder heads. Carefully, set the gasket in place. New gaskets are flat and must be bent into position before installation. Use the old gasket/pan as a guide.

The gaskets have alignment notches that must be positioned underneath the cylinder head. This keeps the gasket aligned with the ports in the cylinder head. Apply a thin layer of RTV to the outside of the gasket at the water-port areas. There should now be a layer of RTV on the inside and outside of the four water ports.

Paper Gaskets

If the gaskets do not already have silicone beads around the water-port areas, apply a thin coating of RTV sealant to the inner and outer areas around the water ports in the gaskets. Secure the gaskets to the cylinder head with Gasgacinch. Align the gasket to

the ports, rather than the bolt holes in the gasket. If necessary, trim the gasket around the bolt holes with a utility knife.

The valley-pan gasket needs to be trimmed around the area of the paper gasket. Leave only a small area around the end bolt holes. Those should be the only places where the valley tray overlaps the paper gasket. Apply a small amount of RTV in this area to ensure a good seal at this point of overlap. Set the valley tray in place.

All Gaskets

Install the intake manifold end seals and/or RTV (as you determined by the test-fit). Carefully lower the intake manifold in place.

Tighten the bolts by hand. Then, use a socket and a breaker bar to gradually tighten the bolts about a half turn at a time in the sequence that is shown. When the bolts begin getting tight, switch from using a breaker bar to a torque wrench and tighten the bolts in the sequence shown to the torque that is listed in the appendix.

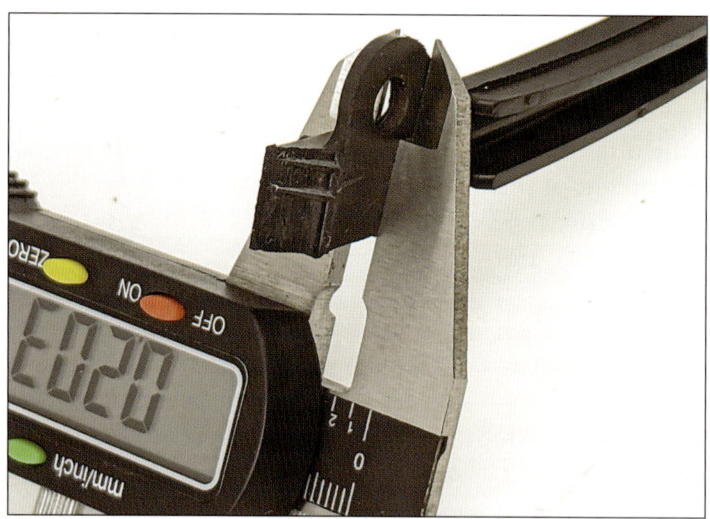

Measure the thickness of the intake-manifold end seals. Using these two measurements can determine the best method for sealing the manifold ends. Details are in the text.

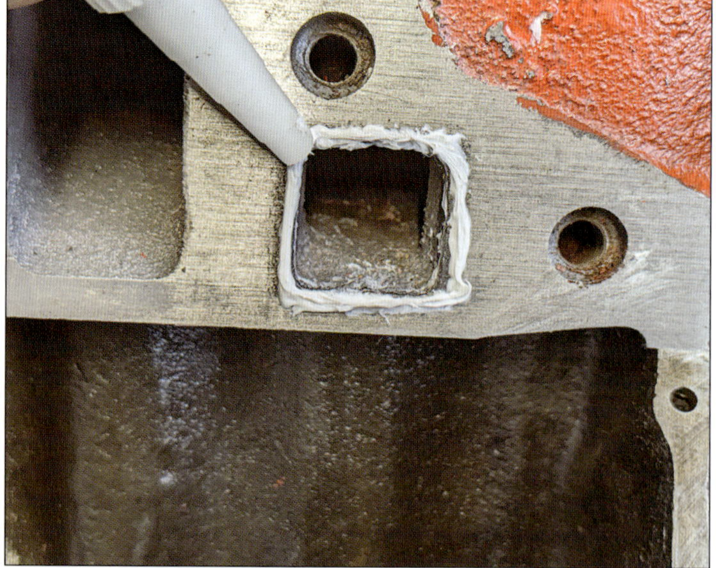

If steel gaskets are used, apply RTV sealant at the four coolant passages at the ends of the cylinder heads.

Apply a light coating of RTV sealant around the coolant-passage openings on the outside surface of the intake-manifold gaskets.

A small dab of RTV sealant at each of the four corners helps to prevent leaks.

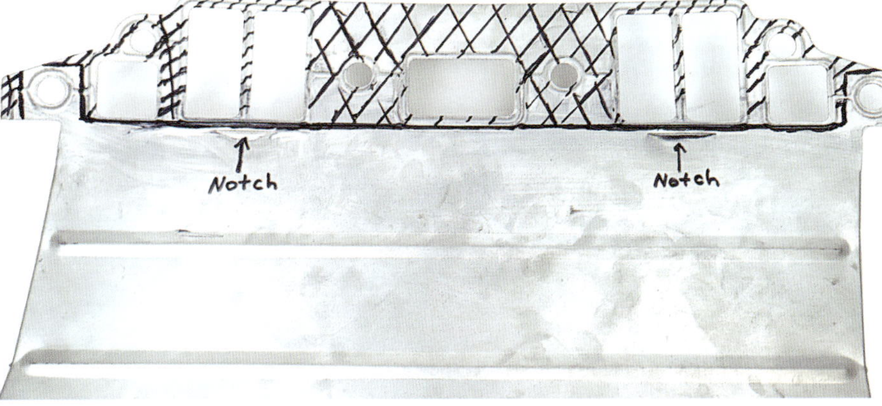

If you are using paper gaskets, trim away the cross-hatched area on each side. Basically, you're cutting away the area where the paper gaskets go except for the areas around each end bolt. Leave a bit above the notches to allow the notches to engage properly against the cylinder head.

Intake-manifold end seals have one side that fits over a dowel pin in the block. The other end has a protrusion that fits into a hole in the block. If you have trouble getting the protrusion into the hole, there's probably a bit of old rubber in the hole. Ask me how I know!

Tighten the intake-manifold bolts following the sequence that is shown here to the torque that is listed in the appendix. Don't tighten the bolts all at once. Instead, work up to the final torque in three stages, increasing the torque each time that you go through the sequence.

Thermostat and Housing

Attach the thermostat housing gasket to the thermostat housing with Gasgacinch. Place the thermostat in place in the intake manifold and spread a thin coat of RTV sealant on top of the gasket. Install the two bolts and tighten them to the torque that is listed in the appendix.

Leak Checking

Thoroughly inspect the exterior of the engine, looking for points of potential leakage. It's easy to miss installing a plug or forget to tighten something. In a darkened room, use a bright flashlight directed into openings such as the distributor opening. Look carefully at all gasket sealing points (at all angles). If a little light is getting through, it will probably have a leak.

The advent of powerful flashlights has provided a new leak-detection tool. Attach the end of a flashlight to an opening in the engine. Then, in a darkened room, inspect for light showing through at gasket surfaces. Move a piece of white paper across the gasket surfaces to help you see the light "leak."

Pre-Oiling the Engine

It is strongly recommended to pre-oil the engine prior to installing it in the vehicle. To do so, fill the engine with oil and install the oil filter. This brings us into the discussion of what type of oil and/or additives to use during engine break-in, which is covered in chapter 8.

If you want to monitor oil pressure during the pre-oiling process, connect a mechanical pressure gauge in place of the oil-pressure sending unit.

Special tools are available for pre-oiling the engine and are relatively inexpensive. In addition, one can be made out of an old distributor. To do so, grind off the distributor drive-gear teeth and modify the top of the shaft so that a drill chuck can be put on it.

Set the drill to run clockwise. Then, operate the drill, using a slow speed at first. This is precautionary to keep the oil from spraying everywhere if there is a leak. Run the drill at a low speed while inspecting the engine to be sure that there are no leaks. Now, raise the speed of the drill to about 1,000 rpm, which will simulate 2,000 engine rpm. Strong resistance should be felt as this is done. For reference, most heavy-duty drills have a loaded speed in the 1,500-rpm range.

Continue operating the drill for several minutes, looking for oil to appear around the lifters and at the pushrod end of the rocker arms. If you don't see oil at the rocker arms for a minute or two, that's normal. In addition, oil might not appear at all of the rocker arms. That is also normal. Often, the crankshaft will need to be rotated to obtain oil flow to all of the pushrods and rocker arms.

Oiling at all of the rocker arms is important to verify, as there is always a possibility that there is a plugged

For pre-oiling, use a special tool that has been designed specifically for that purpose, such as the one that is shown. It is possible to fabricate a tool using an old distributor housing, but it's usually more trouble than it's worth to locate the part.

The special tool engages the pump driveshaft slot and also encircles the shaft. Bushings at the top and bottom keep the shaft stable during operation.

When oil is flowing into the rocker arms, that means the oiling system is developing good pressure. It may take a while for this to happen and the oil likely won't flow evenly on every rocker arm. Rotate the crankshaft periodically to even things out.

passageway or a different problem in the block. The rocker arms are the high point in the lubrication system, so if there is oil there, assume that there is oil throughout the engine.

Distributor

Install a new O-ring on the distributor housing. If the crankshaft has not been disturbed since the valvetrain was installed, the number-1 piston should be at its TDC firing position. This is where it should be when installing the distributor. Mark the distributor housing underneath the number-1 wire terminal, which is usually at the passenger's side of the engine when the distributor is installed.

The distributor drive gear is ground at an angle, so the rotor will move a bit when the distributor is lowered into place. The installation process is complicated further by the alignment of the oil pump driveshaft. It may be necessary to rotate the driveshaft a bit to get the distributor to seat completely. Installing the distributor always takes some trial and error. The goal is to have the rotor pointing to the mark on the distributor base, which should be at the passenger's side of the engine. Once that is done, install the distributor hold-down clamp but leave it loose at this time.

Rotate the crankshaft slightly clockwise while observing the ignition timing marks. Position the timing marks to indicate 12 degrees before top dead center (BTDC). Realign the distributor rotor with the mark on the base. Then, tighten the hold-down clamp securely. Don't overtighten the clamp bolt because it will need to be loosened again after starting the engine. Install the distributor cap.

You have now set the ignition timing for 12 degrees BTDC. This may be

When installing the distributor, mark the aluminum base below the terminal for the number-1 cylinder. Align the rotor with this mark during distributor installation.

more timing than was specified for the engine, but a few extra degrees of timing can help with starting the engine. Once the engine has started and has run, reset the timing.

Valve Covers

Install the valve covers. Do not overtighten the nuts. If you do, it is possible to dent the cover and crush the gasket. The factory torque specification is less than 5 ft-lbs.

Engine Mounts

Install new engine mounts. They're relatively inexpensive and difficult to replace after the engine has been installed in the car. The new engine will most likely have more torque than the old one did, so it could break a mount the first time that you step hard on the gas. It's better to be safe than sorry. The mount bolts do not have a specific torque value. Make sure they're good and tight.

Most valve-cover gaskets have tabs that interlock with the valve cover. These hold the gaskets in place during installation. The valve-cover gaskets are designed to be installed dry with no sealant.

Exhaust Manifolds

If you use the original exhaust manifolds, the mounting face may be warped or the bolt holes may no longer line up correctly. Surface warpage can be accommodated by using a thick exhaust gasket. The misalignment of bolt holes can be corrected with a reamer to make the holes bigger. If the manifolds are badly warped, the mating surfaces can be machined flat. Cracked manifolds must be replaced.

Exhaust-manifold gaskets are designed to be installed with the metallic side out. The design of these gaskets allows the exhaust manifold to expand and contract slightly without disturbing the seal.

INSTALLING AND STARTING THE ENGINE

Now that the overhaul project is complete, it's time to get the engine installed and running. Once again, take the time to make sure each task is performed correctly as you work through each step. The work at this stage of the project is just as critical as it is during any of the previous stages.

Preparing the Engine and Engine Compartment

The assembled engine should be spotless, and now is the time to paint it. Most Buicks came from the factory painted red, but some mid-1970s-and-later engines were painted GM Corporate Blue. Do some research regarding what color was used on your vehicle. However, don't be constrained by originality! Engine paint comes in a rainbow of colors. For practicality, darker colors are better because they don't show dirt as much as light colors.

Use engine degreaser to remove all of the gunk in the engine compartment, particularly on the cross-member under the engine. It is important to have all areas around the engine clean to help diagnose any possible oil leaks.

The engine compartment should also be organized. Move tubes, hoses, and wiring harnesses out of the way to accommodate engine installation and to allow for easy identification of the connectors after the engine is installed.

Flush the radiator with water. Place a garden hose into the top radiator-hose fitting and let water flow out the bottom radiator fitting until the water comes out clean.

If you are working on a collector car, do the correct engine-compartment detailing, as it will be easier to do with the engine removed.

Engine paint has a higher temperature rating than normal household paint or even standard automotive paint. It's usually rated to handle 500°F or more. That's enough for the engine block and heads but not enough for exhaust components. Never use standard paint on an engine. It will not last.

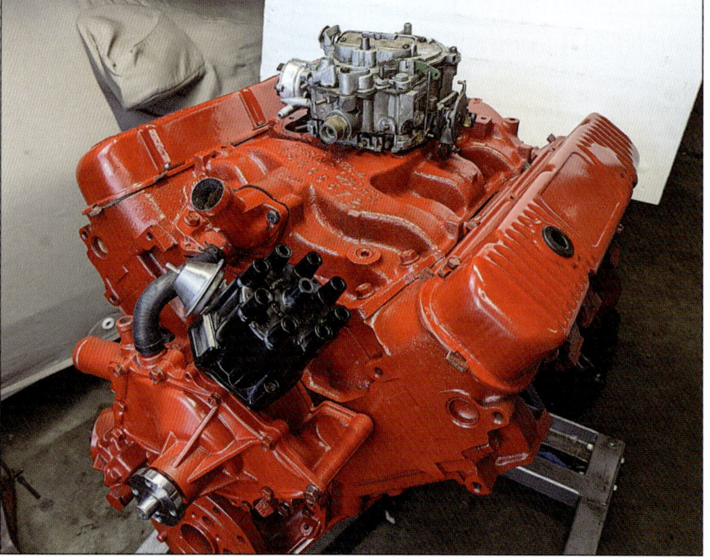

Most Buick engines were painted red, although Buick Red is difficult to find. I used Dupli-Color DE1653, which is a pretty close match to the original color. Some later engines were painted GM Corporate Blue, which is much easier to find.

Header paint (right) is available in various colors, but the most popular colors are silver and black. This header paint can handle between 1,300 and 2,000°F and can be used on exhaust manifolds as well. Exhaust manifold paint (left) is designed to handle 1,200°F and provides a thick, durable coating. It is available in a gray color that simulates the original, raw cast-iron look of an exhaust manifold.

On any car, it is a good practice to paint under the hood to give the engine compartment a fresh look and to prevent rust. This will also help when you are identifying leaks, particularly coolant leaks, as they tend to leave dry residue on paint. Before painting, mask around the engine compartment, particularly the hood, fenders, and front of the vehicle. You'd be surprised how far overspray can travel—even from a spray can.

Give the firewall, fender liners, and crossmember a fresh coat of paint. This not only improves the appearance but also can help you track down potential leaks. Although engine paint is not required for these areas, use a quality paint. Flat black is usually the best choice. When painting the engine brackets, use engine paint because anything that is attached to the engine will get very hot.

In a full vehicle restoration, all wiring, hoses, and other components in the engine compartment are removed and replaced with new or restored parts when the vehicle is reassembled. For most rebuilds, these items stay in place. This can create challenges when masking prior to painting.

Masking tape and newspaper can be used to cover most components, but they are difficult to apply to hoses and wiring. In addition, masking tape is often difficult to remove from hoses and wiring after the paint has dried. Household aluminum foil is perfect for wrapping around these awkward-shaped items.

Paint the accessory mounting brackets that bolt onto the engine. Engine paint will need to be used because components that are directly attached to the engine can reach high temperatures.

Installing the Engine

Before installing the engine, check everything again to be sure that the fasteners are tight and that all vacuum hoses and fuel lines are properly connected. You already checked that there were no serious oil leaks when you pre-oiled the engine. However, there is still the possibility of a coolant leak if you forgot to install a coolant plug, sending unit, or other thermostatic-control switch. Hopefully, you took many photos during engine removal, which will be very helpful at this point.

Decide which accessories and other external components to

To avoid installing a beautiful engine into an ugly engine compartment, thoroughly clean the engine compartment with engine degreaser. Be careful to not get the wiring connectors wet when spraying the degreaser off with water. Use sandpaper to remove any rusty spots.

Transmission Front Seal and Bushing

If your vehicle has an automatic transmission, it's wise to remove the torque converter and have it inspected at a transmission shop. If there's any doubt about the condition of the torque converter, replace it.

While the torque converter is removed, replace the front seal and the bushing that goes behind it. It's common to find that there is a leak at the front of the transmission that has gone unnoticed due to leaks from the engine. You don't want to find the leak after the engine is installed.

If your vehicle has a manual transmission, inspect the clutch pressure plate, clutch disc, flywheel, release bearing, and pilot bushing. It's wise to replace the clutch components and have the flywheel surfaced at the time of an overhaul. There will be no enjoyment of the smooth power of a new engine if it has a slipping clutch. ■

The torque-converter hub has two cutouts that engage the lugs on the transmission pump. When reinstalling the torque converter, make sure that it is fully engaged on the transmission's input shaft, stator shaft, and pump drive lugs. These three engagements are usually felt separately as the converter is pushed and rotated into place. Getting the converter engaged can take some time and effort.

It's common for the transmission's front seal to develop a leak over time. Remove the torque converter to get to the seal. Behind the seal, there is a bronze bushing that should also be replaced, as a worn bushing contributes to seal failure. In addition, note the two lugs that drive the transmission front pump.

attach to the engine during installation. Most people want to keep the momentum going and finish assembly while the engine is on the stand. It makes for nice photos on social media accounts. However, be strategic. Some components are easy to install while the engine is on the stand, and other components make it more difficult to guide the engine into place and are not any more difficult to install in the engine compartment.

I recommend not installing the carburetor at this point because it's relatively fragile and the engine-hoist chain is near it during installation.

In addition, the distributor cap is vulnerable to damage during installation. At a minimum, disengage the distributor-cap retainers so that the cap can move if it contacts the installation chain or other obstructions during the engine installation.

Install the spark plugs and route the spark-plug wires at this point. It's much easier to do this on the engine stand. Use clips to make sure that the wires are kept away from the headers or exhaust manifolds, which will soon be very hot. Don't forget that the distributor shaft on a Buick engine rotates clockwise.

When you are ready to put the engine into place, raise the vehicle, support it securely on jack stands, set

I recommend leaving the carburetor off the engine during installation. The chance of damaging the carburetor outweighs the slight amount of extra effort that is involved with installing the carburetor while the engine is in the vehicle. Tape over the carburetor opening to prevent debris falling into the engine during installation.

Take a final look over the engine compartment to ensure that all hoses, lines, electrical wiring, and connectors are positioned out of the way and will not interfere with the installation. It's common for electrical wires to get caught up in the engine, leading to broken wires and connectors. Hoses and lines are also common places for the engine to get hung up. An engine should lower into place evenly. If that's not happening at any point, inspect the engine carefully at all points, including underneath, to be sure that it is free to move.

The final stages of engine installation must be done with precision. The engine must fit tightly and evenly against the transmission bellhousing. Rotate the engine a bit to make it level with the transmission. Watch the mounting surfaces of the engine and transmission and make sure that they are aligned vertically. The transmission can be lifted up and down with the floor jack to get this alignment correct.

Apply some pressure at the front of the engine to get the engine and transmission to seat against each other. There are dowel pins on the engine to help with this. What usually gets the dowel pins into place is a combination of light rearward pressure on the engine, a slight rotation of the engine, and small up-and-down movements of the transmission.

After the transmission is in place on the dowel pins, install two transmission-to-engine bolts (one on each side). Make sure that it is possible to engage at least three threads of the bolts with only the force of your fingers. At this point, do the final seating of the engine against the transmission by tightening the bolts.

Double-check that there are no wires or hoses trapped between the

the parking brake, and block the rear wheels.

Remember that safety is important when maneuvering heavy components. It's easy to get a finger trapped between a loaded engine mount and a bracket or between the engine block and the transmission. These are minor compared to the severe injuries you will have if the engine, transmission, or vehicle are not safely supported at all times.

Place a floor jack under the transmission bellhousing and raise the transmission until it is at or above its normal height with the engine installed. Remove any supports that were in place for the transmission and exhaust components. Allow the pipes to hang freely.

Firing Order:
1-8-4-3-6-5-7-2

Refer to this graphic when you route the spark-plug wires.

The American Petroleum Institute (API) rates oils regarding their ability to handle high temperatures, neutralize contaminants, and resist molecular breakdown. The newer grades do not have high levels of zinc dithiophosphate (ZDDP), or zinc dialkyldithiophosphates (ZDTPs), as a part of their additive packages because it's assumed that the oil will be used in newer engines with roller lifters. This can create an issue if the engine has conventional flat-foot lifters.

Help, Please!

Have an assistant available during the engine installation so that the process can be carefully monitored. Watch every inch of movement to ensure that there are no obstructions and that the front of the engine is in alignment with the engine mounts and transmission bellhousing.

Installation is not always straight down. You'll often need to maneuver the engine to clear obstacles and angle it so that it properly fits over the engine mounts and flush with the transmission mounting surface. As the engine is lowered and maneuvered, it commonly sways. Hold it tightly during these times to prevent it from hitting vulnerable components, such as the wiper motor. ■

engine and transmission. Then, slowly tighten the bolts a half turn at a time, moving back and forth between them. If resistance is felt, stop and find the obstruction. The bolts should pull the transmission up against the engine very easily without much force. Once the engine and transmission are flush, install and tighten the remaining transmission-to-engine bolts and tighten them to 35 ft-lbs. Remove the floor jack.

Now, guide the engine mounts over the brackets on the frame. Some rearward movement of the engine and transmission is usually necessary. Sometimes, it's difficult to get both mounts to seat evenly over the brackets so that both through-bolt holes align. If this is the case, position the engine so that one of the through-bolts can be installed. Then, use the hoist to position the engine

so that the other bolt will go into place. Tighten the bolts to 50 ft-lbs.

With the engine now solidly in place, install the remaining components by reversing the disassembly procedures that are outlined in chapter 4. Refer to the appendix for torque specifications.

Fill the cooling system with a 50-50 mixture of coolant and distilled water. All Buick V-8s came from the factory filled with ethylene glycol coolant. Today, long-life coolants are available that have a service life of up to 100,000 miles, so consider updating the coolant.

Check for leaks in the cooling system. If there is the slightest drip now, it will become a significant leak after the engine gets warm and the cooling system develops pressure. Fix any leaks now because you don't want to stop the engine until the 20-minute break-in procedure is complete.

It is advisable to pressurize the cooling system to the listed maximum pressure rating to ensure that there will be no leaks. This test requires a cooling-system pressure tester. While a tester such as this can be expensive, it will be useful in the future for diagnosing coolant leaks.

Choosing Oil

Do not use synthetic oils during the break-in period. Even if you plan to run synthetic oil, start with non-synthetic oil for at least the first 1,000 miles.

Engine oils are rated as to their service grade and viscosity. The American Petroleum Institute (API) has a rating system for the service grade that rates the ability of an oil to operate properly under high-stress conditions. The rating system has progressed over time, starting with SA in the 1930s and con-

tinuing through SN at the time of this book's publication. The farther along in the alphabet, the better the oil. However, the latest API formulations do not have zinc, which is essential for break-in and for conventional lifters.

Viscosity is an oil's resistance to pouring. The higher the number, the thicker (or more viscous) the oil is. Oils with a higher viscosity result in higher oil pressure. Select an oil with the viscosity that has the best chance of achieving the oil pressure that is specified for your engine (see the appendix).

Bearing clearance plays a large role in the oil pressure. The more bearing clearance there is, the less pressure can be developed by a particular viscosity of oil. For break-in, SAE 30 oil is appropriate for a stock rebuild with bearing clearances within new engine tolerances. This assumes that a standard-volume oil pump is used. If the bearing clearances are more than stock, the engine may need an oil with a higher viscosity, such as SAE 40. If you are in doubt, a machine shop should

Even with roller lifters, a break-in additive is recommended for the first oil fill. Break-in additives supplement the oil with zinc and other high-pressure lubricants that are needed during the initial high-wear start-up phase.

With conventional lifters, use oil with zinc over the life of the engine. While it is somewhat more expensive than standard oil, it's cheap insurance, considering that catastrophic damage can happen if a camshaft or lifter fails, sending debris throughout the engine.

be able to provide a recommendation based on bearing clearances.

After break-in, use a multi-viscosity oil that allows the oil to flow better at lower temperatures, such as when the car is first started on a cold day. For most engines, 10W-30 or 10W-40 works well. For an engine with stock bearing clearances, 10W-30 works well, while an engine with more bearing clearance may prefer 10W-40.

If the engine has conventional flat-foot lifters, there is something else to consider. Modern automotive oils do not contain high-pressure additives that are required for conventional lifters. The missing additive is zinc, which was removed from modern oils due to environmental concerns. However, oils containing high-pressure lubricants are still available.

An early solution was to use heavy-duty diesel oils because they still contain zinc. However, diesel oil is formulated differently than automo-

tive oils. There are now many specialty automotive oils available that contain zinc and are designed for use with conventional lifters. When you first start the new engine, use a break-in additive. Break-in oils contain supplemental additives that will further protect the camshaft and lifters.

Starting the Engine

Starting the engine is the big moment where all of your hard work pays off. You may be eager to turn the key, but you need to take enough time to get your engine and yourself fully prepared.

Have at least one assistant during the first start-up. He or she will provide another set of eyes to identify any issues once the engine starts. Select someone with mechanical knowledge who can identify problems and make adjustments.

Perform one final inspection of the engine compartment. Look for tools, rolls of tape, dipsticks, filler caps, or anything else that may have been left under the hood. Make sure that the battery is fully charged and check the fluids one more time. It's common to find a low coolant level after the engine sits for a while. This is due to trapped air finding its way out of the engine. The coolant level often drops more after starting when coolant circulation brings out more air. It's best to have your assistant monitor the coolant level for a few minutes after starting before installing the radiator cap.

If it can be done safely, fill the

carburetor float bowl with gas. This will allow fuel to flow immediately into the engine once you start cranking the engine. If this isn't done, the engine will have to run for several seconds before the fuel pump primes and starts delivering fuel to the carburetor.

Leave the air cleaner off the engine and locate a fire extinguisher. It's often helpful to spray a bit of engine-starting fluid into the carburetor. This is especially important if you are trying to start the engine with a dry carburetor.

Attempt to start the engine. It should start immediately. Bring the engine speed to about 2,000 rpm.

If the engine has conventional lifters, it's essential that the engine gets to 2,000 rpm immediately and then varies between 1,500 and 2,000 rpm for 20 minutes. This ensures that oil flows freely over the lifters and camshaft while the lifters are breaking in.

Allow the engine to idle. Adjust the carburetor and ignition timing. Turn off the engine, check for leaks, and add fluids as necessary. Change the oil and filter. If metal bits are in the oil, do not operate the engine until you can determine the origin of this debris and have corrected the problem.

If the engine does not start, make sure that all the spark-plug wires are in place and that the distributor cap is tight. If you can't identify the problem, test for spark using a spark tester.

Sputtering and backfiring can be the result of incorrect ignition timing or the ignition firing order being wrong. Double-check these items. If backfiring continues, check for vacuum leaks and then try advancing the ignition timing a few degrees.

If it can be done safely and easily, fill the carburetor float bowl with gas. Here, I'm filling the carburetor through the float-bowl vent. Add fuel slowly. Most float bowls only hold a few ounces of fuel.

Engine starting fluid is made from ether, which is highly volatile, meaning that it mixes with air more easily than gasoline. Open the choke and throttle plates. Then, spray starting fluid into the intake manifold for about a second. This virtually guarantees a quick start, assuming that everything else has been done correctly. If the carburetor is dry and is starting to die from fuel starvation, have an assistant ready to spray more starting fluid.

If the engine makes excessive noise, shut it down and try to find the source. Clunking noises after a first start are often related to loose torque-converter bolts or a loose vibration damper. A shrieking noise is most likely a loose belt. Check that the fan bolts are tight. A loud whining noise is probably coming from the torque converter or power-steering pump. It's common for these fluid levels to be low, since there's usually some fluid leakage from the transmission-cooler lines and power-steering pump during engine removal.

It's normal to hear clattering noise from the lifters during the first minute or two after start-up. This is caused by the lifters not having enough oil in them to work properly. The noise should go away quickly when the lifters fill with oil. If the clattering continues, it could be caused by low oil pressure. Shut down the engine and determine the cause of the low oil pressure.

Breaking in the Engine

Install a new oil filter and add the appropriate oil to the engine. Choose a multi-viscosity oil, either 10W-30 or 10W-40. Base that decision on the oil pressure that was noticed during break-in. If the oil pressure was well within specification, use 10W-30. If the oil pressure was low, use 10W-40. Drive about 500 miles and then change the oil again.

Break-in is the process through which the new piston rings and honed cylinder walls wear into each other and create a tight seal. The process can be compared to polishing. During this process, the engine temperature may be slightly higher than usual. This is a result of the friction created by the break-in process. During break-in, don't drive the car hard but also don't baby it. Too much friction and heat can damage the rings and leave scoring in the cylinders. If not enough friction is created during this early stage, a glaze can form in the cylinders that will cause the rings to seat poorly.

Oil Consumption

After an overhaul, oil consumption is usually a little higher than on an engine that has been fully broken in. This is usually not very noticeable, but it is something to keep in mind. The reason for the oil consumption is that non-seated piston rings are more prone to allowing oil to get past them.

If oil-consumption issues persist after the first thousand miles or so, there may be a problem. Here are common causes of excessive oil consumption after an overhaul: 1) the piston rings were not installed properly, 2) the piston rings are not seating correctly, 3) there is an internal intake-manifold vacuum leak, or 4) the valve seals are not sealing correctly. Chapter 3 can help with diagnosis.

Maintenance

After break-in, change conventional oil at intervals of no more than 5,000 miles. Always change the oil filter at the same time. Change the air filter, PCV valve, and PCV filters at the interval that Buick recommends for the vehicle. Replace the spark plugs every 12,000 miles if you are using points-type ignition or every 50,000 miles if you are using an HEI ignition. Staying current on these basic maintenance items can greatly extend the life of the engine.

PERFORMANCE AND ECONOMY MODIFICATIONS

Most of today's Buick enthusiasts are primarily interested in maintaining the reliability and drivability of their classic automobile, which is the main focus of this book. Many are interested in improving engine performance, and some are interested in racing and street performance. This chapter addresses those of us with the need for speed.

Ways to improve the fuel efficiency of the Buick engine for long cruises are also covered. Some modifications can improve both performance and fuel economy and should be considered by all enthusiasts.

How is it that Buick engines didn't come from the factory with the performance modifications that are detailed in this chapter? The answer is that engine design is based on many factors, chief among them are cost and exceptional drivability under all conditions. It is necessary to trade some engine performance to achieve these drivability characteristics. Remember, the average Buick was not purchased by an enthusiast. Instead, it was purchased by someone looking primarily for reliable daily transportation. Perhaps sadly, most engines were destined to be installed in commuter cars.

Any engine is essentially a pump that inhales an air/fuel mixture and exhales exhaust gases. Most modifications improve horsepower by better enabling this essential flow of gases

Daily commuting is not a normal use for most classic Buicks, so cold-weather starting, perfectly smooth idling, and fuel economy aren't priorities. You want to enjoy the drive, and spirited performance makes the drive more fun! Buick V-8s respond well to performance modifications, but upgrades have trade-offs—both in cost and drivability. Understand the trade-offs before getting started.

Get expert advice with any level of performance upgrades. Parts manufacturers, as well as some retailers, maintain a staff of experts to help you make the right decisions. These experts are less interested in upselling than in making sure that you are a happy customer.

Stock steel connecting rods are okay for mild performance applications, but they require upgrades, including high-strength bolts.

through the engine. The greater the flow, the higher the horsepower. The horsepower increase from such modifications is made by allowing the engine to operate more efficiently at higher RPM.

Some modifications increase power through increasing the engine's displacement, which improves both horsepower and torque. Your neck will snap harder when you step on the gas pedal, but the gas tank will be drained quicker.

Although this chapter discusses engine modifications separately, it is important to understand that modifications need to be matched with the engine and other components for the best performance. If components are not matched properly, power can be reduced and drivability can be worsened. Similarly, if you installed four different sizes of tires on a car, it would not corner well—no matter how high quality the individual tires are.

So, when selecting parts, speak with performance experts and parts manufacturers to get their educated insight. Be sure that they understand your performance goals and other modifications that you plan.

Safety

Most of the performance modifications that are discussed in this chapter are primarily about making power. This should be distinguished from any modifications that are related to an engine surviving in service when it's pushed toward its horsepower limits, such as with a racing engine.

Durability modifications usually include forged pistons and forged connecting rods. For big-block engines, a girdle to reinforce the bottom of the block is wise to use.

For serious street performance and racing, forged billet crankshafts and aluminum blocks are

This set of domed pistons was designed for ultra-high compression. Stock cast-aluminum pistons don't have the strength for serious performance engines. Forged pistons are stronger and are required for a boosted engine. With Buick V-8s, there are more forged-piston options than cast-piston options, so using forged pistons can help you get the compression ratio and deck clearance that you desire.

When building a serious performance engine, forged-steel connecting rods are needed. These are the I-beam type, which is the strongest. The lower-cost H-beam rods are priced competitively with properly upgraded stock rods. The additional cost of the I-beam rods is easily justified when considering the major engine damage that a broken rod can cause.

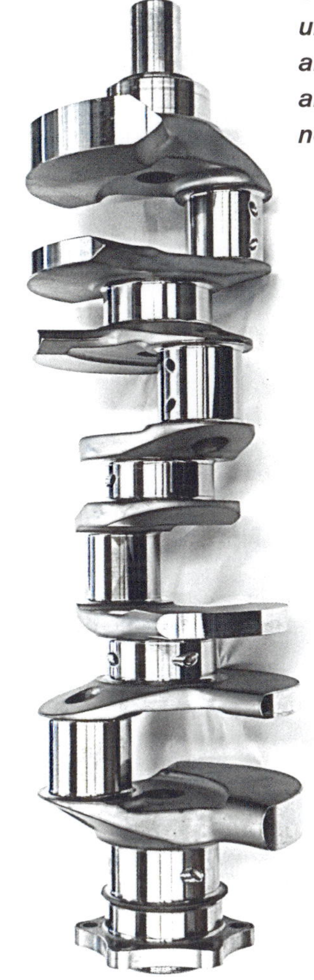

Billet-steel crankshafts (shown here) are the ultimate in strength and can handle massive amounts of horsepower. Unfortunately, they are also very expensive. For that reason, they are not appropriate for most performance builds.

If you are planning a maximum-effort race engine to stomp on the Bowtie and Blue Oval contenders, start with this high-strength aluminum 455 block from TA Performance. It has far greater strength than a stock iron block and many upgrades, such as four-bolt main bearing caps.

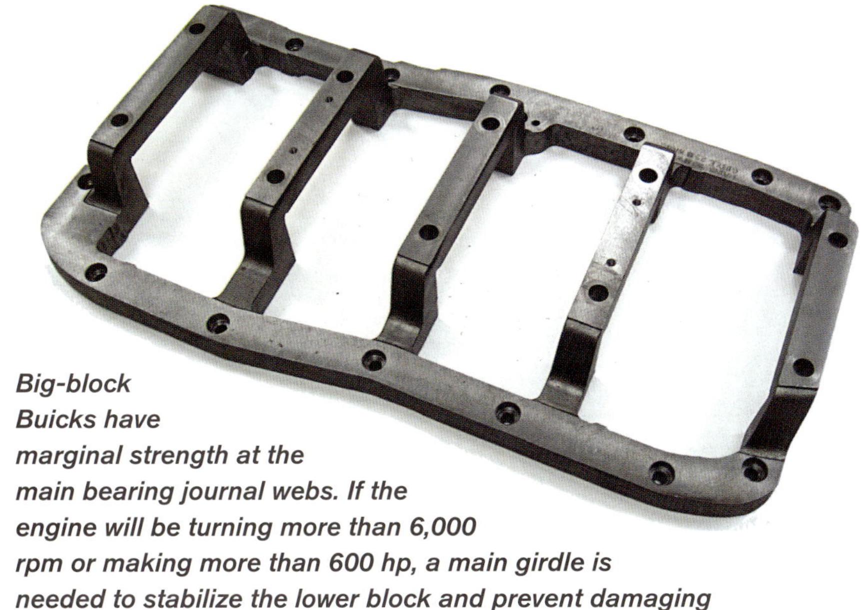

Big-block Buicks have marginal strength at the main bearing journal webs. If the engine will be turning more than 6,000 rpm or making more than 600 hp, a main girdle is needed to stabilize the lower block and prevent damaging oscillation at the main caps.

available, although they are quite expensive. Such modifications should not be needed for a typical street-performance build. Consult with Buick engine experts as to the durability upgrades that your build will require (see the source guide).

Displacement

The result of increased displacement is additional horsepower and torque, which is why it's usually best to design a street-performance engine with the largest displacement that is practical. The downside is that increased displacement usually leads to a decrease in fuel economy (assuming that all other factors are the same).

For most people, the budget of the engine build is the main factor that limits displacement. Performance Buick engine builders usually want to start with a 455 block to get the largest cylinder bore that is available (4.3125 inches).

Overboring can provide some additional displacement, but avoid going beyond a 0.030-inch overbore unless the block is sonic checked. Sonic checking reveals any issues with "core shift," which is slight misalignment of the cylinder bores that occurs during manufacturing. Core shift is common, and it can cause the cylinder walls to be thin in critical areas.

Sonic checking will reveal if there's enough material around the bore to safely make the hole larger. If you're planning a large overbore or horsepower above approximately 500, talk to the machine shop about sonic checking.

To get even more displacement, increase the stroke. All big-block Buicks share the same stroke (3.9 inches). TA Performance sells modified stock crankshafts that can get to about 500 ci. Beyond that are custom billet-steel crankshafts that can get to 523 ci, but these are very expensive and not really appropriate unless you are building a race engine.

Compression Ratio

The compression ratio expresses the amount that the air/fuel mixture is compressed when a piston rises from bottom dead center (BDC) to top dead center (TDC) during the compression stroke. The first number in the ratio represents the volume above the piston at BDC. The second number represents the volume at TDC. A 10:1 ratio means that the piston is compressing the air/fuel ratio into an area that is 1/10 the size when it travels from BDC to TDC. The concept is simple, but the compression ratio's effect on an engine's operating characteristics is complicated and often misunderstood.

More compression improves an engine's power and efficiency. However, its effect is not linear, which means that an increase in compression ratio from 7:1 to 8:1 will have a greater effect on efficiency than increasing compression ratio from 10:1 to 11:1. From a power and efficiency standpoint, you want to raise the compression ratio as high as possible. Unfortunately, destructive engine "knock" will occur if compression ratios are too high.

When deciding on a compression ratio, always err on the side of caution. The slight gain in power from an extra point of compression (usually just a few horsepower) isn't worth it if the result is a melted piston!

During the 1960s and up to 1970, performance engines had compression ratios in the range of 10:1, and some were as high as 11:1. The high-octane fuels that were available at the time permitted these high compression ratios. Such fuels are now very expensive and are not commonly available at gas stations.

As a general rule, there is a risk of engine damage if commonly available "pump gas" is run in an iron-headed Buick engine with a compression ratio that exceeds 9:1. If you are running aluminum cylinder heads, the compression can be higher. I'll discuss the other virtues of aluminum heads later in this chapter, but for now, aluminum is

Engine Swaps

If your Buick has a 350 engine, consider swapping it for a big-block to get more displacement. Even a potent 350 does not match a 455 in terms of torque, which is critical to street performance in a heavy car. In addition, finding performance parts will be more difficult for the 350 because the aftermarket focused its parts-development efforts on big-blocks.

The good news for 350 owners is that swapping in a big-block is not extraordinarily difficult. The main issue is that the big-block is a physically longer engine, so the frame mounting pads are in different locations than they are for the 350. Replacement mounting plates can be installed to get the 455 to sit in the correct location in your Buick's engine bay. In addition, the 455 engine is heavier, so stiffer front suspension springs are needed to get the vehicle ride height correct. A bigger radiator and the proper fan shroud will also be needed.

There are a number of other considerations, but the details for this swap are outside the scope of this book. TA Performance is a great resource for parts and advice, and reputable internet forums, such as v8buick.com, can be helpful as well. ■

This chart shows how the compression ratio impacts horsepower. The numbers on the horizontal axis represent the amount of horsepower lost versus a theoretical engine with an infinitely high compression ratio. Note how the bigger gains come at the lower end of the compression-ratio range. The gain between 9:1 and 10:1 is less than 2 percent.

better at dispersing heat than iron, so aluminum heads enable an engine to tolerate higher compression ratios without knock or detonation. Generally speaking, an engine can run up to 1.5 points of compression higher with aluminum heads than iron heads.

The preceding information describes the static compression ratio, which does not consider the effects of high-performance camshafts. It's normal for the intake valve to remain slightly open as the piston starts traveling upward on the compression stroke. Compression does not begin until the valve is fully closed.

Performance camshafts usually close the intake valve later than stock camshafts, thus reducing the amount of compression. The term "dynamic compression ratio" is used to factor in the variable of the intake valve closing. If you use a high-performance camshaft, the static compression ratio can sometimes be increased a bit further without risking detonation.

You should now have enough information for an informed discussion with an experienced Buick engine builder concerning how much compression can be run in your performance engine. The source guide in this book identifies Buick engine experts who can help to optimize your build. Use their knowledge to the fullest.

If your plan is to stay with the stock iron heads, an engine overhaul provides an opportunity to reduce the compression ratio as needed to keep it in the 9:1 range. Any change that adds volume above the piston

will reduce the compression ratio. Common methods of reducing the compression ratio include using thicker head gaskets, pistons with a large dish area, and pistons with a lowered compression height (they sit lower in the cylinder at TDC). The best performance and efficiency are achieved when a piston at TDC is flush with the engine-block deck. This is referred to as "zero deck clearance."

Buick engine builder Jim Weise cautions that replacement pistons for Buick V-8s often have significantly lowered compression height, which can set the piston excessively low in the cylinder, sometimes as low as 0.080 inch at TDC. The result can be a poor-running, detonation-prone engine. Consult Buick engine experts and shop carefully for pistons that achieve the desired compression ratio with the piston as close as possible to zero deck clearance.

Forced Induction

Superchargers and turbochargers force the intake charge into the cylinders. This adds power by making the charge denser than if it was simply drawn into the cylinder by the vacuum created by the piston moving down during the intake stroke. It is possible to add a lot of power using forced induction, but the engine would need to be built differently than it would for a naturally aspirated engine. Specifically, a forced-induction engine requires the use of forged pistons and probably runs a lower compression ratio. Special head gaskets, such as multi-layer steel (MLS), will be necessary, even at low boost levels. High boost levels usually require machining for O-ring seals around the cylinder bores.

Determining the Compression Ratio

As a part of any engine overhaul, measure the compression ratio before it's assembled. For this job, you need the following items:

- A flat block of Plexiglas about 5 inches square with a 3/8-inch hole drilled
- A way to measure liquid in cubic centimeters (a scientific burette or syringe is generally used.)
- Petroleum jelly
- A low-viscosity liquid (Some use alcohol, but water works fine as long as the metal surfaces are dried off quickly afterward to prevent rust.)

There are three necessary measurements: 1) cylinder-head combustion-chamber volume, 2) engine-block deck volume, and 3) head-gasket volume. Follow the photos and captions to gather these measurements.

Once you have the measurements, plug them into the formula:

$$\text{Constant volume} + \text{Swept Volume} \div \text{Swept Volume} = \text{Compression Ratio}$$

Constant volume is the total of the three numbers that you measured: combustion-chamber volume, block deck volume, and head-gasket volume.

Swept volume is the volume that a piston displaces when traveling from BDC to TDC. To determine the swept volume, use the high-school geometry formula πr^2 (pi x radius squared) x the stroke. The radius being squared is the cylinder bore diameter.

Example

Calculating the compression ratio of a newly rebuilt 455:
Bore = 4.3425 inches (stock bore plus a 0.030 overbore)

The cylinder heads must be overhauled, assembled, and ready for installation. Install a spark plug and then seal a block of Plexiglas over the combustion chamber using petroleum jelly. Then, slowly introduce a carefully measured liquid. Record how many CC's were needed to fill up the combustion chamber.

Use the same measuring technique to determine the volume below the block deck with the piston at TDC. The crankshaft, pistons, piston rings, and bearings must be installed. Wipe a bit of petroleum jelly into the gap between the piston and the cylinder wall, which will prevent leakage past the rings.

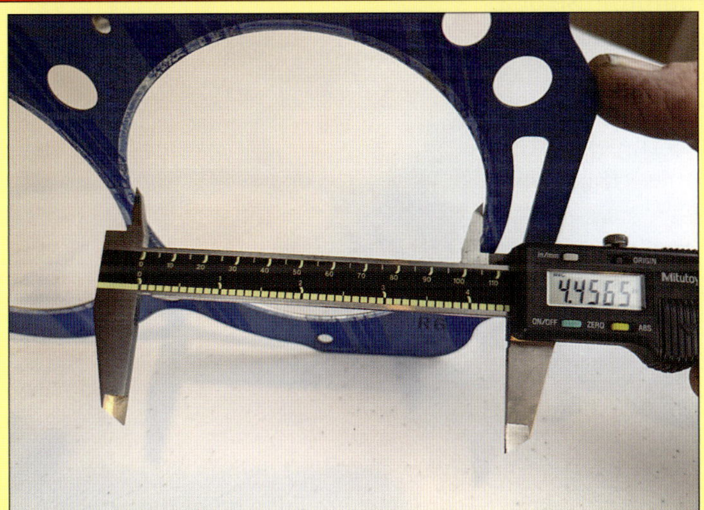

Determine the head-gasket volume. Manufacturers provide specifications for their gaskets (either the volume in CC's or the compressed thickness). If the compressed thickness of the gasket and the gasket bore diameter are known, you can determine the volume.

After determining the numbers, some math must be done. However, it's not difficult. There are also compression-ratio calculators online that will do the math for you. Some calculators even consider camshaft specifications to determine the dynamic compression ratio. When it comes to the compression-ratio calculation, you can never be too precise.

Stroke = 3.9 inches
Cylinder-head combustion-chamber volume: 68
Cylinder deck volume: 25 cc's
Head-gasket volume = 13 cc's

Calculating Swept Volume

4.3425 ÷ 2 (This provides the radius, which is expressed as "r.")

= 2.1713 inches

2.1713 x 2.1713 (This is "r^2," which is simply the radius multiplied by itself.)

= 4.7145 inches

4.7145 x 3.1416 (Here, I'm multiplying by ϖ, rounded to 4 decimal points.)

= 14.8110 inches

14.8110 x 3.9 (Here, I'm multiplying the area by the stroke to determine the volume.)

= 57.7629 ci (the volume of one cylinder)

57.7629 x 16.3871 (Here, I'm converting from cubic inches to cubic centimeters [cc's.])

= 946.5664 cc's of swept volume

Calculating Constant Volume

As was mentioned previously, the constant volume is simply all of the volume above the piston. Add the cylinder deck volume, head-gasket volume, and combustion-chamber volume. In this case, the constant volume is 68+25+13 = 106 cc's.

The Answer

Now, apply the formula:

Swept volume + constant volume ÷ swept volume

1,052.5664 ÷ 106 = 9.93:1.

Place a ":1" after the number to express it as a ratio, and 9.9299:1 is the compression ratio (just under 10:1). So, in this example, if you are running aluminum heads, you should be at a safe ratio. If you are running stock iron heads, add some volume above the cylinder to achieve a lower ratio. The easiest way to make small adjustments is to use a thicker head gasket. If you can find a thicker gasket with double the volume (26 cc's instead of 13 cc's), you can drop the ratio about one point:

1,065.5664 ÷ 119 = 8.95:1, which is just about as high as is desired on a street engine with iron heads.

Caution: When using thicker or thinner head gaskets, other parts are affected. Using thinner head gaskets may require machining the intake manifold–to–cylinder head surfaces so that the ports and mounting bolt holes align correctly. In addition, shorter pushrods may need to be used to achieve the correct lifter preload. Thicker head gaskets may require thicker intake-manifold gaskets for correct port alignment, and longer pushrods may be required. ■

Boosted cars require specialized equipment and tuning, which is outside the scope of this book. If you want to supercharge or turbocharge your Buick V-8, do the research and consult with experts.

Camshaft

No single modification changes the operating characteristics of an engine as much as the camshaft. In simple terms, the camshaft is a mechanical computer that determines when the valves open and how much they open. The lobes on a camshaft are precision machined to accomplish a specific pattern of flow through the cylinder heads as well as the intake and exhaust systems.

The profile and spacing of the camshaft lobes are determined through hundreds of mathematical calculations that determine how an engine will perform. It's important to understand that (as with any other aspect of engine performance) there isn't "good," "better," or "best." As an extreme example, a stock camshaft is unsuitable for racing, and a racing camshaft is unsuitable for street use.

Camshafts are a compromise of a multitude of performance characteristics. Selecting a camshaft requires considering all other components of the engine as well as the expected operating characteristics that you want from the engine.

Fortunately for Buick enthusiasts, many great camshaft options are available. TA Performance has a complete line of cams and the expertise to help buyers choose the best option. In addition, major camshaft manufacturers produce camshafts for Buicks: Comp Cams, Crower, Iskenderian, and Howard's Cams.

Specifications

When you shop for a camshaft, there are a number of specifications to contemplate. For the novice, the information can be difficult to interpret. Fortunately, most camshaft manufacturers provide information about the operating characteristics that can be expected with their cam designs, which are also known as "profiles" or "grinds."

I recommend contacting the technical department of the camshaft manufacturer, which will help you select the correct camshaft. Be prepared to provide all of the information about your engine build, including the cylinder heads, intake-manifold design, header/exhaust-system design, gear ratios,

Every camshaft comes with a cam card that provides all of the specifications of that particular camshaft. Don't throw this away! The other components for the engine build need to work within these parameters. If any substantial changes are made at a later time, the cam specs will need to be considered again.

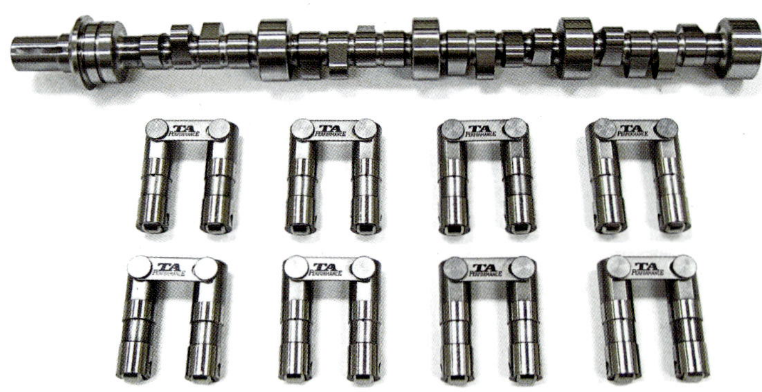

Selecting the right camshaft for a build is critical for meeting performance and drivability goals. Before selecting a camshaft, know the planned engine displacement, compression ratio, and operating RPM range. You should also know which cylinder heads, intake manifold, and headers you're planning to use.

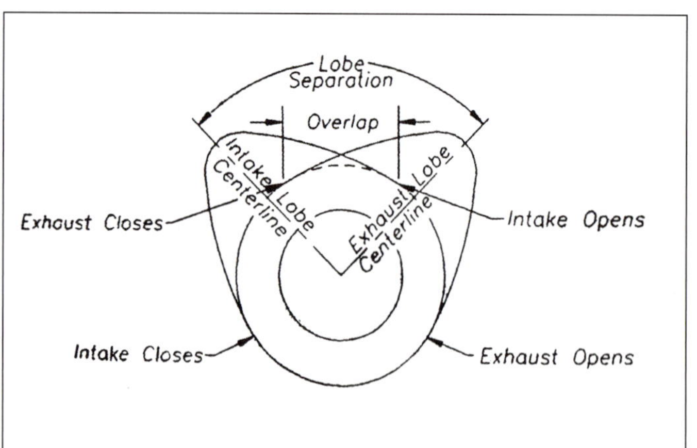

Camshafts may look simple, but they are extremely precise mechanical computers. This graphic provides a visual explanation of the terminology that you need to know.

and torque-converter type (for an automatic transmission).

Certain specifications of the cam design can provide an abundance of information about how it will perform in an engine. It's helpful to review these specifications to select the correct camshaft for the engine.

Lift

The term "lift" is the maximum distance (measured in inches) that the valve is lifted off its seat during operation. A stock camshaft might lift a valve about 0.410 inch off its seat. Often, intake and exhaust valves have slightly different lifts for the intake and exhaust (the exhaust is a bit higher than the intake). A serious race engine may have lift as high as 0.700 inch.

Street-performance engines generally have lift in the 0.500-inch range. As with so many other aspects of engine performance, more is not always better. The lift does not need to be higher than the point where maximum flow is achieved through the ports in the cylinder head.

Stock heads tend to max out flow at relatively low lift, so putting a 0.700-lift cam in a stock engine will not improve performance because lifting the valves more than the point of maximum flow is of no value. On the other hand, cylinder heads that have been designed for high performance and racing tend to flow more at higher lifts, so 0.700 lift might be appropriate for an all-out race engine. The important thing to remember about valve lift is that it should be matched to the performance characteristics of the cylinder head.

Duration

The duration is the amount of time that a valve stays open, and it is measured in degrees of crankshaft rotation. Generally speaking, a cam with long duration will have better operating characteristics at higher RPM at the expense of low-end torque, fuel economy, and drivability on the street.

Camshaft manufacturers generally provide two duration measurements for their cams: 1) advertised duration and 2) duration at 0.050-inch lift. The latter provides a more accurate way of comparing various cams, and I recommend seeking out the duration at 0.050-inch lift.

Generally speaking, a stock engine has a duration of about 200 to 210 degrees at 0.050-inch lift. On a street-performance engine, it is about 215 to 245 degrees at 0.050-inch lift. Race engines tend to be in the 250- to 275-degree range.

Lifters for cams above 245 degrees at 0.050-inch lift will almost always be solid (flat or roller). The reason for this is that even the best hydraulic lifters can become inconsistent at high RPM, and racers prefer the strength and durability.

Overlap

All camshafts have overlap, which is the period of time during which the intake and exhaust valve are both open. To put it simply, this overlap time is needed to ensure efficient filling of the cylinder, particularly at high RPM. More overlap provides better high-RPM performance but results in lower compression and vacuum at low RPM, particularly at idle.

The familiar "lope" of a high-performance engine is primarily caused by high overlap. Generally, stock engines have 15 to 30 degrees of overlap, street-performance engines have 25 to 55 degrees, and race engines have 60 to as much as 100 degrees.

Overlap is closely related to other factors, such as lobe separation angle (LSA), which cam manufacturers commonly give as a specification. A wide separation of the intake and exhaust lobes results in less overlap and therefore better low-RPM performance. A tighter LSA is associated with high-performance and racing engines.

Lifters

The camshaft selection also determines what type of lifter is used because camshaft and lifter types cannot be interchanged. Nevertheless, it's important to understand the various lifter types because each has advantages and disadvantages that can become a part of the decision-making regarding the cam/lifter package.

A roller lifter (right) has a wheel at the end that rolls smoothly on roller bearings. Roller lifters are superior to flat lifters. They reduce friction and permit the use of camshafts with faster ramps.

Conventional Hydraulic Lifters

Stock Buick engines came equipped with hydraulic lifters that have a flat area of contact with the camshaft. This type of lifter provides a simple, reliable, and inexpensive way of transmitting motion to open and close the valves. The main body of the lifter is essentially a hollow cylinder filled with pressurized oil (from the oil pump). A piston in the cylinder rides atop the column of pressurized oil that transmits the lift of the camshaft to the pushrod.

The design of hydraulic lifters makes them self-adjusting, so they do not normally require any servicing. In addition, hydraulic lifters tend to operate more quietly than solid lifters. The primary disadvantage of hydraulic lifters is that they are somewhat RPM-limiting. Their inherent operating characteristics are associated with a condition known as "pump-up," which contributes to unstable valve actuation at high RPM (generally higher than 5,500 rpm).

Solid Lifters

Solid lifters, which are also known as "mechanical lifters," are barrel-shaped, solid-steel components that ride on the camshaft lobes and raise the pushrods through direct mechanical action. Unlike hydraulic lifters, solid lifters do not compress or extend during operation. Therefore, solid lifters provide stable, precise operation throughout the RPM range. Solid lifters are mostly used in high-RPM race applications and street/strip engines.

The main disadvantages of solid lifters are that they require periodic adjustment to maintain maximum performance and they are prone to be noisy. Another disadvantage is that solid lifters operate more harshly than hydraulic lifters, so stiffer springs are required and valvetrain components tend to wear out more quickly.

Solid-Roller Lifters

Solid-roller lifters are used in the highest performance applications, usually racing engines. The most obvious advantage is that the spinning wheel at the foot of the lifter reduces friction compared to the flat contact surface on the lifters that were discussed previously. Equally (if not more) important is that the wheel allows more aggressive camshaft profiles to be used.

Roller lifters are known for their ability to operate on camshafts with fast "ramps," which refers to how much valve lift is delivered for a given amount of camshaft rotation. Flat-bottom lifters are limited in terms of how much ramp speed they can handle before the edge of the lifter foot digs into side of the cam lobe. Roller lifters can operate on camshaft lobes that are closer to being square in profile, permitting the valve to obtain high lift quickly.

Since solid-roller lifters are used primarily on fast-ramp cams, one downside is that the associated rapid opening and closing of the valves leads to increased wear on valvetrain components, particularly the valves and the valve seats. Another disad-

vantage of roller lifters is that they are significantly more expensive than flat-bottom lifters.

Hydraulic-Roller Lifters

Hydraulic-roller lifters represent the highest level of development for street-driven vehicles and are standard equipment on virtually all new vehicles with a cam-in-block design. They offer the advantage of reduced friction and the ability to use cams with faster ramps. They're also easier on valvetrain components and just as quiet as hydraulic flat-bottom lifters.

Typically, a hydraulic-roller cam provides a smoother idle and better low-speed operating characteristics than a flat-bottom lifter of the same specifications. The main disadvantage of hydraulic rollers is that they are more expensive. However, with more widespread use, the prices have been reduced to the point that they are an option for all but the most budget-oriented build.

Valve Springs

Camshafts with aggressive profiles that are designed to be operated

A high-performance camshaft must be accompanied by upgraded valve springs. The springs must be strong enough to keep the lifter on the camshaft lobe with no bounce at high RPM. High spring pressures usually require stronger pushrods and rocker arms.

at high RPM require upgrades to other valvetrain components. Most importantly, stiffer valve springs are needed to keep the lifters tight against the camshaft lobes at high RPM.

A basic set of springs for a near-stock cam should provide about 100 pounds of pressure when the valve is seated and 250 pounds of pressure at maximum lift. A moderate hydraulic-roller cam needs about 130 pounds of pressure seated and 350 pounds of pressure open. Solid-lifter cams for racing often have 200 pounds of seated pressure and 500 pounds of open pressure.

Keeping within the guidelines from the camshaft manufacturer, err on the side of stiffer springs to prevent the valves from floating and potentially contacting the pistons. Just make sure that all of the other valvetrain components are up to the task.

Pushrods

Adequate pushrod strength is commonly overlooked during an engine build. The pushrods must be able to overcome the maximum spring pressure without deflection. Be sure that the pushrods that you selected are rated for the pressure of the springs that are being used.

Don't go overboard, as stronger pushrods are also heavier, and excess weight can contribute to valve float at high RPM. Chromoly steel is a good compromise for strength and light weight, but chromoly pushrods are more expensive than pushrods made from standard steel.

Rocker Arms

If the valve springs will be significantly stiffer than stock, use upgraded rocker arms. Stock stamped-steel rocker arms can be overloaded easily, resulting in deflection and excess wear. Performance rocker arms provide better strength to avoid deflection. Most have roller tips, which offer greater precision and help to reduce friction.

The best rocker arms also have roller bearings at the fulcrum to reduce friction and handle high spring loads. Most modern performance rocker arms are made from aluminum, which offers lighter weight than steel rockers. As with pushrods, it's desirable to reduce the weight of the valvetrain components in a high-RPM engine.

Another factor in rocker-arm selection is the rocker-arm ratio.

A stock stamped-steel rocker arm (bottom) is not strong enough to handle high valve-spring pressures. In addition to being lighter in weight, a good aftermarket aluminum rocker arm (top) can handle spring pressures that would bend a stock rocker. The best rockers are made from high-strength aluminum and use roller bearings at the tip and the fulcrum point.

Stock Buick engines have ratios that range from 1.55 to 1.6 (see the specifications at the end of this book). A 1.55 ratio multiplies the camshaft lobe lift by 1.55. So, if a camshaft lobe raises the valve lifter by 0.400, the valve will be lifted 0.62 off the seat due to the lift multiplication provided by the rocker arm.

Aftermarket rocker arms can have ratios as high as 1.7:1. Increasing the rocker-arm ratio is a way to increase the valve lift without moving to a cam with a higher lift. The aforementioned 0.400-lift cam would have 0.680 lift with a 1.7:1 rocker. Consider the specifications of all components when designing the valvetrain.

Critical Valvetrain Safety Checks

On a stock or near-stock engine where camshaft specifications run within narrow ranges, usually it is

These chromoly pushrods from TA Performance are much stronger than stock pushrods and feature the additional benefit of being adjustable. It is easy to adjust for the perfect preload on hydraulic lifters or the lash on solid lifters.

possible to just install the valvetrain components and not worry about anything bad happening. However, high-performance engines vary greatly as to their camshaft specifications and valvetrain design. Thoroughly check the valvetrain to make sure there are no issues that will damage the engine.

Valve Spring Coil Bind

Coil bind is when a spring's coils contact each other and stack solid at or before the point of full valve lift. With a high-lift camshaft, it's important to be sure that this point will not be reached during engine operation, otherwise damage to the valvetrain will occur.

Spring manufacturers provide a specification for the height of the spring when it reaches the point of bind, which is also known as the "solid height." Always check to be sure that there is adequate clearance to avoid coil bind. To make the calculation, subtract the valve lift from the spring installed height (see the specifications). The resulting number should be at least 0.060 inch more than the coil-bind specification. The 0.060 inch measurement is a safety factor that considers inertia effects at high RPM.

Valve Retainer-to-Guide Clearance

A similar phenomenon happens when a valve retainer contacts a valve guide before full lift is achieved. To check for this type of interference, install a valve without the spring in place and allow the retainer and guide to come into contact. Measure the distance between the valve-spring seat and the retainer. This measurement should be at least 0.060 inch more than the spring installed height minus the valve-lift specification.

Piston-to-Valve Clearance

High-lift/duration cams can cause the valves to come into contact with the pistons. Camshaft manufacturers can confirm whether there's a possibility of this happening with their cams, but there is no easy way to calculate this possibility. The only way to be sure is with a dynamic measurement method that requires the engine to be temporarily assembled.

With the cylinder head off, press modeling clay onto the top of the piston. Install the cylinder head with an old gasket that has the same thickness as the gasket you're planning to use. Rotate the crankshaft through at least two full revolutions. Remove the cylinder head and use a razor blade to slice through the clay. Measure the thickness of the clay at its thinnest point. The measurement should be at least 0.100 inch to prevent potential valve-to-piston contact during engine operation.

Exhaust Manifolds

Your Buick engine left the factory with cast-iron exhaust manifolds that were designed to provide quiet and reliable operation. If you're planning a mild-to-moderate engine build, cast-iron manifolds have several advantages over tubular headers:

- Cast-iron manifolds do not become warped or damaged as easily as headers.
- Exhaust manifolds encapsulate heat better than headers. Since headers have more surface area, they disperse more heat in the engine compartment. Manifolds do a better job of containing the heat and channeling it out through the exhaust system.
- Exhaust manifolds have less of a tendency to develop exhaust leaks.

- Exhaust manifolds tend to be quieter, reducing noise in the engine compartment.
- Headers are often difficult to install and occupy more space under the hood. This can make access to the starter and other components more difficult. Additionally, the starter's life may be reduced when using headers due to greater heat being generated in closer proximity compared to exhaust manifolds that radiate less heat and are farther away from the starter.

The preceding bullet points are not intended to keep anyone from buying a good set of headers. I just want you to make an informed decision and understand the trade-offs that are involved with headers. For a mild engine build, factory cast-iron manifolds may be the best choice. However, increasing the horsepower more than 20 percent or so pushes the limit of most factory manifolds. Remember that performance is all about flowing as much air as possible through the engine. A restriction at any point reduces the overall flow, regardless of how capable other components may be.

Headers

Most performance engine builds benefit from the use of steel-tube headers. They can increase horsepower without reducing fuel economy or affecting drivability. Headers allow exhaust gases to flow out of the engine more easily, using a phenomenon known as "scavenging." The gases flowing through the tubes create inertia that causes a low-pressure area at the exhaust port in the cylinder head. The low pressure pulls the exhaust out of the engine more efficiently.

Headers are available from multiple manufacturers with various designs and sizes depending on the clearance that is available and the type of performance that you're seeking. It's best to contact the technical departments of the manufacturers and discuss your build with experts who can help you select the right design for your engine.

TA Performance offers a complete line of quality headers and the expertise to identify what's best for your application. In addition, Doug's and Hooker offer quality parts.

Types

The most common type of header consists of four long steel tubes that join at a collector. Known as "four-into-one headers," they produce high-RPM power but are less effective in the low and mid RPM ranges.

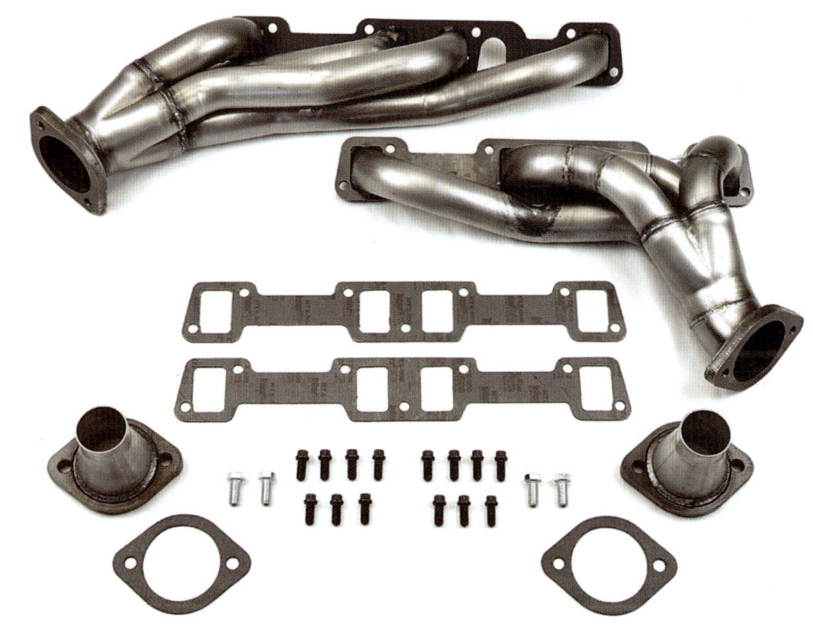

Shorty headers take up less space in the engine compartment but are more restrictive, providing only small horsepower gains when compared to exhaust manifolds.

Tri-Y headers are aptly named for their appearance. The four pipes merge into two pipes, which are again paired at the collector. Try-Y headers sacrifice a slight amount of power in the high-RPM range when compared with four-into-one headers, but they provide excellent power and torque in the low and mid RPM ranges.

Short-tube headers, which are also known as "shorty headers," are usually used when clearance is limited or emissions requirements won't allow the use of full-length headers. Shorty headers are often more efficient than stock cast-iron manifolds, but they do not perform as well as long-tube headers.

Length and Diameter

As a general rule, longer tubes produce more power. However, 40-inch tubes are usually the longest. Shorter tubes are used where clearance is an issue or where emissions requirements do not permit long tubes.

The tube diameter is another important consideration, and it's

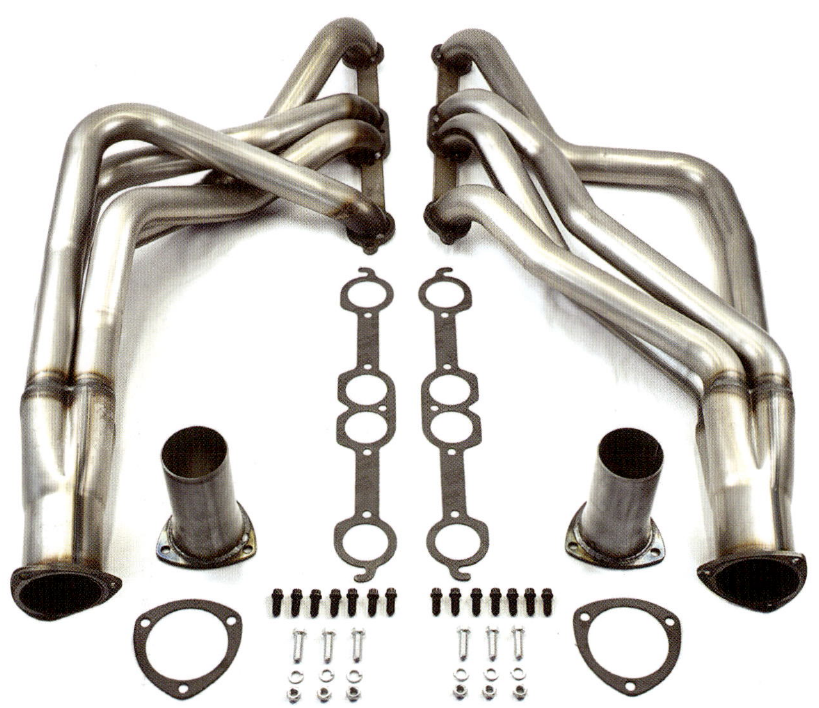

Four-into-one headers are the most common type. They vary in flow capacity based on the tube diameter and length. Larger tube diameters permit better flow. Longer tubes prevent turbulence and promote scavenging.

not a "bigger is better" proposition. Instead, select the tube diameter carefully based on the engine displacement and level of performance that you expect. For example, a small-block engine built for street use will generally do best with a header-tube diameter of $1^5/_8$ inch. A big-block or high-performance small-block may do best with a $1^7/_8$-inch tube. Engines built for racing often have a tube diameter of 2 inches.

Installing headers with 2-inch tubes on a street-driven small-block engine will result in reduced performance compared to using a $1^5/_8$-inch tube. This is because the exhaust flow is insufficient to allow scavenging in such a long tube. It's best to consult with header manufacturers to determine what's best for your engine.

Buying Tips

Flange thickness is a significant consideration, as the thicker the flange, the better the cylinder head-to-header flange will seal under high pressures. Cast-iron manifolds have a surface that's machined flat and will seal better than a header. Most headers are mild steel and have a thickness of 5/16 or 3/8 inch. It's best to choose a header with a thicker flange. It will hold its shape better, especially if the bolts get over-torqued.

Don't buy cheap header gaskets—particularly the flange gaskets. Headers are susceptible to leakage at this point, so choose gaskets that will resist blow-out. Racers often use solid copper gaskets with a coating of high-temperature RTV at the ports. These will resist high pressures, particularly those run in boosted applications.

After installing headers, the air/fuel mixture may be a bit leaner. It may be necessary to use bigger jets in the carburetor. An air/fuel-ratio (AFR) gauge can be used to determine if a jet change is needed.

Exhaust Systems

Most Buicks came from the factory with an exhaust system that compromised power and fuel economy to achieve quiet operation. The exhaust-system components were adequate for the stock performance level, but an increase in power causes the pipes and mufflers to restrict the higher exhaust flow.

Most factory-installed exhaust systems have a two-into-one "Y" pipe. A single pipe carried all of the exhaust to the rear of the car, where the single muffler was located. This worked well for a stock performance level, but a dual-exhaust system improves performance and economy on almost any application.

The higher the horsepower and exhaust flow, the more the car will benefit from an exhaust upgrade. However, there's no benefit to going overboard. Installing a 3-inch exhaust system with straight-through mufflers on a car with a mildly built engine will result in more noise but no additional power. For most people, this extra money can be better spent elsewhere.

For performance and racing applications, the pipe diameter should be at least 2¼ inches for moderate performance, 2½ inches for high

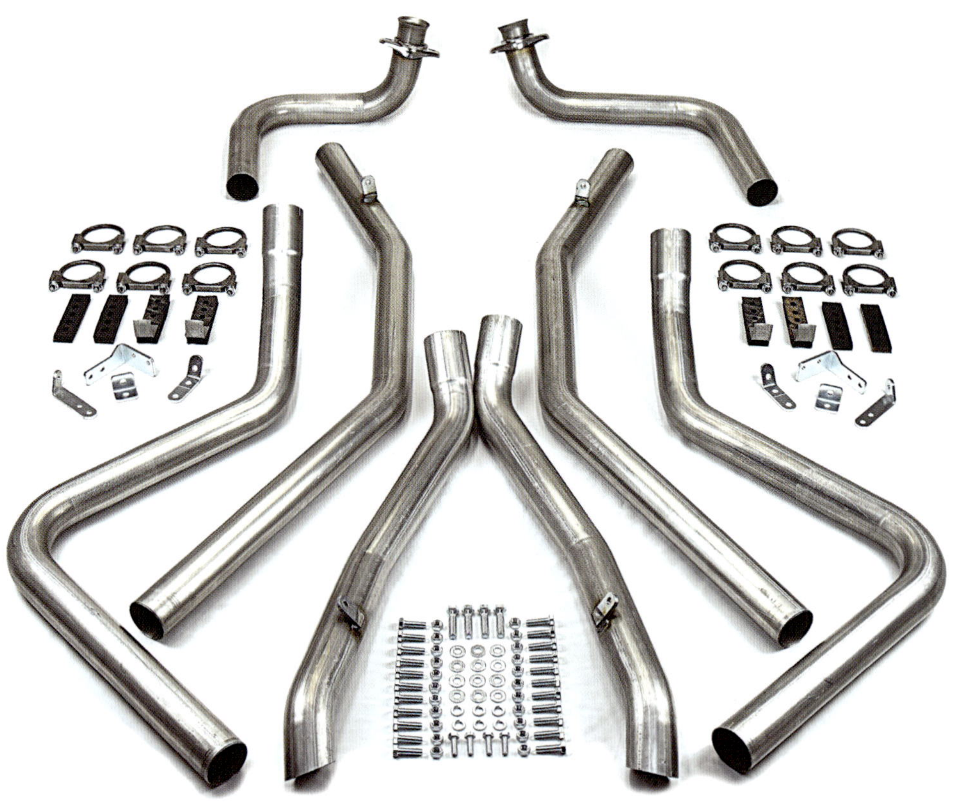

A dual-exhaust system with large pipes reduces backpressure and can increase horsepower. As with headers, the higher that an engine's horsepower potential is, the bigger the losses are if the exhaust system is restricted.

performance, and 3 inches for maximum street performance and racing. Larger pipes are often more difficult to fit on the car and can increase noise, but pipes that are excessively large for the application will not reduce performance.

The 1975-and-later Buicks were equipped with catalytic converters, which significantly reduce emissions. The car must retain a catalytic converter to be legal on the road. Be sure to consider this as you plan your build. Even if you currently live in an area that does not have an emissions-inspection program, laws can change, and you might move to a different state.

Mufflers

Many mufflers are on the market that promise to improve the performance of the vehicle, and most of them deliver on that promise. When selecting mufflers, consider these five factors: fitment, flow, noise level, tone, and price.

Muffler fitment is the most important issue. Make sure that the car has the space for the mufflers and that they fit well. Universal mufflers require modifying and fabricating exhaust hangers. Better mufflers are designed for precise fitment on your car, but they tend to be more expensive.

The amount of exhaust gases that a muffler will flow is rated in cubic feet per minute (CFM). The major muffler manufacturers provide this specification. Comparing the mufflers on the basis of flow helps with decision making.

Sometimes (but not always), the best performing mufflers are also loud. For a street-driven vehicle, be sure that the sound level, which is measured in decibels, is legal in your

community. State noise laws are often more generous than local ordinances and homeowners' associations. Be sure to understand the legal limitations—as well as your neighbor's tolerance!

For many enthusiasts, the exhaust tone is one of the most important considerations. The car should sound as good as it performs. Once the choices have been narrowed down in terms of fitment, flow, and noise level, compare them on the basis of tone. Manufacturers provide sound clips of their mufflers on their websites, and other enthusiasts are usually happy to provide videos of their cars.

Ignition Systems

Pre-1975-model engines used point-type distributors. Standard models came with single-point distributors, while high-performance models sometimes had dual-point versions. If your engine has a point-type distributor, it will probably benefit from an electronic ignition system.

Electronic ignition systems, including those that are available in the aftermarket as well as those that have been installed by the factory since 1975, make conventional point-type distributors outdated. It's

easy to convert from point-type ignition to electronic ignition, particularly if you are using the reasonably priced kits that are available.

Whether or not you convert to electronic ignition, power can generally be gained by optimizing the distributor's advance curve. Within certain limits, the more ignition advance that can be achieved at a particular RPM without preignition (pinging), the better the engine will perform. Optimizing the timing will often improve fuel economy, and there's generally no downside if it is done with care.

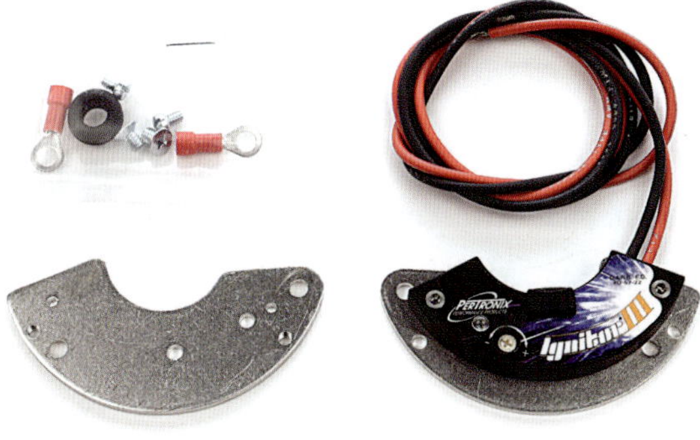

If you have a 1974-or-earlier engine and want to ditch the ignition points but maintain an original look, this PerTronix system is a great solution. It fits inside the stock distributor and is the simplest and easiest way to get an electronic ignition system.

HEI distributors debuted on 1975 Buicks. They represented a huge improvement over points ignition systems and are still a great choice for performance builds.

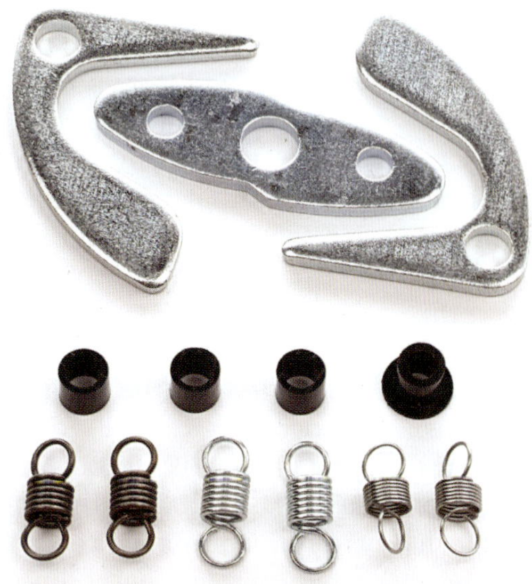

This simple, inexpensive kit allows buyers to change the distributor's mechanical advance curve. The kit's instructions identify which springs and weights to use to achieve the desired curve.

Dial-type timing lights allow DIYers to check the advance curve of their ignition system. These are more expensive than standard-type timing lights, but if you need to purchase a timing light anyway, consider spending a little extra money to get this helpful added feature.

During wide-open-throttle performance, the ignition advance is determined by the initial advance and the mechanical (also known as "centrifugal") advance. Initial advance is what is checked at tune-up time with a timing light.

The factory specification is usually somewhere between 5 to 12 degrees BTDC. The initial advance can usually be increased to 14 to 18 degrees without issues. However, if the engine is harder to crank or it idles poorly when the initial timing is increased, dial back the initial timing a degree or two until the issues go away.

Mechanical advance adds timing as engine RPM increases, adding about 20 degrees BTDC, depending on the application. Adding the initial advance to the mechanical advance provides the total advance, which should not exceed about 36 to 38 degrees BTDC.

Another consideration is the RPM where total advance is achieved. Most stock distributors hold out total advance until about 3,500 rpm. In most cases, the distributor can be set up to achieve total advance at about 2,500 rpm, which improves mid-range performance.

Optimizing the ignition curve can be done by using a "dial-back" timing light that allows the observation of all aspects of the distributor's advance curve while the engine is running. A quality dial-back timing light is a great investment for performance tuning as well as conventional tuning and troubleshooting.

A radical street engine or a race engine can benefit from a multiple-spark ignition system. This

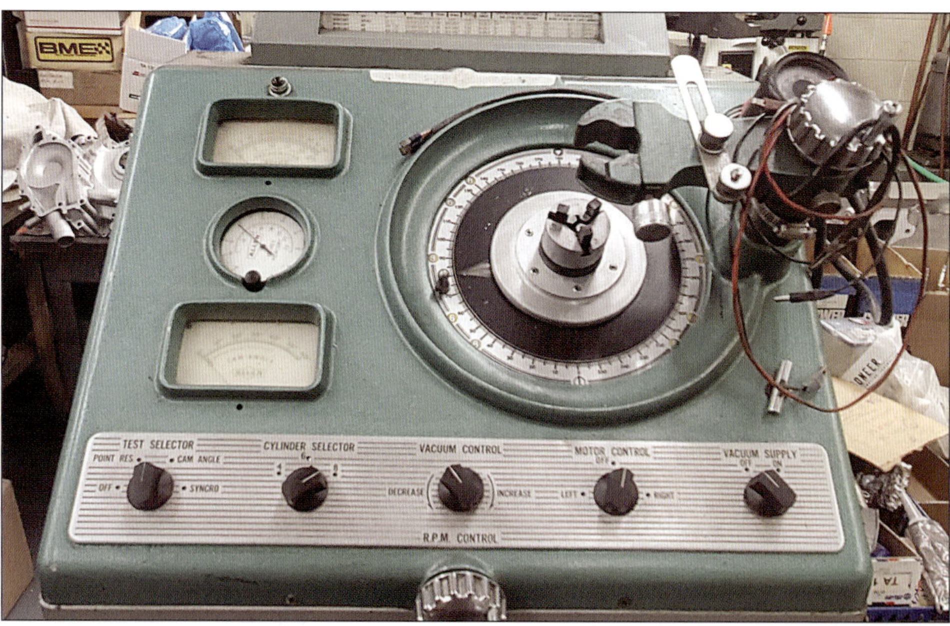

It's wise to have a properly equipped shop set up the distributor so that it can deliver the correct advance under all conditions. This machine simulates engine RPM and vacuum to allow quick and precise adjustments.

On engines with high-overlap camshafts, an ignition box with multi-spark capability will keep the engine running more efficiently at idle and low RPM. This is the PerTronix Digital HP, which is one of the latest entries into the market, competing with companies such as MSD and Mallory.

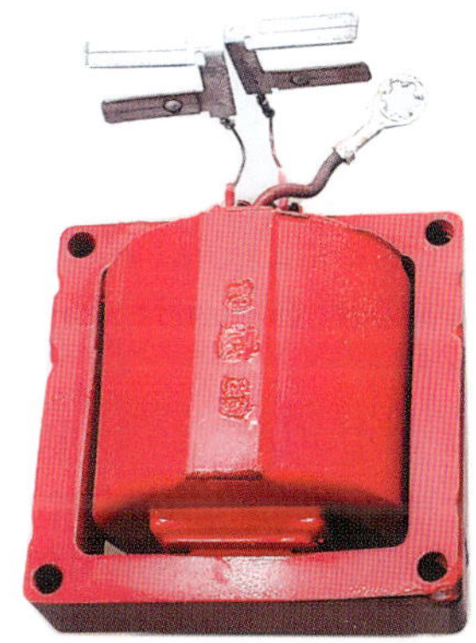

High-performance ignition coils that fit directly into the HEI distributor cap are available. A coil upgrade is recommended for any engine that will see more than 5,500 rpm. Adapters are available for remote coils that allow you to use an HEI distributor with an external coil.

If an electronic ignition system upgrade kit is chosen for a 1974-or-earlier vehicle, get a high-performance coil to go with it. Canister-style performance coils keep the original look but can handle higher RPM levels.

system delivers a stronger spark with the additional benefit that the timed spark is actually delivered in multiple pulses, which helps to overcome ignition issues arising from high-overlap camshafts.

As a general rule, engines with camshafts that have a duration of 240 degrees at 0.050 inch or more benefit from a multiple-spark system. It's a common misconception that a multiple-spark system will cause an engine to run better at higher RPM. This is not necessarily the case. In fact, many of the popular ignition systems do not deliver multiple sparks at high RPM.

The primary advantage of a multiple-spark system is that it allows better performance at low RPM. Long-duration camshafts bleed off cylinder pressure at low RPM, and the air/fuel mixture can mix with the outgoing exhaust gases. This makes complete combustion more difficult and increases the possibility of a misfire.

A multiple-spark system allows the engine to run more efficiently at idle and low RPM, which helps to keep the plugs from getting carbon fouled and may help to smooth out the idle.

Another ignition-system upgrade that is necessary at high performance levels is a high-output ignition coil. The factory HEI system that was used on 1975-and-later engines provided a huge improvement over points-type ignition systems.

HEI is an abbreviation for "high energy ignition." Those who began servicing these systems in the late 1970s were shocked to discover just how significant the improvement was. What was not well understood is that increases in engine RPM cause coil output to be reduced.

Up to 5,500 rpm or so, the standard HEI coil can deliver a strong spark for full combustion. As RPM increases, that output is reduced. If you're building an engine that will see engine speeds over 5,500 rpm, it is essential that you select a coil that's up to the task. The better coils will deliver a strong spark through 10,000 rpm. They are pricey but worth every penny for high-RPM engines.

Cylinder Heads

The cylinder heads that you select for an engine are the primary determinant of how much power the engine can generate. Airflow through cylinder heads must make directional changes that slow the flow of the gases. The sizes of the ports in the heads are restricted in some areas to clear nearby components, and turbulence can develop in these areas. Performance improvements in the cylinder heads come primarily by straightening the flow of gases and reducing restrictions.

In the past, the only way to get more flow from Buick cylinder heads was to port the factory original heads. Porting cast-iron heads is difficult and time-consuming. It is also a bit of a lost art these days. For most performance engine builds, aftermarket aluminum heads are the best option. Aftermarket heads often flow better out of the box than the best ported cast-iron heads.

Aftermarket heads can look like a bargain when considering the cost of porting factory heads. In addition to flow improvement, aluminum heads are much lighter and can handle a significantly higher compression ratio without detonation.

With its full line of performance aluminum cylinder heads, TA Performance offers everything from basic street performance to all-out racing. Its heads are designed to use the stock shaft-type rocker-arm system, which is generally more stable than stud-mounted rocker arms. TA Performance offers its heads "as cast" or fully ported. The appearance of the fully ported heads is very similar to the factory design.

Edelbrock is a top name in the manufacturing of aluminum cylinder heads, covering most domestic V-8 engines. Its quality Buick cylinder heads are a great replacement for stock cast-iron heads, supporting up to 500 hp.

It's important to note that Edelbrock heads must use the Chevrolet/Pontiac–style stud-mounted rocker arms. In addition, Edelbrock heads have an outward appearance that is noticeably different than the factory cylinder-head design.

If you're restoring your car and want to keep things "all Buick," porting the factory heads might be an option. However, don't expect a huge improvement in airflow. Porting should be carried out by a shop with Buick engine experts.

Intake Manifolds

Contrary to what some think, Buick did not intend to make its intake manifolds heavy and restrictive. Its designs reflected a compromise of requirements, and high performance was not at the top of the list. Primary consid-

erations were for reliability and smooth engine operation under all conditions, including extremes in temperature.

Cast iron is a heavy material, but it is dimensionally stable (does not warp easily) and has an excellent heat-retention capability. This allows the factory heat-riser system to bring up manifold temperature quickly on a -20°F winter morning. However, today's Buick enthusiasts aren't very interested in cold weather starting performance or perfect drivability in all conditions. Performance is at the top of the list—and compromises be damned!

Today, there is a greater selection of Buick aftermarket intake manifolds than ever before. The design of modern intake manifolds takes advantage of decades of racing data. Modern computer-modeling has taken intake manifold design to an even higher level. The materials and machining capabilities that are available today could have only been dreamed of when Buick engines were originally designed.

The point is that factory intake manifolds are mostly obsolete from a performance standpoint. Unless the main goal is to keep a factory muscle car all original, I recommend that serious performance builds include an aftermarket aluminum intake manifold that was designed for the performance level that you intend.

Careful selection of an intake manifold is essential to achieving maximum performance, fuel economy, and drivability. Selecting the most appropriate manifold for the application will show gains in all of these areas. An additional benefit of an aftermarket performance intake manifold is that it is made from aluminum, which will save weight over

Aftermarket aluminum cylinder heads are the best choice for most performance builds. These TA Performance heads maintain the original look and also use the stock shaft-type rocker-arm system.

the cast-iron manifold that was used on virtually all Buick engines.

As with cylinder heads, TA Performance and Edelbrock are the main players. They both provide a full line of up-to-date designs to suit all types of engine builds. In addition, Offenhauser is a company with a long tradition of making great manifolds, including classic dual-quad manifolds.

Dual-Plane Manifolds

For street performance, get a dual-plane intake manifold. The shared-runner design of a the dual-plane manifold maintains higher intake velocity at lower RPM. A well-matched dual-plane intake manifold improves power across the RPM range while maintaining good fuel economy and drivability.

Factors that affect low and mid RPM performance include the runner volume and the velocity of the intake gases. Runners are the tunnels in the intake manifold that run from the plenum area under the carburetor to each intake port in the cylinder head. Most dual-plane intakes that are designed for street performance use runners that are moderately sized and maintain high velocity in the runners.

Higher velocity benefits low and mid RPM performance. Why is that? Well, engineers could bore you to death with discussions of fluid dynamics. However, to put it simply: flowing gases have inertia, and the greater the velocity, the greater the inertial force that is available to fill a cylinder when the intake valve opens.

Single-Plane Manifolds

Single-plane manifolds are best suited for racing and maximum-performance street applications. These manifolds require higher airflow to achieve their maximum efficiency. Compared to a dual-plane manifold, a single-plane manifold will not perform as well at low and mid RPM.

Regarding intake manifolds, as is the case with most other performance parts, bigger is not always better. If the manifold is too big (meaning that the interior volume is too much for the application), it will not achieve your power goals and the engine will run poorly in the low and mid RPM ranges.

Many manifolds are available for Buick engines, and they are all designed to deliver performance in certain RPM ranges with complimenting performance upgrades elsewhere on the engine. Contact parts manufacturers and other Buick performance enthusiasts to select the right manifold for your engine.

Tunnel-Ram Manifolds

Tunnel-ram intake manifolds are excellent eye candy and attract lots of attention at cruise nights. However, do they add any power to the engine? Well, actually, yes! In fact, for a radical street engine or a drag-race

For street-driven vehicles, a dual-plane intake manifold is a great option because it provides great low and midrange performance.

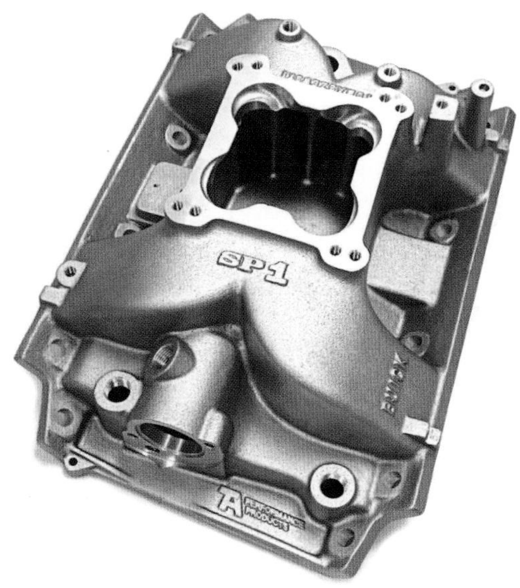

Single-plane intake manifolds should be reserved for engines that will regularly see high RPM. The only real advantage to using a single-plane intake manifold is a slight improvement in airflow at high RPM.

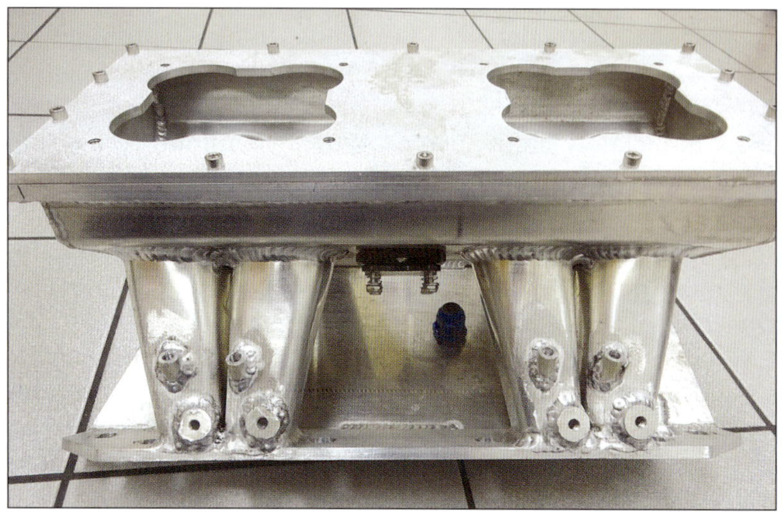

Tunnel rams look really cool and produce more power than the single-plane or dual-plane manifold types. Since they have the complexity of multiple carburetors and are exposed to the elements, they really aren't practical for most people. They're best suited for race engines.

High-flow air cleaners offer better performance, and they can improve hood clearance compared to a stock air cleaner.

engine, the tunnel ram is probably the setup that will provide the most power (not including turbocharging or supercharging systems).

The main disadvantages are obvious. Not many people want to remove their hood or cut a hole in it. In addition, having the induction system exposed to the elements is probably not a good thing. Engine starting might be more difficult due to the long distance between the carburetor and cylinder head. However, if you like the tunnel-ram appearance, want the ultimate naturally aspirated performance, store the car in a garage, and don't drive it in the rain, this might be the setup for you.

Fitting an Intake Manifold

Moving onward from theories to practicality, not every intake manifold will physically fit under every hood or have all the provisions in regard to accessory brackets, vacuum ports, and emissions components.

One of the biggest considerations

when selecting an intake manifold for street use is hood clearance. Manifolds designed for maximum performance will often not fit under the hood of a Buick without modification. Most enthusiasts want to maintain the original flat hood on their car, so some intake choices are eliminated right out of the gate.

Intake-manifold manufacturers list the critical dimensions of their

intake manifolds on their websites. Compare their dimensions to the dimensions on your current manifold and check the clearance that is available with your current air cleaner in place.

Carburetor Flanges

If you are running the stock-type Quadrajet carburetor on your engine, find a manifold to match its unique

If you are using a Quadrajet carburetor, make sure that the intake manifold you selected accommodates the "spread-bore" mounting flange. A Quadrajet cannot be installed onto a square-bore manifold without an adapter. Many modern manifold designs have a compromised design that accepts the square-bore and spread-bore styles. Check with the manufacturer before purchasing a manifold.

"spread-bore" design. Most manifolds are designed with four equally sized holes for the throttle plates (known as the "square-bore" design). While adapters are available to fit a Quadrajet onto a square-bore manifold, they increase the effective height of the manifold and potentially cause issues with hood clearance.

Emissions Devices

Beginning in the late 1960s, an ever-increasing trend began toward more vacuum-controlled devices as well as thermostatic devices, primarily for emissions-control systems. These devices frequently tapped into intake-manifold vacuum and the hot coolant flowing through the cross-over passages in the intake manifold. Many performance intake manifolds do not have provisions for all of the factory devices. Make sure the intake manifold supports all of the systems that you need to maintain.

Carburetors

If you're planning to make performance upgrades and your engine was originally equipped with a 2-barrel carburetor, upgrade to a 4-barrel carburetor and intake manifold. The additional two "barrels" of a 4-barrel carburetor open only under hard acceleration and provide additional airflow, which allows the engine to generate more horsepower at higher RPM.

The most common aftermarket carburetors are based on proven designs that were originally offered by major automotive manufacturers. Different methods are used to open the secondary barrels on the various designs, providing either better fuel economy or faster throttle response. High-performance and racing carburetors provide a range of optional features that improve the ability to tune for performance and drivability on race engines that are notoriously finicky.

Holley

Holley has the most popular carburetor designs that are used on high-performance and racing engines. The primary advantage of the Holley designs is that they are in widespread use. Therefore, they are well understood in the world of high performance. Tuning parts and expertise are easily available.

Holley-type carburetors are available in a myriad of airflow ranges (measured in CFM) and configurations. For high-performance and racing engines, you can select a precise set of features, including specialty features that are not available on some other carburetor designs. Holley carburetors range in price from about $300 to more than $1,500. The higher-priced carburetors flow more air and have more features that allow the carburetor to be more precisely tuned to the application.

One potential disadvantage of using a Holley-type carburetor is that it has a square-bore design, while almost all Buick factory intake manifolds used a spread-bore design that will accept only a Quadrajet-type carburetor. Although adapter plates are available, it's usually best to use a Quadrajet carburetor on a stock intake manifold. Many aftermarket intake manifolds have a standard bore design, so a Holley or AFB/AVS carburetor is usually preferred.

The most common Holley designs use vacuum secondaries. Vacuum-secondary carburetors are available in a variety of flow ratings, with 600 cfm being the most popular. A vacuum diaphragm delays the opening of the secondary throttle plates under hard acceleration, which prevents engine bog. By using springs of varying tension above the vacuum diaphragm, the rate of opening of the secondary throttle valves can be adjusted to tune them precisely to a particular engine and vehicle combination.

Keep in mind that carburetor tuning varies by vehicle weight and other factors. Vacuum-secondary carburetors are well suited to street use and achieve similar fuel economy as the Quadrajet type. Inexpensive and versatile, the vacuum-secondary design is a great choice for mildly modified street cars, where fuel economy is a consideration. These carburetors usually have choke valves, and aftermarket versions usually use an electric choke that is easy to set up.

Holley carburetors with vacuum-controlled secondary throttles usually deliver better fuel economy than double-pumpers. The popular universal variants include an electric choke for easy installation.

Holley's mechanical-secondary designs (commonly referred to as double-pumpers) are best suited for racing and high-level street-performance applications. They are available in ratings from 480 to 950 cfm. While vacuum-secondary carburetors open the secondary throttle plates slowly to prevent engine bog, mechanical-secondary carburetors open all four barrels simultaneously.

The bog is overcome by squirting extra fuel into the secondaries while the throttles are opened. The name "double-pumper" refers to the second accelerator pump required to achieve this function.

Many mechanical-secondary carburetors have an idle-mixture screw at each of the four throttle plates, which allows a better idle tuning range for engines with high-overlap camshafts. Double-pumpers often have a manual choke or no choke at all by design. The Holley HP series of carburetors does not have a choke. They are designed primarily for race use. HP carburetors are rich in race-tuning features. Those features, of course, come at a higher price.

The Holley Dominator (model 4500) is the ultimate performance model and is available in ratings of 1,050 to 1,400 cfm. These are not street-friendly carburetors and are to be used on only the highest-performance racing engines. Because of their enlarged throttle body, they can only be used on intake manifolds that have been manufactured specifically for Dominators. Unless you're planning to build a race engine with horsepower near the four digits, a Dominator is not needed.

Demon

Demon carburetors have designs, CFM ratings, and features that are similar to Holley. Demon Carburetion is owned by the Holley Performance Group.

While Demon-style carburetors have a more modern appearance than Holley-style carburetors, the Demon-style carburetors operate similarly and use most of the same replacement parts as standard Holleys. In fact, Holley rebuild kits can be used for Demon carburetors. Still, many racers and performance enthusiasts shy away from Demon carburetors because tuning is different than Holley carburetors. For example, Demon carburetors tend to use larger jets to flow the same amount of fuel. Demon carburetors are priced similarly to the Holleys and have loyal fans, including me.

Quadrajet

Quadrajet carburetors were installed as original equipment on GM cars from the 1960s to the 1980s. While they were not as popular in performance circles as other designs, they can support the fuel-system requirements of all but the most powerful racing engines. Since they were designed for street use on passenger cars, they are fuel efficient and work exceptionally well in daily driven street cars.

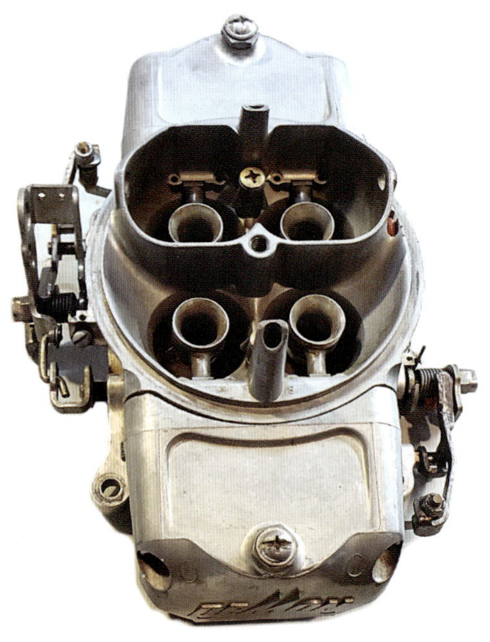

Double-pumpers mechanically open the secondaries through a progressive linkage. To compensate for the sudden drop in vacuum when the gas pedal is punched, a second accelerator pump is needed. The advantage of a double-pumper is that there is no delay when the secondary barrels are opened. The disadvantage is that more fuel is used if you have a heavy foot. This is Demon's version of the double-pumper: the Mighty Demon.

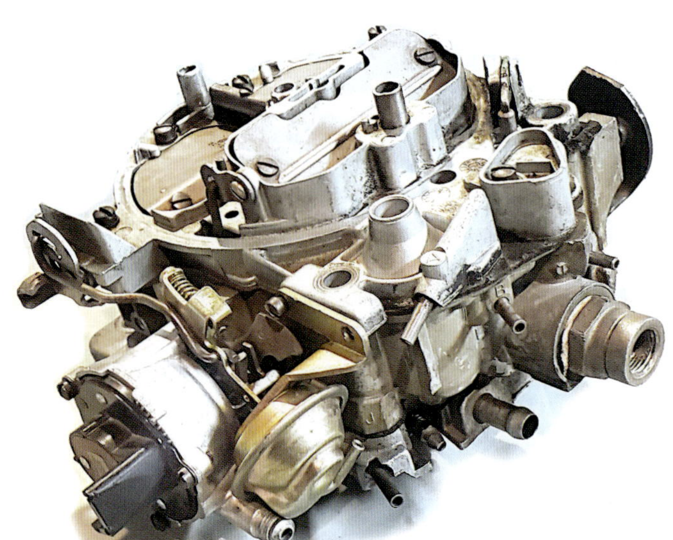

If the Buick engine has an original 4-barrel carburetor, it will almost certainly be a Quadrajet. Quadrajets are good for mild-to-moderate performance engines.

The secondary barrels use an adjustable air valve that prevents bogging under hard acceleration. The air valve does not respond to throttle input as quickly as a Holley double-pumper, but it is as responsive as a Holley vacuum-secondary design when adjusted properly. The main advantage (or disadvantage) of the Quadrajet is that it is a spread-bore design.

To use a Quadrajet carburetor, an intake manifold that is specifically designed for the Quadrajet is required or an adapter plate under the carburetor must be used to adapt it to a standard-bore flange. If you plan to use a stock Buick intake manifold, the Quadrajet is often the preferred design.

The original Carter AVS and AFB designs have been improved upon by Edelbrock and are manufactured in the USA. They come with an electric choke and are great options for a street car.

AVS/AFB

Commonly available in the aftermarket are carburetors based on designs that were originally marketed by Carter and installed on many Chrysler Corporation vehicles in the 1960s and 1970s. Today, Edelbrock manufactures the air valve secondary (AVS) design, and tuning parts are widely available.

The AVS design uses an air valve that functions similarly to the Quadrajet. Unlike the Quadrajet, the AVS has a square-bore throttle body, meaning that it can be installed on most aftermarket intake manifolds. AVS carburetors use electric chokes and are easy to install.

They are popular on street-performance engines and commonly available in 500- and 800-cfm ratings. These carburetors are known for their simplicity and durability. They provide good fuel economy and are relatively inexpensive.

Demon offers carburetors that are loosely based on the AVS design. Marketed as the Street Demon, these carburetors incorporate modern design features and are available in 625- and 750-cfm ratings. Since the Street Demon is a significant departure from the AVS design, parts interchange and availability could be an issue.

Sizing

Select a carburetor that will just meet the airflow requirements of the engine. A carburetor that is too big for the application is not likely to add any power, even in the high-RPM range. In fact, an oversized carburetor will most likely lead to poor performance in the low and mid RPM ranges.

There is little to gain and much to lose when the carburetor is oversized in relation to the engine build. Carburetor manufacturers can provide recommendations as to the best carburetor CFM rating for your engine. They have charts and calculators online that are specific to their carburetor designs.

Electronic Fuel Injection

It is debatable whether your engine will make more power with electronic fuel injection (EFI) compared to a properly sized and tuned carburetor. The main argument for choosing fuel injection is that it can provide improved drivability (particularly when the engine is cold) and fuel economy.

If you're not experienced with carburetor adjustments and tuning, an EFI system with "self-tuning" capabilities can be an attractive option. Tuning changes with EFI don't require mechanical disassembly as they do with a carburetor, and they can be made in real-time while driving. In addition, many EFI systems can automatically compensate for changing weather conditions and altitude.

Although the prices of EFI systems have decreased significantly, they are still significantly more expensive than the average carburetor. They also

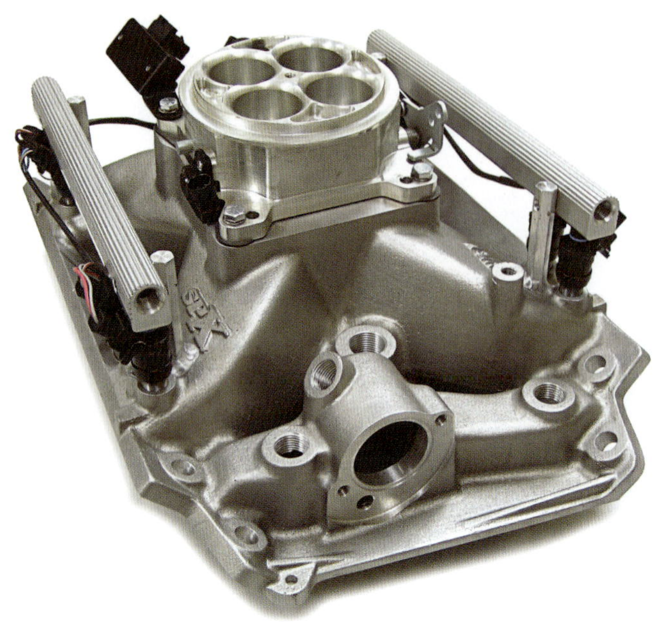

If you want your Buick to start and run as flawlessly as a new car, the best option is to use EFI. Aftermarket EFI systems use an oxygen sensor and have a feedback control loop to maintain the optimal air/fuel ratio (AFR). The AFR updates are continuous, immediately responding to changes in operating conditions. The idle speed and mixture never require adjustment, and you don't have to rely on a finicky choke during a cold start.

require installation of a high-pressure electric fuel pump.

My general recommendation is that if you're familiar with carburetor tuning and you mainly drive your car at the racetrack and/or an occasional drive around town on nice days, using a carburetor is a logical choice. However, if the car is driven every day or on long cruises, it will benefit from the improvement in fuel economy and drivability that fuel injection can provide.

As with carburetors, it's important to select an EFI system that's matched to the expected performance level of the engine. Many of the less-expensive systems are limited as to the airflow that they support. A low-end system might not meet the needs of a hot street engine.

How Does It Run?

After the engine has been rebuilt and the performance modifications have been made, you'll be eager to see if the engine performs as you expected. Don't be discouraged if the initial performance is not spectacular. Most performance builds require tuning to achieve their full potential.

It's common to "find" an additional 50 hp just through basic tuning that includes optimizing the air-fuel ratio and ignition timing curve. This is best done on a chassis dynamometer and with the aid of a tuning expert. Get recommendations from other performance enthusiasts in your area to find a good tuner. The cost of the services may seem high, but they're often the best value in the engine build.

SPECIFICATIONS

350-ci Small-Block V-8 Engines	
General Details	
Displacement	350 ci
Bore	3.8 inches
Stroke	3.85 inches
Rod length	6.387 inches
Rod/stroke ratio	1.6514 inches
Bore/stroke ratio	0.987 inch
Cylinder-bore center to cylinder-bore center spacing	4.24 inches
Crankshaft-bore center to block deck height	10.187 inches
Firing order	1-8-4-3-6-5-7-2
Cylinder numbering: Left (driver's) side	1-3-5-7
Cylinder numbering: Right (passenger's) side	2-4-6-8

Torque Specifications	Ft-lbs (Unless Otherwise Indicated)
Spark plugs	15
Crankshaft bearing caps to cylinder block	95
Connecting-rod cap nuts	
—Nuts (1968–1972)	35
—Bolts (1973–newer)	50
Cylinder head to engine-block bolts	75
Harmonic balancer to crankshaft bolts	120 (minimum)
Crankshaft pulley bolts	23
Flywheel to crankshaft bolts (auto and manual transmission)	60
Oil pan to engine block	14
Oil pan drain plug	30
Oil pump cover to timing chain cover	10
Oil pump pressure regulator retainer	35
Oil pickup tube/screen to block bolts	96 in-lbs
Oil pan windage tray to cylinder block bolts	11
Oil galley plugs	25
Oil-pressure sending unit to cylinder block	23
Timing cover to block bolt	20
Water pump to timing-cover bolts	84 in-lbs
Cooling fan pulley	20
Thermostat housing to intake manifold	20
Automatic choke cover to cylinder-head bolts	96 in-lbs
Intake manifold to cylinder head	55
Exhaust manifold to cylinder head	18
Carburetor to intake-manifold bolts	156 in-lbs
Fuel pump to cylinder-block bolts	20
Engine-mount insulator to engine-block bolts	63
Fuel-pump eccentric to timing-chain sprocket bolt	48
Rocker-arm shaft to cylinder-head bolts	25
Torque-converter cover bolts	48 in-lbs
Transmission to engine bolts	35
Valve-cover bolts	48 in-lbs

Note: 12 in-lbs is equivalent to 1 ft-lb. Measurements in in-lbs are more accurate for small torque measurements

Camshaft	
Material	Cast-alloy iron
Bearings	Steel-backed Babbitt
Number of bearings	5
Drive	Chain
Number of links	54
Crankshaft sprocket	Sintered iron
Camshaft sprocket	Nylon-coated aluminum
Bearing journal diameter	
—No. 1	1.785 to 1.786 inches
—No. 2	1.785 to 1.786 inches
—No. 3	1.785 to 1.786 inches
—No. 4	1.785 to 1.786 inches
—No. 5	1.785 to 1.786 inches
Journal clearance in bearings	
—No. 1	0.0005 to 0.0035 inch
—Nos. 2, 3, 4, and 5	0.0005 to 0.0035 inch
Crankshaft	
Material	Nodular iron
Thrust bearing location	No. 3 main bearing cap/saddle
Endplay (measured at thrust bearing)	0.003 to 0.009 inch
Main bearing journal diameter	2.9995 inches
Crank pin journal diameter	2 inches
Main bearing to journal (oil) clearance	0.0004 to 0.0015 inch
Lubrication System	
Normal oil pressure	37 pounds at 2,600 rpm
Main, connecting rod, and camshaft bearing lubrication	Pressurized
Oil pump type	Gear driven

Piston pin and cylinder wall lubrication	Splash and nozzle spray
Crankcase Capacity	
—With filter	5 quarts
—Without filter	4 quarts
Pistons	
Piston-to-bore clearance	
—At top ring land	0.027 to 0.036 inch
—At top of piston skirt	0.0008 to 0.0020 inch
—At bottom of piston skirt	0.0013 to 0.0035 inch
Ring width	
—No. 1 compression ring	0.0770 to 0.0880 inch
—No. 2 compression ring	0.0770 to 0.0780 inch
—No. 3 oil ring	0.1810 to 0.1870 inch
Ring end gap	
—No. 1 compression ring	0.010 to 0.020 inch
—No. 2 compression ring	0.010 to 0.020 inch
—No. 3 oil ring	0.015 to 0.035 inch
Piston pin	
—Length	3.06 inches
—Diameter	0.9394 to 0.9397 inch
—Clearance in piston	0.0004 to 0.0007 inch
—Clearance in rod	0.00075 to 0.00125 inch interference fit
Direction and amount offset in piston	0.040 on major thrust side
Connecting Rods	
Bearing (oil) clearance (limit)	0.0023 inch
Endplay (total for both rods)	0.006 to 0.020 inch
Valvetrain	
Rocker-arm ratio	1.55 to 1
Rocker arm-to-shaft clearance	0.0022 to 0.0037 inch
Valve lifter mechanism	Hydraulic
Valve lifter diameter	0.8422 to 0.8427 inch
Valve lifter-to-bore clearance	0.0008 to 0.0023 inch
Pushrod length	9.65 inches*
*Check lifter preload, as described in chapter 6	
Intake Valve	
Overall length	4.994 to 5.024 inches
Head diameter	1.870 to 1.880 inches
Seat angle	45 degrees
Stem diameter	0.3723 to 0.3730 inch
Stem taper	0.003 inch total
Clearance in guide	0.0015 to 0.0025 inch
Exhaust Valve	
Overall length	5.014 to 5.044 inches
Head diameter	1.495 to 1.505 inches
Seat angle	45 degrees
Stem diameter	0.3723 to 0.3730 inch
Clearance in guide	0.0015 to 0.0032 inch
Valve Springs	
Valve closed pressure at length	70 to 80 pounds at 1.727 inches
Valve open pressure at length	175 to 187 pounds at 1.340 inches
Installed height	1.727 inches

400, 430, and 455 Big-Block Engines

General Details	
Displacement	400, 430, and 455 ci
Cylinder bore	
—400	4.04 inches
—430	4.1875 inches
—455	4.3125 inches
Stroke (all)	3.9 inches
Rod length	6.607 inches
Rod/stroke ratio	1.6923 to 1
Bore/stroke ratio	
—400	1.0359 to 1
—430	1.0737 to 1
—455	1.1058 to 1
Cylinder-bore center to bore-center spacing	4.75 inches
Crankshaft-bore center to block deck height	10.57 inches
Firing order	1-8-4-3-6-5-7-2
Cylinder numbering: Left (driver's) side	1-3-5-7
Cylinder numbering: Right (passenger's) side	2-4-6-8

Torque Specifications	**Ft-lbs** (Unless Otherwise Indicated)
Spark plugs	15
Crankshaft main bearing cap bolts	100
Connecting-rod cap nuts	45
Cylinder head to engine block bolts	100
Harmonic balancer to crankshaft bolts	200 minimum
Crankshaft pulley bolt	23
Flywheel to crankshaft bolts (auto and manual transmission)	60
Oil pan to engine block	14
Oil-pan drain plug	30
Oil-pump cover to timing chain cover	10
Oil-pump pressure regulator retainer	
—400 and 430	25
—455	35
Oil pickup tube/screen to block bolts	96 in-lbs
Oil-pan windage tray to cylinder-block bolts	
—400 and 430	96 in-lbs
—455	156 in-lbs
Oil-pressure sending unit to cylinder block	25
Oil-gallery plugs	25
Timing cover to block bolts	20
Water pump to timing-cover bolts	84 in-lbs
Cooling-fan pulley	20
Thermostat housing to intake manifold	20
Automatic choke cover to cylinder head bolts	96 in-lbs
Intake manifold to cylinder head bolts	
—400 and 430	50
—455	55
Exhaust manifold to cylinder head	18

Carburetor to intake-manifold bolts	156 in-lbs
Fuel pump to cylinder-block bolts	20
Engine-mount insulator to engine-block bolts	70
Timing-chain sprocket to camshaft bolts	22
Rocker-arm shaft to cylinder-head bolts	
—400 and 430	30
—455	25
Torque-converter cover bolts	48 in-lbs
Transmission to engine bolts	35
Valve-cover bolts	48 in-lbs

Note: 12 in-lbs is equivalent to 1 ft-lb. Measurements in in-lbs are more accurate for small torque measurements.

Camshaft

Material	Cast-alloy iron
Bearings	Steel-backed babbitt
Number of bearings	5
Drive	Chain
Number of links	48
Crankshaft sprocket	Sintered iron
Camshaft sprocket	Nylon-coated aluminum
Bearing journal diameter	
—No. 1	1.785 to 1.786 inches
—No. 2	1.785 to 1.786 inches
—No. 3	1.785 to 1.786 inches
—No. 4	1.785 to 1.786 inches
—No. 5	1.785 to 1.786 inches
Journal clearance in bearings	
—No. 1	0.0005 to 0.0025 inch
—Nos. 2, 3, 4, and 5	0.0005 to 0.0035 inch

Crankshaft

Material	Nodular iron
Thrust bearing location	No. 3 main bearing cap/ saddle
Endplay (measured at thrust bearing)	0.003 to 0.009 inch
Main bearing journal diameter	3.25 inches
Crank pin journal diameter	2.249 to 2.250 inches
Main bearing-to-journal (oil) clearance	0.0007 to 0.0018 inch

Lubrication System

Normal oil pressure	40 psi at 2,400 rpm
Main, connecting rod, and camshaft bearing lubrication	Pressurized
Piston pin and cylinder-wall lubrication	Splash and nozzle spray
Oil pump type	Gear driven
Crankcase capacity	
—With filter	5 quarts
—Without filter	4 quarts

Pistons

Piston-to-bore clearance	
—At top of ring land	0.0343 to 0.0423 inch
—At top of piston skirt	0.0007 to 0.0013 inch
—At bottom of piston skirt	0.0017 to 0.0033 inch
Piston ring groove	
—No. 1 compression ring	0.2090 to 0.2165 inch
—No. 2 compression ring	0.210 to 0.2190 inch
—No. 3 oil ring	0.1815 to 0.1890 inch
Piston ring width	
—No. 1 compression ring	0.077 to 0.078 inch
—No. 2 compression ring	0.077 to 0.078 inch
—No. 3 oil ring	0.1815 to 0.1890 inch
Piston ring end gap	
—No. 1 compression ring	0.013 to 0.023 inch
—No. 2 compression ring	0.013 to 0.023 inch
—No. 3 oil ring	0.015 to 0.055 inch
Piston pin	
—Length	3.52 inches
—Diameter	0.9994 to 0.9997 inch
—Clearance in piston	0.0004 to 0.0007 inch
—Clearance in rod	0.00075 to 0.00125 inch interference fit
Direction and amount offset in piston	0.060 on major thrust side

Connecting Rods

Bearing (oil) clearance (limit)	0.0020 to 0.0023 inch
Endplay (total for both rods)	0.005 to 0.012 inch

Valvetrain

Rocker-arm ratio	
—1967 and 1968 (cast aluminum)	1.59 to 1
—1969 and 1970 (stamped steel)	1.54 to 1
—1971 and later (stamped steel)	1.6 to 1
Rocker arm-to-shaft clearance	0.0015 to 0.00330 inch
Valve lifter mechanism	Hydraulic
Valve lifter diameter	0.8422 to 0.8427 inch
Valve lifter-to-bore clearance	0.0008 to 0.0023 inch
Pushrod length	9.378 inches*

*Check lifter preload, as described in chapter 6.

Intake Valve

Overall length	4.994 to 5.024 inches
Head diameter	2.0 inches
Seat angle	45 degrees
Stem diameter	0.3720 to 0.3730 inch
Stem taper	0.003 inch total
Clearance in guide	0.0015 to 0.0025 inch

Exhaust Valve

Overall length	5.014 to 5.044 inches
Head diameter	1.625 inches
Seat angle	45 degrees
Stem diameter	0.3723 to 0.3730 inch
Clearance in guide	0.0015 to 0.0032 inch

Valve Springs

Valve closed pressure at length	67 to 77 pounds at 1.890 inches
Valve open pressure at length	170 to 184 pounds at 1.450 inches
Installed height	1.727 inches

Accel Performance Ignition
1801 Russelville Rd.
Bowling Green, KY 42101
866-464-6553
holley.com/brands/accel

Chicago Muscle Car Parts
912 E. Burnett Rd.
Island Lake, IL 60042
847-526-2200
chicagomusclecarparts.com

Cloyes Gear & Products
7800 Ball Rd.
Fort Smith, AR 72908
479-646-1662
cloyes.com

CNC Motorsports
118 Front St.
Brookings, SD 57006
605-692-1697
cnc-motorsports.com

Comp Cams
8649 Hack Cross Rd.
Olive Branch, MS 38654
800-365-9145
compcams.com

Demon Carburetion
1801 Russelville Rd.
Bowling Green, KY 42101
866-464-6553
holley.com/brands/demon

Doug's Headers
440 E. Arrow Hwy.
San Dimas, CA 91773
909-599-5955
pertronixbrands.com/pages/
dougs-headers

Edelbrock Performance
8649 Hack Cross Rd.
Olive Branch, MS 38654
800-416-8628
edelbrock.com

Enginetech
1205 W. Crosby Rd.
Carrollton, TX 7500
800-869-8711
enginetech.com

Erson Cams
7301 Global Dr.
Louisville, KY 40258
800-588-9608
pbm-erson.com

Flowtech Exhaust
1801 Russelville Rd.
Bowling Green, KY 42101
866-464-6553
holley.com/brands/flowtech

Hedman Hedders
12438 Putnam St.
Whittier, CA 90602
562-921-0404
hedman.com

Holley Performance Products
1801 Russelville Rd.
Bowling Green, KY 42101
270-781-9741
holley.com

Hooker Headers
1801 Russelville Rd.
Bowling Green, KY 42101
866-464-6553
holley.com/brands/hooker

Howards Cams & Racing
Components
280 W. 35th Ave.
Oshkosh, WI 54902
920-233-5228
howardscams.com

Iskenderian (Isky) Racing Cams
16020 S. Broadway
Gardena, CA 90248
310-217-9232
iskycams.com

Jasper Engines
P.O. Box 650
Jasper, IN 47547-0650
800-827-7455
jasperengines.com

Jegs Performance
101 Jegs Pl.
Delaware, OH 43015
614-294-5454
jegs.com

Jet Hot Coatings
2611 LaVista Dr.
Burlington, NC 27215
800-432-3379
jet-hot.com

Kenny Betts Racing
7 High St. Unit B
Newport, Maine 04953
951-541-4750
buickracingparts.com

Lunati Performance Parts
8649 Hacks Cross Rd.
Olive Branch, MS 38654
662-892-1500
lunatipower.com

Melling Engine Parts
2620 Saradan Dr.
Jackson, MI 49204
517 787-8172
melling.com

Molnar Rods Motorsports Parts
Corporation
6520 Boundary Run Dr.
Mechanicsville, VA 23111
804-779-0888
molnarrods.com

Moroso Performance
80 Carter Dr.
Guilford, CT 06437
203-458-0542
moroso.com

MSD Ignition
1801 Russelville Rd.
Bowling Green, KY 42101
866-464-6553
holley.com/brands/msd

Northern Auto Parts
801 Lewis Blvd.
Sioux City, IA 51105
800-831-0884
northernautoparts.com

Offenhauser
5300 Alhambra Ave.
Los Angeles, CA 90032
323-225-1307
offenhauser.co

Original Parts Group
1770 Saturn Way
Seal Beach, CA 90740
800-243-8355
opgi.com

PerTronix Performance Products
440 E. Arrow Hwy.
San Dimas, CA 91773
909-599-5955
pertronix.com

Powertrain Products Inc.
520 Thompson Creek Rd.
Stevensville, MD 21666
888-842-0023
powertrainproducts.net

Rock Auto Parts
6418 Normandy Ln., Ste. 100
Madison, WI 53719
608-661-1376
rockauto.com

Speedmaster
1101 W. Rialto Ave.
Rialto, CA 92376
310-361-0020
speedmaster79.com

Speedway Motors
340 Victory Ln.
Lincoln, NE 68528
800-979-0122
speedwaymotors.com

S&J Engines
3808 N. Sullivan Rd.,
Bldg. 7-C
Spokane Valley, WA 99216
800-942-7800
sandjengines.com

Summit Racing
1200 Southeast Ave.
Tallmadge, Ohio 44278
800-230-3030
summitracing.com

TA Performance Products
16167 N. 81st St.
Scottsdale, AZ 85260
480-922-6807
taperformance.com

Tri-Shield Performance
11771 Tigua Rd.
Pine City, MN 55063
320-629-8999

Weiand
1801 Russelville Rd.
Bowling Green, KY 42101
866-464-6553
holley.com/brands/weiand

Year One
1001 Cherry Dr., Unit 1
Braselton, GA 30517
800-932-7663
yearone.com